PRAISE FOR *Organic Revolutionary*

Organic Revolutionary *is an important message about the historic and current place of organic agriculture in the good food movement, how the integrity of organic has been challenged, and the opportunity that organic agriculture holds to promote planetary health.*

**Enid Wonnacott, Executive Director NOFA-Vermont**

*I hold Grace in high regard as a leader in the organic movement because of the depth of her thinking and writing combined with the highest of motives and concern for the future of humanity. ...unless leaders like Grace, and others along the entire agricultural production chain, can collaborate using a holistic framework we will fail to address the web of social, cultural, economic and environmental complexity that can help us avoid global catastrophe.*

**Allan Savory, President, Savory Institute; Chairman, Africa Center for Holistic Management**

*At a dinner party, sometimes one has the good fortune to be seated next to the person who knows the dirt on everyone else there and isn't afraid to talk...Gershuny had a hand in the founding of NOFA, the founding of the OTA, the development of the NOP, and more; she speaks of these important developments, and of the other organic movers and shakers who helped to mold them, from a deeply personal perspective. But the book transcends gossip column status to ask important ongoing questions about the organic movement. Should the organic standards be consumer-driven or farmer-driven? Should they focus on the source of inputs or on the ecological soundness of the practices? Can organic agriculture achieve mainstream status without hanging its principles out to dry? Whether you like Gershuny's answers to these questions or not, you'll enjoy the conversation.*

**Alice Percy, review in *FEDCO/Organic Growers Supply Catalog***

PRAISE FOR *Organic Revolutionary*

*Gershuny is no dispassionate detached observer. The story of organic is the story of her life. Not just her professional and public life; her love life and family life are also inseparable from the broader drama of Organic USA. For this reason, Gershuny's history of organic standards and labeling is necessarily an autobiography—and inversely, she could never tell the story of her life without going through the whole history of the organic movement.*

Carmelo Ruiz-Marrero (1967-2016), journalist and political activist

*Grace Gershuny, a founding member of the American organic agriculture movement and a long-time organic farmer, has written a thoughtfully comprehensive, entertaining, and deeply personal account of her adventures in the movement and on the land.... Her story is an important one and her ultimate conclusions, along with her hopes for the future, are optimistic for the new generation of organic farmers.*

Reeve Lindbergh, author of *Under a Wing* and *The Midnight Farm*

*The book provides a much needed perspective on the process of reconciling radical politics with the world of government administration and the growing organic market being increasingly dominated by big companies. The form of a 'memoir' makes it easy to read. Occasionally, personal matters take over the story, but that is what they do in most peoples' lives. It adds flesh and blood to the book.*

Gunnar Rundgren, founder of Grolink AB and author of *Garden Earth*

*Gershuny's book... is her story of hard-fought successes in food activism, set into the ups and downs of her own personal life... It's an interesting read and an excellent primer on how government regulations are set. It's chock-full of lessons learned that are applicable to today's food system activists, but it's also a story with many parallels to other social and environmental movements, such as Black Lives Matter, gay marriage, global climate change, safe drinking water, or banning plastics.*

Sarah Galbraith, *Vermont Woman*

# ORGANIC
## REVOLUTIONARY

**SECOND EDITION**
WITH NEW PROLOGUE AND REVISED TEXT

# ORGANIC
## REVOLUTIONARY

A MEMOIR OF THE MOVEMENT FOR REAL FOOD,
PLANETARY HEALING, AND HUMAN LIBERATION

## GRACE GERSHUNY

### SECOND EDITION
WITH NEW PROLOGUE AND REVISED TEXT

Organic Revolutionary: A Memoir of the Movement for Real Food, Planetary Healing, and Human Liberation

Second Edition
Copyright © Grace Gershuny 2017
ISBN: 978-0-9972327-2-1

JOES BROOK PRESS
Book design and layout by Marie Hathaway
www.organic-revolutionary.com

*To Miranda Smith and all our children.*

# Contents

✿

✿

# Foreword

Grace Gershuny weaves her personal journey into the fabric of the story of the transition of the organic movement into an organic food industry. She takes up the challenge of turning an ecological philosophy into a federal regulation—a Herculean effort to put a legal framework on a process that flows from seed to table. This effort took us from the wild frontier of disparate fiefdoms to uniformity. *Organic Revolutionary* is the inside story of the people and events that led to the organic market and regulation we have today.

I was homesteading in southern Quebec in the seventies when our paths crossed at the wonderful, annual, Northeast Organic Farmers Association (NOFA) summer conferences. The camaraderie and knowledge-sharing of these events were the epitome of the organic zeitgeist. At the time, I was a partner in an organic fertilizer and compost company and wrote a small pamphlet on soil fertility. One thing led to another and soon Grace and I were collaborating on the Organic Food Production of North America (OFPANA) standards, the development of the Organic Crop Improvement Association (OCIA), and the revision of *The Soul of Soil*.

Organic agriculture has recently received Papal (and Pay Pal) endorsement for its personal and planetary benefits. There is increasing scientific evidence of the benefits of organic farming including, but not limited to, the reduction of oncogenic, toxic, and endocrine-disruptive pesticide residues in humans, the elimination of antibiotics in livestock, the prohibition of GMOs in organic production, higher nutrient density of organic food, and the provision of a carbon sink in agricultural soils via sequestration. It is ironic that the original scientific term "organic" is all about carbon. Organic retail sales continue to grow, adding textiles, cosmetics, and aquaculture to the mix. Consumers are voting for organic at the checkout line, and organic has become a lifestyle choice more than an agricultural methodology. Major global corporations have concluded that ecological can be economical.

Grace's unique perspective as both movement organizer and USDA bureaucrat lifts the veil to reveal how a derided philosophy became an industry regulation. And how an embattled group of people in the bowels of bureaucracy teased a sound blueprint for the organic sector's growth in spite of hostility and neglect from within and contradictory demands from the "so-called" organic community. There are often references to the "organic community," but the historical reality is that the early organic pioneers were usually radicals or renegades from their own community, whether they were Hippies or Posse Comitatus, Mennonite or Hare Krishna, Survivalists or University Professors…hardly a rainbow coalition. While I may differ with Grace on the relative influence of the organic farm groups and the organic businesses, nonetheless an alliance of organic and environmental organizations supported Senator Leahy's congressional efforts and the Organic Food Production Act of 1990 (OFPA) was passed…alea iacta est. This enabling legislation was just the beginning. It took 12 years of "open, transparent, and democratic" debate to get a regulation. This debate soon became polarized between two differing viewpoints of organic production.

Grace cuts to the core of the organic purist versus pragmatist dichotomy. These two solitudes have been warring since the first organic apple was sold. This polarization continues to threaten the organic sector from within. Should perfect be the enemy of good? These days the battle continues on social media, at organic conferences, and in NOSB meetings as the "purists" try to eliminate any farming or processing materials that may be considered synthetic, while the "pragmatists" try to protect tools necessary for efficient production.

Grace alternates her personal story with clear and accessible explanations of the legal and philosophical rationale for the organic regulations as they were developed. This well-crafted rhythm provides a social context of the movement and some welcome respite, for everyone except a few policy wonks, from the burden of following the regulatory story.

There is an old saying that the two things you don't want to see made are sausages and regulations. Grace shows the difficulties of changing a holistic philosophy into a process, not product, guarantee. I used to spend hours composing a cogent and all encompassing paragraph to define organic; now I just say it is CFR 7 Part 205.

This book is essential reading for anyone seeking to understand the events and ideas pivotal to the growth of the organic sector in the US.

**Joe Smillie**
Founding Member of the International Organic Inspectors Association (IOIA)
Founding Member and past-President of the Organic Trade Association (OTA)
Former member of the National Organic Standards Board (NOSB)
Former Senior Vice-President of Quality Assurance International ( QAI)

**AMS** Agricultural Marketing Service (agency of USDA that includes the NOP)

**APHIS** Animal Plant Health Inspection Service (agency within AMS that regulates GMOs)

**CCOF** California Certified Organic Farmers (certifier)

**CSL** Corn steep liquor

**EPA** US Environmental Protection Agency

**FACA** Federal Advisory Committees Act

**FDA** US Food & Drug Administration

**FSIS** Food Safety Inspection Service (agency within AMS responsible for meat, dairy and poultry inspection)

**FVO** Farm Verified Organic

**GOTS** Global Organic Textile Standard

**GMOs** Genetically Modified Organisms

**HACCP** Hazard Analysis of Critical Control Points

**IFOAM** International Federation of Organic Agriculture Movements

**ISO** International Standards Organization

**NCAT** National Center for Appropriate Technology

**NEFCO** New England Food Coop Association

**NESFI** New England Small Farms Institute

**NOC** National Organic Coalition

**NOFA** Northeast Organic Farming Association (previously Natural Organic Farmers Association)

**NOP** National Organic Program

**NOSB** National Organic Standards Board

**OCA** Organic Consumers Association

**OCIA** Organic Crop Improvement Association (certifier)

**OFAC** Organic Farmers Associations Council

**OFAWG** Organic Foods Act Working Group

**OFPA** Organic Foods Production Act of 1990 (the organic law)

**OFPANA** Organic Foods Production Association of North America (now OTA)

**OGBA** Organic Growers & Buyers Association

**OGC** Office of General Counsel (legal staff for any federal agency)

**OMB** Office of Management & Budget (White House)

**OTA** Organic Trade Association

**QAI** Quality Assurance International (certifier)

**SOFAH** System of organic farming and handling—the definition that formed the basis for the first proposed rule

**USDA** United States Department of Agriculture

**VNGC** Vermont Northern Growers Cooperative

**VOF** Vermont Organic Farmers (certifier)

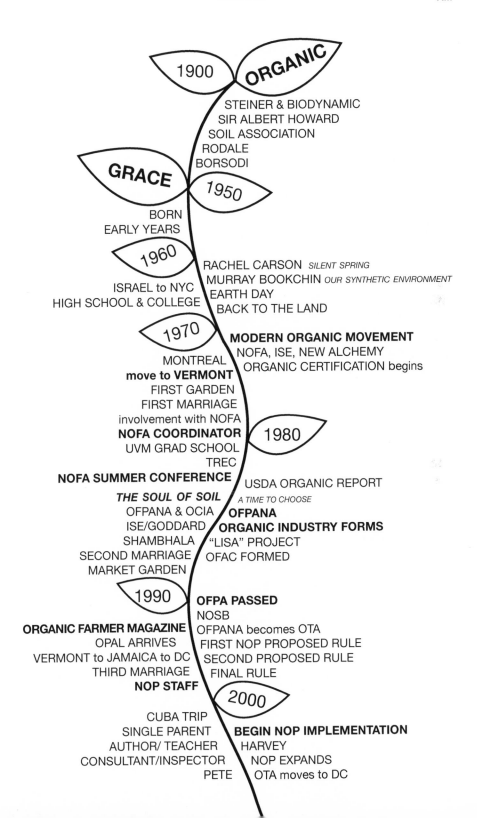

1900 **ORGANIC**

STEINER & BIODYNAMIC
SIR ALBERT HOWARD
SOIL ASSOCIATION
RODALE
BORSODI

**GRACE** 1950

BORN
EARLY YEARS

1960

ISRAEL to NYC
HIGH SCHOOL & COLLEGE

RACHEL CARSON *SILENT SPRING*
MURRAY BOOKCHIN *OUR SYNTHETIC ENVIRONMENT*
EARTH DAY
BACK TO THE LAND

1970

MONTREAL
**move to VERMONT**
FIRST GARDEN
FIRST MARRIAGE
involvement with NOFA
**NOFA COORDINATOR**
UVM GRAD SCHOOL
TREC

**MODERN ORGANIC MOVEMENT**
NOFA, ISE, NEW ALCHEMY
ORGANIC CERTIFICATION begins

1980

**NOFA SUMMER CONFERENCE**
*THE SOUL OF SOIL*
OFPANA & OCIA
ISE/GODDARD
SHAMBHALA
SECOND MARRIAGE
MARKET GARDEN

USDA ORGANIC REPORT
*A TIME TO CHOOSE*
**OFPANA**
**ORGANIC INDUSTRY FORMS**
"LISA" PROJECT
OFAC FORMED

1990

**ORGANIC FARMER MAGAZINE**
OPAL ARRIVES
VERMONT to JAMAICA to DC
THIRD MARRIAGE
**NOP STAFF**

**OFPA PASSED**
NOSB
OFPANA becomes OTA
FIRST NOP PROPOSED RULE
SECOND PROPOSED RULE
FINAL RULE

2000

CUBA TRIP
SINGLE PARENT
AUTHOR/ TEACHER
CONSULTANT/INSPECTOR
PETE

**BEGIN NOP IMPLEMENTATION**
HARVEY
NOP EXPANDS
OTA moves to DC

# Prologue—Summer 2015:

*It takes courage to ask people to think critically about ideas so taken for granted as to be like the air they breathe... Rather than fearing mistakes, courage requires that we continually test new concepts as we seek to learn—ever willing to admit error, correct our course, and move forward.*
—Frances Moore Lappé & Joseph Collins
*World Hunger: Ten Myths*

While drought devastates the nation's salad bowl in California, this has been a very rainy season in Vermont. Our forty-odd heirloom apple trees are heavily laden, and a couple of large limbs have actually broken under the weight of the ripening fruit. The garden is bursting with tropical lushness, and it took until mid-July for our neighbor to find enough dry days in a row to hay our field. Flowers are blooming wildly, buzzing with pollinators. Our five hens give us all the eggs we can use or give away, with yolks deep yellow from the weeds and bugs they eat along with the food scraps we deposit in the chicken yard, while commercial egg supplies are squeezed by the outbreak of avian influenza that has decimated mega-poultry farms in the Midwest.

I feel grateful and privileged to live here, surrounded by such beauty in every season, confident in the bounty that pours out of the earth to nourish us. Growing older, I'm heartened by younger generations of farmers and gardeners, builders and tinkerers, smart people with the skills to stay warm and well fed through this region's long and bitter winters. Taking stock of the great blessings life has brought me, I can assure you that the story you are about to read has a happy ending, at least for its protagonist. The rest of the world—well, that's another matter.

It seems that, despite the best efforts of many of us of the "boomer" generation, the situation—whether environmental, social, economic, or political—seems to become scarier by the month. Though we who live in this rural paradise count ourselves fortunate, we fear for the future of our children and grandchildren, for the refugees risking their lives to flee brutal wars, for the island dwellers who watch the seas rise and threaten their homes, and for the many who live in drought-stricken areas where water is no longer a given. We cringe as the oil rigs wend their way to the Arctic, soon to be devoid of summer sea ice. We join climate marches, protest against oil pipelines, install solar panels, and support our local farmers. We get involved in politics, work to raise public awareness, and proclaim that Black Lives Matter. And we pray that our efforts have not been too little, too late.

## Why This Book?

In the fifteen years it has taken me to write this book, the real food revolution that began with the advent of a government-approved, USDA-regulated organic label has rapidly gained momentum. Popular movements promoting local food, food sovereignty, and food justice, along with a host of eco-label schemes such as fair trade, animal welfare, and non-GMO, have exploded throughout the country and the world. However, despite the resounding success of the now $39 billion organic market[i] organic production still accounts for less than 1% of domestic land in agriculture in 2015–twenty-five years after the Organic Foods Production Act (the organic law) was enacted and fifteen years after the National Organic Program was established.

I was a principal author of the USDA's first proposed National Organic regulation, and left the National Organic Program staff shortly before the final rule was published. The story of this process, which consumed much of my life for five years, is interwoven here with the story of my movement along my own personal timeline before, during, and after this arduous federal process. It's the story of how the organic revolution became rooted well before the federal government cared to notice, and the personal, political, and practical struggles that ensued in the heroic effort to move it beyond farmers' markets and into supermarkets.

When I accepted a staff position with USDA's National Organic Program in 1994, Washington, D.C. was the last place on earth I expected to find myself. For over twenty years I had devoted my life to advocating for organic agriculture, most recently as editor of a fairly influential national publication called *Organic Farmer: The Digest of Sustainable Agriculture*. I had also earned part of my living for several years as a market gardener in Northeastern Vermont, which I've called home for over forty years now. One of my goals in taking on this work for the USDA was to help introduce more organic-friendly thinking within this huge bureaucracy, second only to the Pentagon in size. Never again, I swore, would an organic farmer walk into an Extension Service office and be scoffed at. Once this law was implemented, every federal agricultural agency would have to offer assistance, be it technical, marketing or financial, to producers interested in using organic methods. I saw the sanctioning of organic farming by its former arch-enemy as a turning point in the radical transformation of American agriculture. Naively ambitious as this goal might have been, it was, ironically enough, undermined in the end not so much by the barriers erected by a recalcitrant establishment, but by the community of organic activists themselves.

It took three years of almost superhuman effort after I joined the NOP staff for the USDA to finally publish a draft organic regulation, seven years after its authorizing legislation was enacted. The public responded to this proposed rule (which offered the first-ever opportunity to submit comments via the Internet) with a record-breaking number of negative comments. Reflecting the widespread belief that previously high organic standards had been corrupted by the agribusiness-dominated USDA, and that the proposal would allow organic food to be produced using genetically engineered seeds, irradiation, and sewage sludge, many of these comments were full of outrage and venomous anger.

The public response to our work, especially coming from some people I'd worked with closely over the years, disturbed me deeply. What really made me angry was my belief that organic advocates had subverted their own revolution; in the immortal words of Pogo, "We have met the enemy and it is us." The messages coming from many activists seemed contrary to the organic principles that we all claimed to espouse, and the demand that the standards must be as high as possible actually played into the likely agribusiness agenda of preventing organic agriculture from becoming any threat to business as usual by limiting it to a tiny niche market. This is the story behind the evolution of the USDA organic standards, what happened to derail them from reflecting organic principles, and what it will take to lead the American food system along a more organic path.

A central belief that has guided my journey is that the Great Transformation of our culture, society, and politics that is needed if we are to head off global catastrophe has already begun.[ii] The possibility of transforming American agriculture to predominantly organic methods can be a powerful force in improving the health of the whole planet, and the organic revolution is now in full bloom. But the vast majority of American agriculture is still dependent on environmentally destructive methods, which result in soil degradation, water depletion and pollution, the manufacture and dispersal of toxic substances, and wildlife habitat destruction, to name a few well-chronicled examples.[iii] Many of these practices, chief among them nitrogen fertilizer manufacture, result in the emission of a significant quantity of greenhouse gases. A study published in *Nature* in 2012 estimates that about one-third of all greenhouse gas emissions can be attributed to the global food system, of which "agricultural production provides the lion's share," according to its authors.[iv]

Given the well-documented benefits of organic production (which does not permit use of synthesized nitrogen fertilizer) for crucial planetary life-support systems like biodiversity, water quality, and carbon sequestration,[v] it seems that the transition of as many acres as possible as rapidly as possible to organic management is more urgent than ever. It is no longer, as many of us believed thirty or forty years ago, only about producing healthy, nourishing, nontoxic food using methods that protect the environment, grown as close as possible to where it will be consumed and readily available to all people. It is also about an eminently practical means of helping to reverse the momentum toward mass suicide on a scale not previously imagined, even at the height of Cold War fears of nuclear Armageddon.[vi]

So I have persisted in polishing this story, offered in the hope that the growing revolution in producing, preserving, and distributing food will continue picking up steam—without picking fights that could ultimately undermine its success.

## How Has the Story Evolved?

It has taken me endless soul searching to tell this story. Soon after my employment with the National Organic Program ended in the year 2000 I began working on telling the story of what had just transpired, giving it the title *The Organic Revolution*. It was a much different book than the one in front of you, full of philosophy, politics, and polemic. It was angry and more than a little bitter, born of my own need to set the record straight and chastise those who had got it all wrong.

I assumed that this story would readily be picked up by a mainstream publisher and find an eager mass audience as a result of the increased public attention to organic food once the USDA organic seal began to appear on grocery shelves. I quickly engaged an outstanding literary agent who specialized in environmental writing, and then won a spot in a free two-week writers retreat for environmental authors. An editor for a respected environmental publisher expressed strong interest, but it was later nixed by their marketing department—a scenario that was repeated several times with different potential publishers. After a few more fruitless efforts to place *The Organic Revolution*, my agent reluctantly gave up.

While working for the organic industry as a consultant for the ensuing decade, I continually encountered distorted misconceptions about how USDA had stolen organic from its rightful owners, and then watered down the standards at the behest of corporate agribusiness. As I gravitated more toward higher education, I found that students and young farmers who considered themselves food system activists had accepted these oft-repeated distortions as undisputed fact. Even respected academics who wrote articles and books about organic history and food politics repeated the same story, citing each other to support these "facts." In the midst of trying to counter the misinformation that was quickly becoming common knowledge, it was damn hard to concentrate on how to tell the story so it could be heard.

In 2010, still floundering for the right approach to present my message, I finally gave up on finding a publisher to take it on and decided that self-publishing was the route to pursue. I knew I needed an editor who had some familiarity with me and my quirky story. Someone who could understand how it felt to be perpetually swimming upstream, challenging conventional wisdom even among the unconventional minority. Of course, that could only be my dear friend and mentor Miranda Smith, to whom this book is dedicated. We had only a few months of working together before her untimely death, but thanks to Miranda's gentle urging and guidance, I was able to find my authentic voice and the confidence to use it.

The idea of telling the story in the form of a memoir was a great relief to the long-suffering members of my writers group. My new title, a double-entendre that would have made Miranda chuckle, was *Reclaiming the 'O' Word: Memoir of an Organic Revolutionary*. Finally getting the space from intense engagement with the ongoing organic controversies, and then finding the help I needed to polish and publish it, I was also advised to drop the somewhat cryptic main title. As I write this, in the final weeks before preparing the manuscript for publication, we have finally settled on *Organic Revolutionary: A Memoir of the Movement for Real Food, Planetary Healing, and Human Liberation* as a succinct encapsulation of the book's core message.

Today's young food activists and aspiring farmers often accept as a given that the organic label, now that it has been taken over by its former enemy, has lost its meaning. They believe that "industrial organic" is no better than conventional chemical-intensive agriculture, and that "local is the new organic." The "O" word, once verboten amongst agricultural policy makers, is now considered meaningless by those who were formerly its passionate advocates. How did this happen, and what can be done to move the organic revolution forward? How can I challenge the young activists' assumptions without defusing the passion and commitment of this burgeoning movement for real food? Why is this important? These questions (and a few others) have kept me determined to tell this story.

## What's Inside?

This book is organized to be roughly chronological, but the chapters follow a somewhat zigzag path through time. For this reason I have included some helpful reference guides up front. An acronym glossary will help in navigating the thicket of abbreviations and initials that seem to arise like black flies in Vermont in May. The accompanying timeline includes key events of both my personal story and the evolution of organic certification to serve as a reference while you're reading. The Appendices include a couple of the lengthier articles and documents that are pivotal to the story, as well as an annotated bibliography for those seeking more background on the subjects discussed.

Although this book is not intended to be an academic treatise, I have endeavored to provide sources in the endnotes for information that did not originate with me or come from personal notes and observations. Throughout the book I have included some more policy-heavy details that are offset as sidebars or text boxes. These are not essential to the story, but will interest those who are concerned with the devilish details of theories, laws, and regulations. If this is not you, feel free to skip over them. I have made every effort to relate events in which I participated as honestly as possible, but acknowledge that my own memories and interpretations of my experience are as subject to personal prejudices and beliefs as anyone's.

Please read this story with an open mind and open heart, and talk about it with your friends. May you follow your own path to a kind, healthy, and abundant future.

Organically yours,
Grace Gershuny

### ENDNOTES

i   2015 figures went up to $43.3 billion

ii   See Joanna Macy, *Active Hope* in Annotated Bibliography.

iii   See Gunnar Rundgren, *Global Eating Disorder* and Frances Moore Lappé & Joseph Collins, *World Hunger: 10 Myths*, 2nd ed. in Annotated Bibliography

iv   http://www.nature.com/news/one-third-of-our-greenhouse-gas-emissions-come-from-agriculture-1.11708 accessed December 9, 2015

v   See for example Rodale Institute's paper, "Regenerative Organic Agriculture and Climate Change" at http://rodaleinstitute.org/assets/RegenOrgAgricultureAndClimateChange_20140418.pdf accessed December 9, 2015

vi   Klein, Naomi. *This Changes Everything: Capitalism vs the Climate* (see Annotated Bibliography)

# UPDATE FOR THE SECOND EDITION — SUMMER 2017

In the two years since I finished writing *Organic Revolutionary*, a great deal has changed in the world at large as well as the world of alternative agriculture and organic food.

The 2016 election woke a lot of people up to the precarious times in which we live. The interrelated spectres of political upheaval, economic disintegration, and environmental deterioration offer few glimmers of hope. Many now believe that it is already too late to save "civilization as we know it," and our task must be to preserve cultural remnants in communities where people are able to procure the necessities of life without depending on the global supply chain.

Paradoxically, there are many signs of hope. The organic industry—including the number of new farmers and land under organic management—continues to grow. Retail organic sales approached $50 billion in 2016, and organic acreage finally reached 1 percent of US farmland. This growth has not been without some pain. Early in 2017 a widely publicized scandal involving freighter loads of fraudulently labeled "organic" feed grain was blamed for depressing organic farm prices and stalling transition plans on the part of midwestern grain growers, as well as giving ammunition to those who denounce the very concept of organic agriculture.

Among the more inspiring changes I have noticed recently is the increased visibility of people of color as leaders of the organic revolution. They are reclaiming their agricultural heritage, advocating for food justice, and organizing workers throughout the food system—among the lowest paid and most vulnerable to the depredations of political and climate chaos. This has underlined my long held belief that leadership must come from people generally characterized as "Global South," whether they are descendants of slaves in the Americas or indigenous communities fighting corporate land-grabs in Africa and Asia.

Other heartening developments relate to a perceptible increase in public awareness of the connection between how food is grown and climate change. Both the potential to draw down carbon from the atmosphere through the miracle of photsynthesis, and the elimination of synthetic nitrogen from our crop production toolkit are among the immediate benefits that even "industrial organic" offers. This message has become a focal point of the many conversations I have been having since publication of this book.

My own life has remained remarkably stable and intact, and for this foundation of community, abundant harvests, good health, and love I am eternally grateful.

After more than a year of running around the country, speaking to people at conferences, trade shows, small libraries and book stores, I have learned a ton. Connecting with people who share my concerns about what we are eating, how we are growing it, and the increasing incidence of climate-related disasters has fueled my sense of urgency about the need for the message of *Organic Revolutionary*.

I am grateful also for the opportunity to make these connections, whether in person or on-line through podcasts and webinars. Though my focus this year is now shifting to working more deeply on the local level with some remarkable people in this paradise that I am privileged to call home, I fully intend to continue reaching out to a wider audience for some time to come.

Please check out the various media and press appearances listed on www.organic-revolutionary.com, and read any blog posts that interest you. I will continue sending out occasional newsletters, and sound off on social media when the impulse strikes. If you feel inclined, do get in touch and ask to be on my email list.

I am always interested in what you are thinking, dear reader. What ideas do you take issue with, and what do you think I am not seeing? Please invite me to come to your community to talk about the history and promise of the organic revolution. I will do my best to get there.

With hope for a culture of regeneration,
Grace
Barnet, Vermont
September, 2017

# ORGANIC REVOLUTIONARY

# 1 How a City Girl Learned to Love the Dirt

*Everything is a circle. If you stay behind long enough, sooner or later you'll be ahead.* — Win Way[1]

In 1973, at the age of 23, I grew my first garden and discovered my life's work. I had just moved to a remote and beautiful community in Northeastern Vermont after spending a couple of years in an urban commune in Montreal, to which I had fled after graduating from college in New York City. The commune had fallen apart the previous winter, but now my dream of a land-based life where I could learn to grow healthy food, working with like-minded friends to build a better world, was about to be realized.

I moved to this remote and beautiful area to be with Tom, the man I loved. We married in April, and were able to come up with a down payment on an old farm house with a few acres of brushy, swampy land in the town of West Charleston. We moved in that June and wasted no time preparing the only piece of tillable land on our homestead to grow a garden. We hired a local farmer to plow and harrow the half-acre of fertile bottomland that was densely covered with a lush growth of witch grass. This tenacious plant—more accurately known as couch grass—spreads through tough underground rhizomes that sprout a new individual every inch or so of their length, punctuated by a sharp growing tip that can penetrate the most compacted soil. We spent the last two weeks of June furiously planting every inch of the half-acre plot, after raking out as much of the tangle of witch grass roots as we could and digging in a liberal amount of manure. Both physically exhausted and exhilarated by the effort, it felt like utopia was within reach.

That summer I witnessed the miracle of how healthy, vibrant vegetables could emerge from good soil, fertilized by love, sweat, and determination. Everything I had read about in old *Organic Farming & Gardening* magazines proved true; there was no turning back.

## From the Beginning

People often ask how I got involved with organic agriculture since I grew up in an urban environment in a family without any farming experience. My response usually begins with, "It seemed like the only reasonable thing to do at the time." Although my upbringing was mostly urban, my family heritage did include some episodes of yearning for rural independence.

My parents lived in Ozone Park in Queens, New York in 1949 when I was conceived, but packed up my sisters, then ages 11 and 13, to live in a small town just south of Albany, New York. My mother told me she believed that I wanted to be born in the country, but my father had also taken a civil service job that entailed helping adjust landowners' claims for building the New York State Thruway. We moved a little farther south, to a hamlet that is now a neighborhood of Kingston, New York, when I was still an infant. My earliest memories are of this bucolic village that butted up against a cow pasture and was situated down the road from a swimming area on a creek that once fed the Erie Canal. At some point we had a small patch of garden in one of the places we lived during our moving around, but it could not have been very interesting to me as it left no clear impression. For a few years my parents owned a dilapidated farmhouse and about forty acres of land near Lake Ontario in the town of Wolcott, New York; we visited only rarely, but I have often wished they had managed to keep it.

From a young age I wanted to be a scientist. While my playmates wanted dolls and nice clothes, I wanted a chemistry set and a microscope. Among my clearest recollections of elementary school was being asked during fourth or fifth grade what we wanted to be when we grew up. My answer was obvious, but the teacher prodded me to be more specific and asked, "What kind of scientist?" To which I declared, "A scientist of all sciences." With kind condescension, teacher assured me that this was not an option—one had to choose which branch of science to pursue. Specialization could not be avoided. My sense of shame at how presumptuous my goal was never left me, but neither did my sense that this was not only possible, but also necessary.

A tumultuous adolescence in the crucible of the 1960s in New York City derailed my scientific aspirations as much as did the specialization

The Gershuny family, 1959, Brockport, New York: (l-r) Mary, Lee, Grace, Roxanne, Eva (Hyman's mother), Hyman.

doctrine of the educational establishment. My childhood dream of attending the Bronx High School of Science was realized, but my dreams had meanwhile shifted to cultural and social glory in the theater. Always eclectic, my interests later moved toward media literacy and mass media's increasing domination of political discourse during my college years. The connection of mass marketing to the environmental ills of overconsumption appeared obvious. The part of me that loved academic pursuits was overcome by the bureaucratic anonymity of mass higher education; craving the practical, I eventually graduated from Queens College with a major in mass communications. After helping to 'liberate' the college television studio and produce our own reports from the radical front during the protests over the killings at Kent State, I was convinced that the way to save the world was to take over the mass media and change the cultural narrative of competitive consumerism. How that might happen, I didn't have a clue.

## Escape from the Big Apple

In 1971, soon after graduating from college, I awakened to the organic vision of dropping out of dependence on the corrupt "system" and working to heal the earth. Determined to escape New York and live with a group of kindred souls, I headed to Montreal to join a commune where some people I had met the previous summer lived. The Montreal Home for the Mentally Bewildered was where I learned to both cook and stretch food dollars; it's also where I began to learn about food production. Although I had participated in the first Earth Day demonstration in New York in 1970 and was outraged about pollution of all kinds, the connection between the environment and how our food is produced had never really entered my mind.

I soon got involved with the Montreal Natural Foods Coop, largely out of interest in the idea of coops and community ownership of resources. The Coop owned a van, and we would drive out to the rural Eastern Townships region of Quebec in search of fresh organic produce to sell to our customer owners. The Coop also had a pile of back issues of *Organic Farming & Gardening* magazine, the early Rodale flagship publication, which I quickly devoured. Articles that talked about the importance of soil microbiology and how pesticides and synthetic fertilizers damaged it made sense to me. My dormant scientific literacy and understanding of biology, now reawakened, conspired with my college training in deconstructing mass media hype to tune me in to the rip-off perpetrated by corporate fake food. Inspired by the information I found in the Rodale magazines and the emerging alternative press, I saw the increasing arsenal of poisons used to grow food, along with increased environmental exposure to toxic chemicals, as the culprits behind the growing epidemic of cancer and degenerative diseases.

Our house was an old Victorian charmer situated right on the McGill campus. Formerly known as the Crystal Palace for its meth freak inhabitants, it was now populated by an array of youth workers, mental health counselors, crafters, draft dodgers, and activists. Various friends came through, hung out, and sometimes moved in, while two stable couples emerged, both of whom recently celebrated their fortieth wedding anniversaries. Fifty dollars a month was requested of each inhabitant for rent and utilities, plus seven dollars a week for food, and there was always enough surplus remaining to throw a good party. It was here that I first heard of Murray Bookchin, who was to become a major influence in my life. A friend and housemate who went by the name of "cual," was pursuing a self-directed study of philosophy, and spoke glowingly in his Cuban accent of this guy—"Mooooree Boookchin"—whom he would love to meet. (More than a decade later I would actually meet Murray and begin to study his work.)

Tom Jensen showed up one day on a hardwood buying expedition with a friend of the house who had stayed with him in Vermont while resolving a minor pot bust. I was immediately drawn to his intelligence and kindness as well as his maturity, which was at a level well beyond what I had known with previous lovers.

Around the time we got our six-month notice that we would have to vacate our Montreal home to make way for a new physics building, I began thinking about moving to Vermont to pursue my dream of rural renaissance—and also to pursue Tom, who had recently visited again. A few of us were invited to the home of Dick Hinters, a housemate's former philosophy professor. In the course of the conversation Dick asked each of us to describe our vision of the kind of world we wanted to see, and the kind of work we wanted to do to bring it about. My own ideas were moving in the direction of organic farming and alternative energy and doing credible scientific work—but an expanded science that integrated non-rational modes of understanding nature and that didn't demand a disconnection of mind from body, intellect from emotion, or art from science. Dick immediately whipped out a brochure and handed it to me. It described an organization based on Cape Cod called New Alchemy Institute—one of the founders was his sister-in-law, Nancy Jack Todd. I devoured the little pamphlet, which spoke the same language I had used to express my dream. It was one of those cosmic moments when the next step in your path presents itself. I decided to pay them a visit before making my move to Vermont.

A couple of months later I was on a bus bound for Cape Cod, finally arriving in the town of Falmouth, Massachusetts where I was warmly welcomed by John and Nancy Todd. I only spent a few days at New Alchemy, helping count cabbage worms to evaluate the resistance of different varieties to the voracious little larvae, among other tasks. New Alchemy was a pioneer of what has become known as permaculture, a process of using ecological technologies to design efficient, beautiful, and productive human communities and landscapes based on rigorous scientific observations. John Todd, an oceanographer by training, developed the concept of a "living machine" to treat wastewater, and used the same principles to create integrated aquaculture-hydroponic vegetable production systems enclosed in greenhouses. Such a structure, attached to an energy-efficient dwelling, became known as an "ark." Wind and solar power, geodesic dome design, and other sophisticated

Montreal group portrait, 1971. Front (l-r): Su Baker, Grace Ger-shuny, Roberto (/cual) Delgado. Middle (l-r) Joan Chanin, Shelagh Johnson, Kevin O'Neil. Rear (l-r) Danny Lewis, Mary Ellen O'Neil, Philip Lepine.

technologies played a key role in ongoing research. The signature line in all their publications was "to restore the land, protect the seas, and inform the earth's stewards."

## Transplanted to Vermont with a Slight Detour

Much as the New Alchemy vision and fellowship appealed to me, I was already in love and planning a move to Vermont in the spring of 1973. But first, I had to take a slight detour to visit my parents in Israel. So what were my folks doing in Israel anyway? This was actually their second for-ay to the land of milk and honey, this time to retire and escape Brooklyn. They had made a previous attempt to flee the rat race (about which my father complained endlessly) in 1960 by picking up and moving from our home in Rochester, New York to a kibbutz on the Sea of Galilee when I was ten years old. This had little to do with Zionism and more to do with a parental longing for a cooperative lifestyle on the land. It was not an easy time for the prepubescent me or for my parents, who were quickly disillusioned and turned tail for the States a mere seven months later, landing in a decaying Bronx neighborhood with my Yiddish-speaking grandmother, fiftyish and unemployed—oy vey. However, the longing for

Cover, *Journal of the New Alchemists* #1, 1973

a cooperative lifestyle on the land inserted itself into my psyche, and like-ly helped to inspire my own escape to the commune in Montreal.

My father's quest was not a sudden inspiration either. In the 1930s he had been a follower of Ralph Borsodi, who was an early proponent of living cooperatively on the land as well as decentralism, social and economic justice, and the philosophical underpinnings thereof. Borsodi had started a community in New York State called The School of Living, which influenced the 60s back-to-the-land movement. I know that my dad had some ongoing contact with one of Borsodi's associates named Bob Swann, with whom he had apparently corresponded about his eco-nomic theories. But I never had much interest in my dad's crackpot ideas—at least not when he was around to lecture me about them.

It wasn't until much later in life, when I picked up a biography of the recently deceased Bob Swann, that my family connections became more meaningful. Swann, I learned, was a principled civil rights and peace ac-

Wedding ceremony, Newark, Vermont, April 1973. Tom Jensen, Grace Gershuny with Newark Town Clerk

tivist who, like Borsodi, was strongly influenced by Gandhi while studying in India. He co-founded the Schumacher Society (after Fritz Schumacher, author of *Small Is Beautiful*), based in Western Massachusetts, where he put many of Borsodi's economic ideas such as local currencies and land trusts into practice. I actually met Bob Swann and his partner Susan Witt in the 1980s in my capacity as NOFA Conference organizer. Swann inquired about my dad and asked me to give him his regards—but by this time dad had suffered a stroke and was never to tell me the story of that connection. Reading about Swann's life and work 20 years later gave me an eerie feeling of carrying out an inherited mission that had somehow been encoded in my genes, and yet one I felt I had come to completely on my own.

Their return to Israel in the 1970s was inspired less by visionary zeal and more by my parents' return to their religious roots, which I described by calling them born-again Jews. Being so far from her children was tough on my mother, though, and after five years in the promised land they returned to Brooklyn. Staying in the city to be close to one of my sisters was not an option for them, and my eldest sister was now living in Hawaii with her professor husband and three small children—just too far from the rest of the family. So in 1976 they decided to flee New York for the last time and settle near me, the baby of the family, who was now living out their long-deferred dream.

After that detour to see my parents, I moved in with Tom Jensen in tiny Newark, Vermont in early April of 1973 to begin my own quest for a cooperative lifestyle on the land. Tom's landlady had just decided to renovate the house and seek a higher class of tenants, so we began hunting for another place to live. Tom, who was a childhood polio victim and needed crutches to navigate, finally decided to apply for disability through Social Security (though I always felt that he was one of the least disabled people I knew). His lump sum award for retroactive benefits, combined with my parents' offer of $1,000 if we got married, gave us enough to consider becoming property owners.

The Newark Town Clerk and Justice of the Peace married us a couple of weeks later, and we had just enough for a down payment on a ramshackle old farmhouse about ten miles away in West Charleston, on the banks of the Clyde River. The house was a late 1800s vintage patched-together affair, with an old wood furnace in the dirt-floored basement. Its most attractive feature was the attached garage and barn, all connected so we could avoid having to walk outdoors in winter. It would make a perfect shop area for Tom's business of making hand-carved rosewood dope pipes, and had great potential as a future furniture shop, not to mention barn dances. It needed just a bit of work to be usable.

When we moved in that June we had a half-acre of bottomland plowed and harrowed for a garden—the only reasonably tillable chunk of the seven scrubby, swampy acres wedged between the road and the river that came with the house. Using only shovels, rakes, and hoes, we got the whole garden planted in about two weeks, and I lost about 35 pounds in the course of the season. The growing conditions that summer were close to ideal—hot sunny days and an abundance of rainfall, mostly at night. The combination of freshly tilled sod (a blessing for fertility, a curse for weeds), a good load of cow manure, and our beginner's enthusiasm resulted in an incredible abundance of everything we planted—and I was totally hooked. No doubt we made many silly mistakes that year, but the bounty of my first garden seemed miraculous.

I quickly realized, however, that one could only put up so much of that bounty for the winter, and I tried all the homestead food preservation methods I could. Radishes were one crop we just had too much of—the book we consulted suggested planting them around every squash hill to repel pests. So we had a great many radishes, which I began taking to local country stores in hopes of selling the surplus. It got to the point where they would see me coming and exclaim loudly, "No thanks—we don't need any more radishes!"

The garden was on a well-traveled paved road so our efforts were highly visible in the community. I soon gained a reputation as a knowledgeable gardener, trading advice and experiences with other newcomers in the neighborhood and learning all I could from the local old-timers who found our interest in the old fashioned ways of doing things so amusing. A few miles up the road was a commune called Frog Run Farm, founded by Robert and Mary Houriet. Robert, previously a journalist and political activist, wrote a book called *Getting Back Together* about the country commune movement which inspired quite a few people to come to Vermont and get back to the land. On the strength of my apparent gardening proficiency, he urged me to help organize a farmers market in the nearby town of Newport.

Robert was involved with a loosely organized group of organic farming advocates called the Natural Organic Farmers Association (NOFA), which had secured a small grant to seed similar markets around Vermont. I had been working as a legal secretary for most of the previous year and was confident about my ability to get along with the local establishment. I also had some administrative skills—an important quality for a community organizer. It seemed like a logical step to take, given my frustrated efforts to sell my surplus radishes.

NOFA had its beginnings in the early 1970s, around the same time as New Alchemy, the Institute for Social Ecology in Plainfield, Vermont, and a number of other groups that sought to create positive alternatives to the prevailing system—one whose imminent collapse we were all anticipating, especially after the energy crisis so clearly pointed to the folly of a petroleum-dependent economy. Located mainly in the Northeast and on the West Coast, these groups were, by and large, founded by urban émigrés who shared a passion for the earth and simple living, laced with a strong dose of 60s radicalism.

Early NOFA organizers aimed to distribute produce from organic farmers in Vermont and New Hampshire to activists and food coops in northeastern cities. This entailed costly and time-consuming truck routes to pick up a case of broccoli here and some carrots there, and barely paid the cost of delivery for products of very questionable quality—when payment was even involved. Jake Guest, one of the earliest growers, then based at Wooden Shoe Farm in New Hampshire, tells a story about a load of Chinese cabbage bound for Chinatown in New York City that ends, "That not cabbage, that garbage!" It didn't take too long or too many truck breakdowns to convince the guys (and it was primarily guys at that time) that this was not exactly sustainable.

Despite the prevailing distrust of the profit motive, the more serious growers quickly learned that you can't make a living growing vegetables—you have to sell them. A change of strategy was clearly called for, and the group quickly adopted a new mission of "local food for local markets." The focus would now be on revitalizing agriculture and helping the predominantly dairy farmers in our region diversify by initiating farmers markets and wholesale grower cooperatives. Quite a bit of research and analysis went into discussions about the feasibility of eating more locally and seasonally, along with despair over the lack of infrastructure for accomplishing that goal.

The resurgence of farmers markets in the 70s and 80s is one of the success stories of the early alternative agriculture movement. Farmers markets were at first viewed with suspicion by conservative local merchants, who feared that they would take business away from established grocery stores. "We don't want that kind of people hanging around in public areas," was the response I got in 1975 when I set out to organize a farmers market in Newport, Vermont, about twelve miles from our home. We contented ourselves with a less central location in the neighboring hamlet of Derby, with support from a sympathetic merchant. For two or three years we had only a handful of vendors, including crafts and baked goods. I was the largest produce grower, generating almost $400 from my half-acre garden in my best season—enough to pay the taxes, anyway.

Eventually we were allowed to hold a one-day harvest festival in the Newport town park; it was so successful that the regular Saturday market was relocated there the following year. A VISTA worker (now known as the AmeriCorps program) was later hired to help develop the market and recruit more vendors. More than 35 years later that market is still thriving, touted by the business community as a cultural asset that draws summer visitors into town. Today more than 40 regular farmers markets are established throughout Vermont, with some now operating year round. Similar patterns have been repeated all over the country. The number of farmers markets in the United States has grown steadily from 1,755 markets in 1994, when USDA began to track them, to 8,268 in 2014. There is even a weekly farmers market held in the USDA parking lot in Washington, DC.[2]

## The Roots of the True Organic Vision

To see how this vision grew into the modern organic movement, it may be helpful to review American and European history with this topic in mind. While I read many of the "classics" of organic thought during my early years in Vermont, I didn't fit the pieces together until my involvement deepened and I began teaching about the subject. The excursion that follows offers my own interpretation and selection of events and actors that has helped me to place my own experience in its historical context.

Many people assume that the organic movement had its start with Rachel Carson and the environmental movement of the 60s that inspired farmers to "just say no" to pesticides. The activist uprisings of the 1960s certainly gave rise to the modern organic movement, but the birth of what became known as *organic farming* really occurred in response to the first widespread use of synthetic fertilizers in the early part of the 20th century.

Most of the foundational organic innovators came from Europe, where concerns about the effects of using synthesized chemicals to fertilize crops sprouted a short time after they started being promoted. Around the end of World War I the munitions manufacturers found themselves with large stockpiles of explosives on hand. The Haber process, developed by German scientists, had introduced a cheap technology for manufacturing nitrate-based compounds by using natural gas to turn stable atmospheric nitrogen into ammonia. Although the work of the chemist Justus Von Liebig, a contemporary of Darwin, had been known for some time, up until then it had attracted little commercial interest. Von Liebig demonstrated that plant growth rates could be dramatically increased by adding certain chemical nutrients in synthetic salt form to greenhouse pots. Farmers had long used wood ashes (or pot ash, from which the word potassium comes), crushed bones (high in phosphorus) and, of course, livestock manure (rich in nitrogen) on their cropland, without knowing the scientific explanation for what they were doing. With the advent of cheap synthetic nitrogen and a surplus of it on hand in the form of dynamite, the weapons makers continued the age-old tradition of transferring military technologies to food production. Thus was born the synthetic fertilizer industry.

Although many farmers understood that it was a bad idea to only use synthetic plant nutrients instead of plant- and animal-based fertilizer materials, the results of doing so were too tempting to resist. In place of the backbreaking work of shoveling out stables and barns, loading a wagon and then shoveling it out again in the field, you could just buy a few bags of nitrate fertilizer, sprinkle it over the soil or rig up a device to mix it in with grain seeds during planting, and stand back and watch the crops grow.

A few scientists, including Von Liebig, were not convinced that artificial fertilizers were an unmitigated good. The value of recycling organic materials as a foundation for long term soil health was extensively documented in the early 1900s by F.H. King, head of the USDA's Division of Soil Management. King had traveled through Asia to observe the methods used to maintain highly productive agriculture in the region over the course of 4,000 years, which he described in the landmark work, *Farmers of Forty Centuries*. The multiple benefits of soil humus were well known in Europe, although the central role of soil life in transforming raw organic matter into humus, releasing plant nutrients in the process, was little understood. Darwin had lauded the earthworm as a creator of soil fertility, but little was known about soil microbiology or the devastating effects of high doses of artificial salt fertilizers on soil organisms. Continued use of such fertilizers in place of organic materials clearly resulted in diminished soil humus levels, and some observant farmers reported declines in seed viability and animal reproductive health along with it.

In 1924 a group of farmers in the German state of Silesia got together and asked the renowned seer Rudolph Steiner what to do to counteract the deterioration of crop and livestock health quality that they were observing, which they attributed to the increasing use of artificial fertilizers in place of manure and other organic fertilizers. Steiner obliged them by offering a series of lectures which were transcribed into a small book entitled, *Agriculture*. This marked the origins of the Biodynamic school of agriculture, which remains a highly influential stream of organic agricultural theory and practice.

Steiner was heavily influenced by the German poet and philosopher Johann Wolfgang von Goethe, especially his treatises on botany and the natural sciences. Goethe taught with a holistic viewpoint that emphasizes observation of organisms within their natural context, as opposed to laboratory analysis.[3] Steiner's lectures to the farmers, which are dense with esoteric terminology, draw connections between cosmic forces represented by various planets and the qualities imparted to plants by corresponding minerals. These, he said, play a major role in crop quality (including aroma, flavor, and nutrition, among other things), which is very hard to measure, as opposed to quantity or mass, which is the only factor that is positively affected by synthetic fertilizers. High nitrate fertilization is known to correspond with increased water uptake by crops (and thus increased yields), but correspondingly lower dry matter content—the part with the nutrients.

Steiner also emphasized that farms must be viewed as single organisms, and that all life on the planet forms a single whole that is influenced in countless ways by subtle cosmic forces. One of his *Agriculture* lectures is devoted to detailed instructions for making preparations for the purpose of inoculating compost with the appropriate living energy. Use of these compost preparations, made from various combinations of specific herbs, minerals (particularly silica in the form of ground quartz), and animal parts (such as cow horns and stag bladders), buried or cured in specific ways, form the basis for the current practice of Biodynamic agriculture.[4]

After his death in 1925, Steiner's influence spread throughout Europe and the German fascists, as devotees of esoteric nature mysticism, readily embraced his teachings. This admiration was not mutual for most of Steiner's students, however, many of whom fled the Nazi regime for North and South America as well as Asia and Australia. Among them was Ehrenfried Pfeiffer who came to the US in the late 1930s and helped found the Biodynamic Farming & Gardening Association, living and working for many years at the Anthroposophic[5] community Threefold Farm in Spring Valley, New York.

Although Steiner and his students were the first Europeans to systematize a holistic response to the advent of chemical-intensive agriculture, it is Sir Albert Howard, a British agronomist, who is considered the "father" of modern organic farming. He wasn't the first to use that term, but he was the first to identify the fundamental organic principles and practices, such as the "Law of Return" on the necessity of returning nutrients and organic materials to the soil to compensate for their removal in crops. Much of his work was based on research and observations in India in the 1930s and 1940s, where he was stationed for 26 years in the service of the Empire. Sir Albert later made a point of crediting the Indian peasant farmers with whom he worked for teaching him about their soil improvement practices, including how they made compost by piling different kinds of organic wastes in alternating layers and periodically turning to introduce air. Known as the "Indore" method for the region in India where he learned it, this approach to compost making has become the hallmark of organic practices on both the garden and farm level.

Other examples of indigenous cultures that practiced sophisticated forms of agriculture abound. The organic playbook has borrowed liberally from ancient folk wisdom, including the Asian peasants studied by F.H. King and the Central American chinampas—fertile islands surrounded by complex aquaculture systems. In recent years, anthropologists have rediscovered several more examples of sophisticated ecologically adapted agricultural systems that existed for centuries in the Americas before European conquest.[6] Ancient cultures have also perpetrated some ecologically disastrous farming systems, but the point here is that our revered organic forebears owed much to indigenous ingenuity, coupled with the tools of skilled scientific observation. Europeans may have been the first to articulate the basic precepts of organic methods, but these ideas have found fertile soil to grow into robust movements here in the New World.

Just as the brilliance of indigenous knowledge—the original agricultural revolutionaries—is rarely credited by mainstream agriculture, the contributions made by non-European immigrants to the Americas are often overlooked. Forced migrants, in particular descendants of African slaves such as George Washington Carver, Booker T. Whately, Fannie Lou Hamer and Shirley and Charles Sherrod, practiced and taught improved crop breeding, food sovereignty, and cooperative land management well before the movement that identified itself as "organic" came along.

North America's most influential evangelist of organic farming and gardening was undoubtedly J.I. Rodale, founder of the highly successful publishing company that bears his name. Rodale Press has cranked out a continuous supply of information on the subject since 1942, when the first issue of *Organic Farming & Gardening* magazine was produced, with Sir Albert Howard as Associate Editor. Rodale's contribution to popularizing and disseminating this material, at a time when the promise of "better living through chemistry" was the central principle of the agricultural establishment, has been enormous. While Howard was no fan of

Biodynamics, Rodale was also strongly influenced by Ehrenfried Pfeiffer, whom Rodale visited on several occasions.

J.I. Rodale was both a savvy businessman and a committed seeker of optimum health who was often characterized as a fanatic and worse. Born into an immigrant Jewish family in New York City, young Jerome was by all accounts rather puny and lacking in self-confidence. His focus on the connection between agriculture and health was unfortunately not bolstered by his sudden death of a heart attack while appearing on the Dick Cavett show.

J.I.'s son Robert succeeded him at the helm of the company and initiated a number of worthwhile projects, some of which were well ahead of their time. One such project was the establishment of the well-respected non-profit research farm and institute near Rodale's Emmaus, Pennsylvania headquarters. It was Bob Rodale who sought to popularize the term "regenerative" agriculture in place of "organic." While the idea had some merit, the word just didn't work as a marketing term. Bob was tragically killed in a car accident in Russia in 1990 while working on a joint publication with Russian sustainable agriculture leaders. The Rodale business continues to be family owned and managed and, while the research farm has maintained its standing as a cutting edge scientific institute, the publishing company today betrays little evidence of its agricultural origins, describing itself as "home to some of the most successful and well-regarded health and wellness brands," whose mainstay publications include *Men's Health* and *Prevention*.[7]

Rodale's forte has been in the realm of research and education, but the Rodale enterprise contributed little to expanding the availability of organically produced foods beyond the home gardener. It was entrepreneur Paul Keene, another Pennsylvania-based organic pioneer, who became the first retailer of organic food by founding the mail order company Walnut Acres.

Keene, who died in 2005 at the age of 94, had been a pacifist with a master's degree in mathematics from Yale. He worked as a teacher in India in the late 1930s, where he learned about both Sir Albert Howard and Mohandas Gandhi. After studying at Gandhi's village training school, Keene got involved with the Indian independence movement and traveled for a while with Gandhi's disciple Vinoba Bhave. Returning to the States, he and his wife worked with economist Ralph Borsodi and his associate Bob Swann, whose influence on my own family and journey was noted earlier. After another stint of study, this time with Ehrenfried

Pfeiffer (Steiner's student) at Kimberton Hills Farm, a Pennsylvania bio-dynamic community, the Keenes bought the Walnut Acres farm in Penns Creek, Pennsylvania in 1946 and soon started selling organic apple butter and then peanut butter via mail order. Today Walnut Acres exists only as one of the many brands owned by the Hain Celestial Group, having been sold to that large natural foods distributor in 2003.

"Natural foods" and "health food" are terms that represent the whole purpose of organic agriculture for many, and theories about what constitutes a healthy diet have accompanied the organic movement from the start. The connection between soil health and human and animal health was central to Sir Albert Howard's work, and is similarly emphasized by the biodynamic movement. Indian culture considers food and medicine to be virtually the same; this holistic understanding of the relationship between how food is grown and its nutritional—even spiritual and certainly energetic—qualities continues to be a prime motivator for people concerned about diet and health. The historical movements and theories that are woven together with these concepts form the fabric from which the modern organic movement emerged. The theme of health reappears continually in any discussion of organic philosophy. A universal constant that seems to unite organic farmers and devotees of the new foodie culture is that we all care—and care a lot—about food.

Many early organic advocates started out with the assumption that the only way to obtain a reliable supply of good wholesome food without a trust fund was to grow it ourselves. Early advocates of the nutrition and the health benefits of whole, unrefined foods who also spoke up about the dangers of petrochemically derived food additives comprise another key stream of influence, and their modern counterparts are key to fanning consumer support for the expanding organic market. Authors and scientists such as Weston Price, Adele Davis, Beatrice Trum Hunter, and many others have contributed solid, practical information about why and how to consume the most healthful "nutrient dense" diet. Michio Kushi, founder of the macrobiotic approach, as well as other advocates of vegetarian diets also influenced many aspiring organic practitioners and eaters. The conversation about what constitutes the most healthful diet is interesting and at times heated. While my own food preferences tend towards homegrown omnivore, I firmly believe that everyone has different dietary needs, and the tendency to equate certain food choices with moral superiority (or delinquency) is more than a tad offensive. So I won't get into that discussion here, except to note that some tendency towards "food fascism" is not a big surprise given where the movement comes from.

## Organic's Little-Known Eco-Fascist Roots

The first organic-identified organization was The Soil Association, founded in 1946 by Sir Albert Howard and his friend, Lady Eve Balfour, author of *The Living Soil*. The word "organic" was advocated by another Brit, Lord Walter Northbourne, who described a holistic concept in which the farmer serves as a coordinator of diverse elements of a self-regulating farming system, so as to optimize the cycling of nutrients. It is worth noting that this is not just about the "natural" source of farm inputs, as 21st century organic promoters have led many to believe.

The clash between the emerging "industrial" approach to agriculture and the ideas of Steiner, Howard, and others had political and social implications that were certainly known to early organic theorists. The social aspects of the organic concept were not given much prominence by its founders, but organic farming has never just been about a technological or scientific distinction (just as all technological revolutions have also been profoundly social and political). The social and political context of the early organic movement, and its connection to fascist ideology, is chronicled by Philip Conford in *The Origins of the Organic Movement*.

Among the more persistent myths of the current organic scene is the notion that the modern organic movement sprang from a strictly left-progressive political philosophy. While partially true, it is a mistake to believe that the political left has any claim to ownership of the organic project, or that organic agriculture (or any green technology, for that matter) is inherently politically correct. Rather, the thinking that shaped the organic vision can be traced to both left-wing and right-wing ideologies, and it is apparently the right wing that informed the first consciously organic advocates in Europe. As laid out in excruciating detail by Conford, many of the founders of the Soil Association, with the exception of a few like Sir Albert Howard, were avowed fascists who supported Hitler and Mussolini before these dictators became enemies of the British state.

Steiner's followers in Europe, primarily Germany and Austria, were similarly not all repulsed by the Nazi embrace. Anthroposophy, the spiritual credo founded by Steiner and the basis for his agricultural instructions, "had a powerful practical influence on the so-called 'green wing' of German fascism," according to Social Ecologist Peter Staudenmaier.[8] It was largely, he suggests, through biodynamic agriculture that this influence occurred. The well-known Nazi slogan, "Blood and Soil," was the rallying cry of this green wing, which held that "environmental purity was inseparable from racial purity."

It should go without saying (but still must be said) that none of this means that practitioners of Biodynamic agriculture or avowed Anthroposophists are really fascists at heart. As acknowledged by Staudenmaier and consistent with my own experience, most of those who today espouse Biodynamics, and certainly those who practice its methods without endorsing its religious aspects, tend to be politically liberal, open-minded, and compassionate folks. But I cannot help but shudder at the common emphasis on purity[9] amongst some organic true believers. The enthusiasm of some of the right-wing organic crowd in the US for Biodynamics and its array of mysterious cosmic forces can give one pause as well. We would all do well to acknowledge our ambiguous and not always high-minded histories.

Political and social tributaries of the modern organic movement in North America also spring from some peculiarly American forms of religious fundamentalism and anti-intellectual (i.e., Eastern liberal, often Jewish) sentiment. The Jeffersonian agrarian ideal of the yeoman farmer, as eloquently conveyed by Wendell Berry in *The Unsettling of America*, represents a romantic note that has inspired much of the back to the land movement, myself among them, but that also appeals to the logic of "Blood and Soil." There continues to be a fine line between a heartfelt spiritual reverence for Nature idealized in many forms of new age thought and a tendency toward xenophobic and dogmatic "one and only true way" belief systems.

The populist movement of the late 19th and early 20th century is among the most significant political contributors to the American alternative agriculture stream. One of the best sources for the left-progressive view of this history is *The Corporate Reapers*, a collection of essays by Al Krebs, a founder of the Agribusiness Accountability Project. The democratic, egalitarian ideals of early prairie populism gave rise to a strong rural cooperative movement, state-owned grain elevators and banks (including the sole surviving example in North Dakota), and some of the more constructive farm policies of the New Deal. While Krebs argues convincingly that it was not originally racist or anti-Semitic, the populist movement

eventually was either killed off by World War I era "red scares" or captured by the Democratic Party under the "silverist" William Jennings
Bryan, a great orator famous for his opposition to the teaching of evolution in the Scopes "Monkey Trial."

It is hardly surprising that this strain of agrarianism—which opposes
the capitalist moneyed establishment—has inspired converts to organic
approaches to farming in the mid-20th century. Some of the most respected American organic pioneers emerged from this background, including
the publishers of and many contributors to the influential Kansas City-
based publication, *Acres, USA*, which began publishing in the early 70s
when the modern organic movement was emerging. The populist impulse is also the wellspring of some more sinister organic advocates, including militant neo-Nazi survivalist groups, anti-immigrant vigilantes,
and conspiracy theorists. Among the conspirators in the 1995 Oklahoma
City bombing (in which the explosive material was a synthetic nitrogen
fertilizer) was an organic farmer from Michigan, profiled in Michael
Moore's documentary *Bowling for Columbine*.

## Socialist and Gandhian Influences

Prairie populism was also strongly influenced by socialist writers and organizers, in an era that predated Soviet-style communism. Prince Petr
Kropotkin, calling himself an anarcho-communist, addressed agrarian
issues in tracts such as *The Conquest of Bread*. Kropotkin called for decentralized production of the basic necessities of life, so that staple foods
should be grown close to where they are consumed with only a modest
amount of trade for products that will not grow in a given region. Perhaps the detractors of the first farmers markets in Vermont, who accused
these efforts of being communist, were not as wacky as we thought back
in the 70s.

There were quite a few respectable mainstream leaders who openly identified as socialists in the first decades of the 20th century, some
of whom exerted real influence on US farm policy. The first author to
earn the title of "muckraker" was Upton Sinclair, whose 1906 exposé of
the horrific, unsanitary conditions in the meatpacking industry in *The
Jungle*[10] led directly to the first federal food safety regulations. Oversight
of food safety for livestock, poultry, and dairy products remains to this
day the responsibility of the USDA's Food Safety and Inspection Service

(FSIS), rather than the more recently created Food & Drug Administration (FDA). Sinclair was an avowed socialist, who at one point ran unsuccessfully for Governor of California and was involved in organizing the socialist reform movement called End Poverty in California.

The origins of the Progressive Party have more to do with Theodore Roosevelt's zeal for conservation than with what is today considered progressive politics, but its agrarian-friendly motif has carried over into the present—never mind that traditional conservationists have often been at odds with those concerned with farming. Henry Wallace, who served as FDR's Secretary of Agriculture and then Vice President, later ran for the presidency against Truman on the Progressive Party ticket. Wallace tried to push US agriculture in a more progressive direction, most notably through the first Agricultural Adjustment Act in 1933, which later morphed into the legislative monstrosity called the Farm Bill. While he was not "out" as a socialist, Wallace's disillusionment with the conservative direction of the Democratic Party led him to help revive the Progressive Party, which at various times advocated government ownership of utilities, labor and civil rights, and curbs on monopolies. Some say that his dismal loss to Truman in 1948 was largely due to the Progressive Party's acceptance of support from the Communist Party.[11]

Wallace was also a complex character, who made a fortune as a corn geneticist and founder of the Pioneer-HiBred Corn Company, now owned by DuPont and one of the major developers and promoters of genetically modified seeds. However, the foundation he created with shares of his company's stock has been a key funder of organic and sustainable agriculture work, including the Wallace Institute for Alternative Agriculture founded by Dr. Garth Youngberg, who was the first USDA organic coordinator before the Reagan administration eliminated the position. A similar interest in supporting sustainable agriculture initiatives is found in the foundation endowed in the mid-20th century by W.K. Kellogg, who advocated for the health benefits of whole grains and developed the concept of processing corn into a wildly popular breakfast cereal.

The economic depression of the 1930s coincided with a devastating drought that etched the Dust Bowl in our collective memory, and gave rise to the agricultural reforms advanced by figures such as Henry Wallace. Many recognize the Depression era back-to-the-land movement, the source of some classic homesteading and self-sufficiency treatises, as the basis for the rural renaissance of the 1960s. Scott and Helen Nearing are icons of the modern back-to-the-land movement, revered as models of simple living and self-sufficiency. Their chronicles of building stone houses, eating a vegetarian diet, and living lightly on the land, starting in 1932 in Southern Vermont and later in Maine, were part of the canon of the 60s urban émigrés. Both of the Nearings came from privileged backgrounds and chose a radically different path. Scott lost his faculty position at the prestigious Wharton School of Business of the University of Pennsylvania as a result of his outspoken pacifist and socialist beliefs, including anti-war activism during the First World War. Helen was brought up as a Theosophist (a philosophy closely related to Steiner's Anthroposophy), and was for a time the companion of the renowned "anti-guru" philosopher Krishnamurti. She also maintained ties to Buddhist teachings throughout her life, in addition to her support for Scott's regular writing and lecturing on radical politics.

Ralph Borsodi, whose name inspires puzzled inquiry rather than reverence among most of my contemporaries, has been called the greatest unsung hero of the counterculture movement. The importance of Gandhian thought and practice to the organic movement cannot be overestimated. Like Paul Keene, Borsodi and his associate Bob Swann were also inspired by experiences with Gandhi's disciple Vinoba Bhave. Swann developed the concept of the community land trust modeled after Vinoba's Gramdan villages that were created from land donated by wealthy Indians to be worked cooperatively by the impoverished.

This is of course only a sample of the authors and visionaries who influenced me as I began this journey. The seeds they sowed were rooted in the soil of my own upbringing to propel me forward into the germinating modern organic movement.

## The Sprouting of the Organic Movement

This brings us up to the time of Rachel Carson and the beginning of the environmental movement. As there's no need for me to retell this well-known story here, we'll note the incredible reach of her work and move on to a major influence on my own thinking who also wrote about the problems of contaminated food, air, and water a little while before Carson's *Silent Spring* was released. He was a fellow by the name of Murray Bookchin, about whom I first heard when I lived in Montreal. Writing under the pen name of Lewis Herber, Bookchin published *Our*

*Synthetic Environment* in early 1962. He later teamed up with a young graduate student by the name of Dan Chodorkoff to found the Institute for Social Ecology in Plainfield, Vermont in 1974, forging a new understanding of the relationship between the environmental problems identified in his visionary work and the social ills long decried by Marxists and other political activists.

Once the environmental harm done by modern agricultural chemistry and the injustice of poverty, racism, and violence intersected in the seedbed of the civil rights, environmental, and anti-war movements—to say nothing of the fecundity and creativity of the 60s youth culture—the agricultural and social alternatives seeded by the figures we've met here (and others, to be sure) began to germinate and emerge almost overnight. While there were many motivations for going back to the land, the organizers of the first modern organic groups, at least those on the East and West coasts, emerged from these liberatory movements.

The story is a bit different in the heartland, where the prairie populist-inspired contingent generally eschewed the organic title in favor of "eco-agriculture," and laced their rhetoric with Bible quotes and tirades against eastern bankers and federal bureaucrats. Among the more complex and colorful characters central to the Midwestern alternative agriculture movement was Chuck Walters. Coming from a Kansas farm background, Walters did editorial work for the National Farmers Organization before founding the monthly tabloid *Acres, USA: A Voice for Eco-Agriculture*. Galvanized by Rachel Carson's revelations, Walters "realized how the methodical cheating of small farmers and the enforced swing toward chemical agriculture were gears in the same machine, working in tandem to transform the countryside."[12]

Many of us learned a huge amount through Walters' efforts. Writing in the early 90s, I characterized Walters' tone as "conservative, frankly Christian, anti-Eastern intellectual polemic that makes a lot of us leftish intellectual types uncomfortable." Some of the issues we first read about in the pages of *Acres, USA* included: warnings of global climate shift; destruction of tropical rainforests; the dangers of biotechnology, water fluoridation, mercury amalgam fillings, food irradiation, fossil water depletion; milk pasteurization; hemp legalization; farmers alcohol; free trade; and, of central concern, farm debt, the fight for parity pricing, and economics in general.

## What Does 'Organic' Mean on a Jar of Dilly Beans?

I devoured the words of many of these authors during my first few years in Vermont as I was learning to grow food and became engaged in farmers market organizing. The connections between agriculture, economics, and politics that started coming into focus during my time with the commune in Montreal now expanded more deeply into the soil of my community as I got involved with a new cannery project.

A church foundation funded a project in the mid-70s to set up community canning centers in three different parts of Vermont. The Northeast Kingdom—the area defined by the three northeastern counties, then and still the poorest and most rural part of the state—was identified as one cannery site. A number of food coop members and anti-poverty workers in the town of Barton formed a cannery organizing committee. The object was to develop some kind of commercial value-added product, and then make the small commercial-scale food processing equipment available to local low-income residents to preserve their home garden produce when it was not being used in the enterprise. The cannery was a forerunner of those now widespread incubator facilities, which lease space and food processing equipment to start-up food business entrepreneurs, and was a project that was way ahead of its time. Since high-acid foods such as pickles and fruit are less problematic (and expensive) to process safely than are low-acid staples like corn and spinach, the committee decided on commercial production of three products—pickled beets, apple rosehip butter, and dilly beans—to be sold at upscale gourmet outlets in major cities as organic products. With the addition of funding for a few staff positions through a federal jobs program, the Northeast Kingdom Cooperative Cannery was born.

I was hired to oversee garden production for the beans and beets. The apples and rosehips were all collected from the wild—mostly from overgrown pastures and random trees along some of the prettiest roads imaginable. The garden was a piece of run-down hayfield at Michael and Lisa Weiss' Valhalla Farm in South Albany, Vermont. They had a load of fresh chicken manure dumped and spread on roughly an acre of the field before plowing and harrowing it.

This was a very different kind of experience from my few seasons of tending a home market garden. Though the yield was satisfactory and the work satisfying, the marketing end of things made me think more about what "organic" really meant on that dilly bean label.

If it only meant that no chemical pesticides or herbicides and no synthetic fertilizers were used, we clearly met that standard. But to me this wasn't enough. I thought (still think) that organic should be defined by positive values—what it is that's good, not what it isn't that's bad. And I also understood that "organic by neglect" was not acceptable—just because the apples and rosehips were not being sprayed or fertilized doesn't mean they were any better than orchard-grown fruit, and could actually be of poorer quality. I also didn't really like the term "organic" to describe this kind of agriculture, since the really bad stuff—pesticides and plastic in particular—are categorized scientifically as "organic" compounds. This just means that they contain carbon atoms, generally obtained from a petrochemical refinery.

In my quest to learn to grow the best food I could, I was reading about soil fertility, especially Sir Albert Howard's *The Soil and Health*, and learning what was considered beneficial versus harmful from the organic viewpoint. As I understood it, leaving aside the energy consumption question, raw manure—especially raw chicken manure—is almost as bad for the soil as synthetic nitrogen fertilizer. Both raw manure and synthetic fertilizers release a lot of soluble nitrogen into the soil, which suppresses soil microbes. This is one of the key precepts that differentiate organic from conventional agriculture. The billions of microorganisms that live in every cubic inch of healthy soil are the true source of its fertility, depended upon by organic farmers to feed their crops.

Each type of microbe performs a different function and, as is true of every ecosystem, the waste of one becomes the next one's dinner. Certain soil-dwelling microbes have the ability to break down complex protein molecules into simpler compounds, including soluble nitrates, which they release into the soil at a gradual pace as they reproduce and die. But when these organisms encounter a high concentration of nitrate they shut down; for them it's akin to drowning in excrement. Given constant assaults of this sort they can disappear entirely, leaving biologically dead soil that is dependent on a continual fix of drugs to support a crop. This flush of soluble nitrogen also can end up polluting the water, and while it may make plants grow bigger faster, they will be more susceptible to pests and diseases.

This was the beginning of my lifelong passion for soil—the AHA! moment when my life's mission came into focus. While the true organic vision begins with the soil, it doesn't end there. It became even clearer to me after studying the science of soil that how soil is managed (or mismanaged) affects so much more than how much product can be extracted from it. After reading Wendell Berry and Frances Moore Lappé I began to understand that how we treat soil is not a function of lack of knowledge, but of social, political, and especially economic factors that demand exploitation of the earth and most humans for the sake of enriching a privileged few. Protecting soil demands political action and economic success in addition to a grasp of biology.

The funding for the cannery job ended after a year, and in early 1977 I was again collecting unemployment benefits. Around the same time I noticed a small ad in the mimeographed NOFA newsletter called *The Natural Farmer*, asking for a volunteer to help write standards and develop an organic certification program. This seemed like just the project for me; inasmuch as I was the only one who applied, I got the job.

In the course of pulling together the NOFA certification program I spoke with key leaders and soil gurus around the region. I traveled to Maine to discuss soil testing with the founders of Woods End Laboratory, and spent some time with Samuel Kaymen, the founder of NOFA. All of these conversations confirmed my understanding of the importance of soil health to the health of everyone else who depends on it—meaning all life on earth.

## Into the NOFA Vortex

Taking on the certification position required my attendance at more NOFA meetings and, as I got more involved with the organization, I became infatuated with its purpose and philosophy. I was also impressed with the feminist uprising in the movement, and anyone referring to a farmer as "he" got shouted down at meetings.

My husband took a dim view of this involvement, and it became a point of contention between us. I had to travel long distances to meetings all around Vermont and New Hampshire, and would sometimes stay over rather than drive home in our decrepit car on a cold winter night. Although gas money was usually covered, Tom did not share my zeal to help build a movement.

My yearning for grand accomplishments was ignited by my first NOFA Conference experience in 1978 in New Hampshire, including a legendary party. I was intoxicated by all the Wonderful People Who Knew So Much crowded into one college dorm room, saying hilariously witty things. My infatuation extended both to the ideas I was learning about and to a particular writer who articulated them so elegantly: Jack Cook, the editor of the by this time very impressive NOFA tabloid newsletter, *The Natural Farmer*. By the end of the year my life was completely different, and I emerged in early 1979 as NOFA's first full-time Vermont coordinator and set up housekeeping with Jack, 24 years my senior.

At the same time that I was leaving my marriage, the home that Tom and I had shared and all of our possessions, including the attached barn housing his woodworking business and assorted poultry, were destroyed by a fire on a frigid Valentine's Day. My belongings had been packed and were ready to collect but I could not get my car started to get to the house—the temperature had not climbed above zero degrees Farenheit for more than a week. Thankfully nobody was home when the flames erupted—most likely from a chimney fire. It went quickly, every trace of my old life gone, with almost nothing left from insurance after the bank took its share.

Despite my doubts about what I was doing, I had no choice but to keep putting one foot in front of the other. I moved into an even more ram-shackle and hard-to-heat farmhouse with a new man, took on a new job with huge responsibilities and low pay, had little contact with my former community, and lived with an enormous sense of loss.

Few in my new NOFA community knew what I had been through. I coped with my personal trauma by immersing myself in work, yet felt oppressed by the expectation among some leaders that my personal well-being should be sacrificed for the good of the cause. The idea that personal needs must not be allowed to interfere with the group's larger purpose seems to be a common shortcoming among social change movements. Feeling deprived and barely scraping by, I found myself resenting those I saw as coming from privileged backgrounds, who have the option of an escape route to "normal" society when they got tired of roughing it. I took pains to avoid sharing these feelings as well.

At the time I got involved, NOFA was a bi-state organization with semi-autonomous management of both the Vermont and New Hampshire wings. Civil war appeared imminent; manipulation, mutual suspicion, and power struggles within this tiny and very marginal organization seemed like the epitome of "tempest in a teapot." Seeking common ground, a few of us crafted a new constitution granting each state independence within a loose federation of chapters. Formal NOFA chapters were soon created in other New England states, followed by New York and New Jersey, eventually becoming a seven-state entity and changing its name from the *Natural Organic Farmers Association* to the *Northeast Organic Farming Association*. Today, each state manages its own affairs more or less democratically and also participates in region-wide projects, such as *The Natural Farmer* publication and the summer conference that is now based in Amherst, Massachusetts.

That year I worked like a demon (or maybe a zombie) trying to avoid thinking about the mess I had made of my life. There was plenty to do—organizing and attending endless meetings, hiring staff and recruiting volunteers for multiple projects, and traveling the back roads of Vermont in unreliable vehicles. The annual summer conference, held in Vermont in 1979, was as usual great fun despite a sleep-inducing keynote by a bio-(un)dynamic legend from Germany, whose thickly accented monotone elicited polite applause when it finally stopped. Besides a few farmers markets, we also helped start a root crop growers coop in Hardwick and initiated a political advocacy project that later morphed into its own organization, Rural Vermont. The little time I had for gardening, along with a few key friendships, saved my sanity.

## Challenges and Rewards

This year of intense transition and challenge also marked the start of a deep lifelong connection to Miranda Smith, to whom this book is dedicated. I first heard her name from Robert Houriet, who mentioned her as a potential funder for NOFA's certification program when she was working for the National Center for Appropriate Technology in Montana. I was immediately curious about this person, and a short time later I heard that she had moved to nearby Newport with a group of colleagues, setting up a private consulting group for alternative energy and agriculture. They called themselves The Memphremagog Group after the lake on which Newport sits that bridges Vermont and Quebec. "Wow," I thought, "this is exactly the kind of work I want to do."

Miranda formed close friendships wherever she went, and we hit it off instantly. A year or so later we finally got to work together, when she and her then-husband helped me write a grant to study the potential of making a commercial compost product using chicken manure from a large nearby poultry farm. The raw manure was being spread on cornfields next to the river every year and posing an obvious pollution threat from all the soluble nitrogen and phosphorus it carried. While we didn't get the grant, we did form a bond that endured.

Another key event of that year was an opportunity to testify on behalf of NOFA at hearings held by Jimmy Carter's Secretary of Agriculture, Bob Bergland, on the subject of the structure of agriculture. A lot of academics and agribusiness types were lined up ready to argue for more industrial efficiency and centralized infrastructure to improve the country's food system, following the "get big or get out" philosophy of Nixon's notorious Ag Secretary, Earl Butz. My approach was different and I set out a scenario for a decentralized food system based on the ideas then germinating in the NOFA seedbed. My brief essay depicted a small Vermont town transformed by a thriving local food economy and anchored by a community food processing and distribution center, and was published in a regional farm publication, *The New England Farmer* (now defunct) under the title, "Newville, 1990" (see Appendix). Aside from a few letters to the editor this was my first published article. Remembering it gave me chills thirty-plus years later when I attended the grand opening of the new Food Venture Center in Hardwick, Vermont—a focal point of the economic miracle nicely portrayed by Ben Hewitt in *The Town that Food Saved*.

In the following two years the USDA came out with two pivotal documents. One was the *Report & Recommendations on Organic Farming*,[13] and the other was *A Time to Choose*.[14] The former was a thoughtful look at the current knowledge base and principles of organics and what research might help improve it; along with publication of the study, the USDA allocated a small budget for a part-time organic coordinator. The latter was the outcome of all those "structure of agriculture" hearings, and posed the question of whether we wanted a centralized food system with larger and larger farms, industrial agriculture, and declining rural communities or a diverse, localized agriculture that included farms of all sizes and thriving small towns. Then we held an election in 1980 and are still living with the consequences of that choice. The organic office was disbanded and the report was quickly shredded by the Reagan administration, along with the symbolic act of removing the solar panels from the White House roof. The "O" word became verboten at the USDA for over a decade.

## Moving On

By the end of the year it was clear that my denial strategy could not work much longer. Living with Jack was exciting and stimulating, but way too close to the edge. Once again winter threatened to hold needless and painful struggles with old vehicles and frozen firewood. Our generational difference was another huge obstacle. Truth be told, I missed Tom and was grappling both with guilt over leaving him and what would today be diagnosed as post-traumatic stress disorder. There was also the small matter of a lack of funding past December for my job with NOFA. I just had to get away and sort things out.

My parents, who had by this time relocated to Vermont after their return from Israel, were more than eager to take me in. But I opted instead for refuge with my older sisters in New York and Hawaii, where I could reflect on what I had been through and begin to heal from the sense of loss and guilt that haunted me. I realized that my passion for the organic vision was still central; in hindsight it was probably this passion that Jack represented and that I had fallen in love with the year before. Before I left Vermont we hired Sara Norton as a part-time State Coordinator, and she proved to be an outstanding activator for the organization. Robert convinced me to take over his slot as program developer—a fancy name for grant writer—and the job kept me in touch with what was going on while I was away.

Then a plan took shape to come back to Vermont in the spring and build a little cabin on the property that Tom and I had bought cooperatively with some other friends in West Charleston, and apply to graduate school. My goal was to get a credential that would enable me to help more farmers learn about and try organic practices. University of Vermont (UVM)'s master's program in extension education fit my needs. I was able to write grants for NOFA part-time and use some of my real-world experience to populate various independent study projects. While there wasn't a thesis requirement, one of those independent study projects turned into one of my proudest productions—the now classic manual on ecological soil management called *The Soul of Soil.*

# 2 Finding Soul in the Soil

*In the long run, a fertile soil is just as important for human health as clean air or water.* — Murray Bookchin

*If we try to solve soiciety's problems without overcoming the confusion and aggression in our own state of mind, then our efforts will only contribute to the basic problems, instead of solving them.* — Chögyam Trungpa Rinpoche

The keynote program at the 9th Annual NOFA Conference in 1983 was nothing short of iconic. It was a perfect summer weekend, and the beautiful Johnson State College campus on the edge of the Green Mountains created just the right tableau for our celebration of rural life. More than 100 presenters and 1,000 conference attendees filled the space. The kickoff evening began with an outdoor performance by the acclaimed political activist Bread & Puppet Theater troop from Glover, Vermont. Moving inside to the comfortable college auditorium, the political theme continued. Well-known poet and peace activist Grace Paley opened our hearts with her passion and humor. Next up was radical social ecologist Murray Bookchin, who roused the crowd to replace the corrupt and environmentally destructive market economy with a just and democratic moral economy. In the style of old-time polemicists on street corner soap boxes, he didn't disappoint. Along with Grace Paley, Bread & Puppet's Peter Schumann, and NOFA's founder Samuel Kaymen, Bookchin had been part of the New York radical political milieu, and now all of them were telling us that our vision for organic agriculture represented an important political, ethical, and economic shift. It felt like a moment of luminary convergence, with the activist stars aligned to carry our movement to the next level.

The final speaker was Vermont Senator Patrick Leahy. Though neither a radical nor a New York transplant, he had been a staunch supporter of "alternative agriculture" and an advocate of nuclear disarmament in Congress. In my introduction I suggested that his efforts on behalf of peace and our efforts on behalf of agriculture were related, saying, "Peace

At the NOFA Conference podium with Chuck Cox, NOFA
Council President, July 1983

activists are working to ensure that we have a future. Organic farmers are working to ensure that when we get to the future we can still eat."

The whole process of organizing the event as well as the event itself represented a pinnacle achievement in my life. At the same time, the first edition of my new handbook, *The Soul of Soil*, had just been published by the UVM Extension Service, a year after I completed my master's program. I was overwhelmed and giddy, basking in the praise and admiration from many who had inspired me. Leading up to the ecstatic post-keynote party, a group of the volunteers and farmer leaders who had helped me pull the event together marched to my dorm room, delivering a bouquet of flowers and broccoli and singing Amazing Grace. Even my yearning for a compatible life mate and a place to farm was, it seemed, on the verge of fulfillment.

## Back to School

My decision to pursue a master's degree in Extension Education—even if it was a terminal degree—turned out to be a good one. Before I moved to Burlington to begin my studies at UVM in the fall of 1980, I was able to get a head start by arranging an independent study with a group of consultants in the Eastern Townships region of Quebec just an hour or so away from my newly built cabin. I had heard Joe Smillie and Bart Hall-Beyer speak about ecological soil management at several conferences and was impressed with both their knowledge and their wit. With their associates Angus Curry and Monique Scholz, they formed Eaton Valley Agricultural Services (EVAS) to sell natural soil fertility and pest control supplies, make compost, and provide consulting services to area farmers interested in ecological methods.

Much of the summer was spent following Joe and Bart around as they visited area farms, which were much more diversified than Vermont with its preponderance of dairy. Some days I would just dig through their files and references, and bug them with endless questions. I also interviewed some of the farmers they worked with, including producers of grain, apples, and mixed organic vegetables. Bart and his family put me up during my periodic trips to Quebec. Though I respected Bart's technical knowledge, I found him lacking in the people skills department. It was Joe Smillie who became my lifelong friend and trusted collaborator.

I then expanded my study to include an ecological farming consultant based in the nearby Northeast Kingdom town of Orleans, one whose advice was well respected by the group of organic growers now gaining some experience in building soil fertility. Fred Franklin of Vanguard Farms offered similar services and products to those of EVAS, but with a wildly different style. A self-styled anarchist, Fred had little use for orthodoxy of any kind.

Like EVAS, Fred dispensed natural fertilizers and products such as fish and seaweed emulsions in addition to advice. However, while the EVAS guys had a business-like demeanor and were eager for acceptance by conventional agriculture, Fred dealt strictly in cash and did not hide his disdain for any form of capitulation to conventional wisdom. For example, you could buy rock phosphate in bags from EVAS, but Fred required you to show up at the railroad siding with a shovel and appropriate containers when the bulk phosphate order rolled in. Another distinction: Fred's agricultural philosophy was based on a proprietary formula for balancing soil minerals, including micronutrients, to achieve optimum health, while Joe and Bart were more interested in educating their clients to enable them to make their own decisions about soil fertility needs.

Unfortunately, Fred's silver bullet approach to soil management and health literally proved fatal a few years later. Believing that the trace element boron was a miracle cure for virtually any plant malady, Fred also attempted to treat his own physical maladies by regularly ingesting small amounts of it. There is surely some validity to the idea that a deficiency of boron in soil makes plants more susceptible to insect attack. But too much of any essential nutrient can become a poison, and it doesn't take much to cross that line. Fred's diagnosis of boron poisoning turned into a death sentence. For me it became a horrifying lesson of the folly of trying to reduce health to recipes for nutrient supplements.

Following my summer study I moved to Burlington and became a full time graduate student. Given that town's tight housing market, I decided to accept the opportunity to live on campus in the newly built Living & Learning Center as a participant in an experimental graduate seminar program. This decision was not such a good one. I had never experienced college dorm life during my undergraduate years in New York City, where everyone is a commuter. Now an old lady of 30 with a serious mission in life, I was not accustomed to being treated like an untrustworthy teenager. So I retreated to a room in a group house not far from campus the next semester and drove the two-and-a-half hours to my cabin in West Charleston whenever I could.

My graduate advisors supported my unconventional academic aspirations; once I satisfied a couple of basic requirements, I was free to sample courses from a range of different agricultural disciplines. A few independent study projects rounded out my self-designed concentration in ecological agriculture, and begot more long-term friendships with mentors. I studied rural sociology, agricultural geography, and production economics. The love of my life, though, became soil biology—I can clearly recall the excitement I felt hearing Fred Magdoff talk about mucigel in his introductory soil science course. Sounds a bit icky, perhaps, but if there is any place where the soul of healthy soil may be said to reside it is here, in the gummy stuff that surrounds plant roots and provides ideal habitat for the thousands of beneficial soil dwelling life forms and their myriad symbiotic relationships. The root zone, in all its sublime ecological intricacies, is where healthy plants both create and are created by life in the soil—a miraculous interdependence that nourishes all creatures who depend on both.

My financial aid package included a work-study position at Extension headquarters on campus. Neil Pelsue, an agricultural economist who sometimes gave workshops at NOFA conferences, was my advisor and he

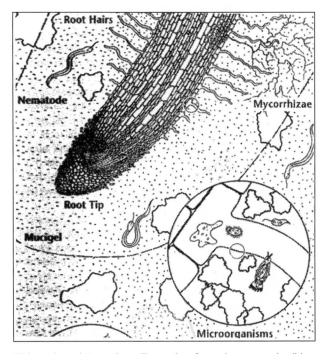

Rhizosphere interactions illustration from the second edition
of *The Soul of Soil* (art by Stewart Hoyt).

suggested that the information I had gathered about ecological soil management would make a valuable publication for Northeastern farmers. It
was an ideal project and I was given a desk with a typewriter in Morrill
Hall, where pamphlets, fact sheets, and information bulletins for farmers
were churned out by the Extension publications office. The hard part was
coming up with a title—I did not want it to sound the least bit flakey. It
was Don McFeeters, my supervisor, who suggested the title "*The Soul of
Soil.*"

After two semesters in the big city of Burlington my coursework was
completed and there remained only one more independent study to wrap
up my program. I moved back to my cabin for the summer and was able
to get by on the income from a small grant-funded project for organizing
a few workshops about farm issues in my home community that had been
passed along to me by a NOFA colleague. My goal for my final graduate
independent study was to gain more hands-on farming experience that
would provide me with more confidence about advising others. I also
needed to complete the book project for which I had received academic
credit, but was still far from finished.

## The Trek to New Hampshire

The grant project wrapped up in the fall. Since my cabin was not habitable in winter and I didn't want to leave the community again, I moved in with friends nearby. There were few opportunities to work on organic farms with someone who could supervise me as a graduate student, but a phone conversation with Samuel Kaymen, NOFA's founder, set me on the next step of my journey. Samuel had set up a school for rural skills and had all kinds of projects going on a hilltop farm in southern New Hampshire. The farm was owned by a wealthy member of a community of biodynamic farmers and anthroposophists, and had recently initiated a small residential program. Many of the leading luminaries of the alternative agriculture movement gave weekend workshops there, including John and Nancy Todd from New Alchemy, Tasmanian ecologist and Permaculture originator Bill Mollison, Vermont herbalist Adele Dawson, and my friend Stuart Hill, a soil ecologist from McGill University. Samuel wanted me to take over running the solar greenhouse and supervising students in the large organic garden, as well as helping with office work and educational programming. There was minimal funding, but he offered room and board with $30 a week spending money and use of the school van for transportation. I jumped at the chance and headed off to Wilton, New Hampshire to join the staff at The Rural Education Center in early January 1982.

My year at TREC (the inevitable acronym for our farm school, whose inhabitants were of course known as Trekkies) was chock full of learning experiences—wonderful and amazing, as well as painful and frustrating. A charismatic visionary, Samuel was multitalented, inspiring, and exuberant, but a bit short on management skills. When he spoke he would hold his audience spellbound, and get us all charged up to build the great new organic society. While not suffering from excess humility, he readily acknowledged his own ignorance and always deferred to his wife Louise before making commitments that might conflict with the needs of their large family.

My notebooks are filled with information about everything from how to make biodynamic preparations to dairy cow nutrition, along with vivid feelings about my life as a barely paid intern with heavy responsibility as the housemother in residence. The cavernous main house included office and classroom space, a kitchen, and dorm rooms for the half dozen or so resident students. The Kaymens' home was a newer wing of the building,

and I had a loft in the still-under-con-
struction bathhouse wing. It was a
drafty old building, and much time
was spent hauling firewood and feeding the various wood stoves.

TREC also provided my final independent study for my graduate
program: an economic analysis of my
experience managing the school's solar greenhouse. Miranda advised me
about the fine points of working with
a solar greenhouse that lacked supple-
mental heat, as her first book, *Green-*
*house Gardening*, had recently been
published by Rodale Press. It was a

At work in the TREC greenhouse.
Photo from "Stirrings" newsletter,
Spring 1982.

joy to learn to produce the vegetable and flower seedlings that we sold to
local garden outlets, and we even returned a small profit to the program.
Growing new seedlings to begin the yearly cycle of gardening remains
one of my favorite spring activities.

Along with everyone else I took an occasional shift on barn chores,
milking our two Jersey and Brown Swiss cows. It was easy to understand
why people become attached to these sweet, gentle animals, but I never
had any desire to tend them day after day. It became abundantly clear
to me that I was not destined to be a dairy farmer after a catastrophic
episode when Samuel was off on a trip and left me and a few students in
charge of chores for a couple of days. His prize Jersey, Maggie, was close
to giving birth, and he left instructions to call a neighbor if we ran into
any problems. Maggie went into labor and we didn't think anything was
amiss until she went down soon after her calf was born—but by then it
was too late. Her pregnancy-related milk fever would have been easily
treatable with a shot of calcium, and the loss was heartbreaking.

By this time I had fulfilled my graduation requirements and received
my diploma, but was still struggling to find time to work on the soil book.
Now that I had my degree, I needed to earn a living and be able to go
back to Vermont regularly to check in on my elderly parents. My father
had had a stroke that June, and was limited in both speech and mobility.
My responsibilities at TREC—along with my new title of Horticultural
Director—were significant enough to demand a real salary, but the best
that could be scraped together was still pitiful. It gave me barely enough

to acquire another vintage Saab in dubious condition.

Nobody was getting rich, to be sure, and Samuel was tired of begging for money from foundations and wealthy donors. A plan began to take shape with help from Gary Hirshberg, one of our Board members and then Executive Director of New Alchemy Institute, to develop a cottage industry that could support TREC financially. Samuel and Louise had previously supplemented their income by selling yogurt they made in their kitchen, and it was a truly superior product. The idea was to make this exquisite organic product from the rich milk from our own cows, and the business would also serve as a hands-on learning experience for our students and interns. Samuel was developing a business plan for the new yogurt company, and I was to be in charge of producing the small fruit— raspberries, strawberries and blueberries—to flavor it, and set about researching this component of the plan. Gary meanwhile came on board to manage TREC's operations, while Samuel oversaw the conversion of a garage that was attached to the farmhouse into a prototype small-scale yogurt factory. The brand name would simply be the farm name, descriptive of the rocky soil that could barely produce enough grass to feed our few bovines: Stonyfield Farm.

It seemed like a real long shot, and it became clear that there simply was no money available to pay staff in the near future. Southern New Hampshire never felt like home and I missed my Vermont community and friends. The next NOFA summer conference was to take place in Vermont again, and I was offered the job of organizing it. With relief I decided to pack up and head back to the other side of the Connecticut River.

Within a few years Stonyfield Farm started becoming a viable enterprise and TREC was no more. Samuel later retired from the company with a comfortable life, and today you can buy organic Stonyfield Farm yogurt in just about any convenience store as well as WalMart. Now owned by the Danone Group, an international conglomerate, it is the poster child for "industrial organic" as portrayed in the film, *Food, Inc.* Gary is now moving away from being the Stonyfield "CE-Yo" to concentrate on political advocacy, including the campaign to require labeling of foods that contain genetically modified organisms (GMOs). Was the demise of the educational non-profit it was originally intended to support an inevitable outcome of the success of the yogurt business? The central question that continues to plague the organic movement is this: Did the success of Stonyfield Farm bring us a step closer to realizing the true organic vision, or does it represent a sellout or co-optation of that vision?

View of Grace's cabin in West Charleston, 1981

## The Way Home

After a year in southern New Hampshire, which was quickly becoming a bedroom community for Boston, I was grateful to be back in Vermont to spend the rest of the winter at the farm where I had worked during the cannery stint. Much was uncertain, but I was able to earn my keep at the farm and begin planning for the big NOFA conference at Johnson State College. I was also still finishing the last bits of my book, which Extension promised to publish if I could get it done soon enough. When spring finally came, I returned to my cabin where I had the essential organizing tools of electricity and telephone. A hose running from my neighbor's house provided running water, and there was a rustic outhouse a few yards into the woods. I grew my own garden for the first time, wrote in my journal, and took long walks.

This was a summer of intense soul searching. For the first time since the Montreal days I was flying solo—living alone and tending my own garden. Now 33 and officially divorced, I saw no prospects for a new life partner on the horizon—eligible males were noticeably scarcer than they were when I arrived in Vermont a decade previously. My conference organizing work occupied most of my attention, but I had little sense of what I would be doing once the conference was over.

I was reading Lovelock & Margulis' treatise on the Gaia hypothesis, named after the Greek earth goddess. Based on biogeochemistry, evolutionary biology, and systems dynamics, the Gaia hypothesis suggests that the entire planet functions as a living, self-regulating organism that has coevolved with its constituent life forms. Biological organisms have, over millennia, altered their environment to be more hospitable to life. We human beings, with our innate capacity to reason and to alter our environment to increase its habitability, are a natural product of evolution. Still seeking the bridge between scientific rationality and non-rational forms of knowledge, I cautiously engaged in my first (and only) solitary psychedelic experience.

That day, roaming the fields and woods near my cabin as the landscape swarmed with life perceived in high definition with the help of the drug, I recognized myself as a voice of the planet, speaking out to help restore her soil-skin to health. Sitting with my hands in the dirt, contemplating the flowering plants growing near the edge of an overgrown field, I could hear the microbial whispers telling me what they needed—what minerals would support the bacterial enzymes and help the legumes to thrive. Perhaps this was the sound of the earth spirits and devas known to so many indigenous cultures and discussed in the biodynamic literature. Finding fresh inspiration in this period of uncertainty and self-doubt, I made a solemn private vow to serve the life of the planet in everything I did.

Much came together for me that summer, reaching a crescendo of intensity as the late July conference time drew near. *The Soul of Soil* was ready for publication, thanks to a professional editor hired by Extension who introduced me to the wonders of word processing. I served as both administrator and program director for the 1983 NOFA Conference, and managed to pull together a magical group of committee volunteers and staff. The experience made me feel like a star and expanded my treasured circle of friendships. Soaking up the glory and the accolades for my book, it felt like I had finally arrived among the ranks of the Wonderful People Who Knew So Much that I first encountered five years earlier. It was also the first summer conference in several years (and as it turned out for nearly the whole decade of the eighties) that actually ended up in the black financially. The potential of this movement seemed infinite, and my leadership role appeared to be a foreshadowing of the great personal accomplishments that awaited. We really might just save the world!

This event heralded several new beginnings for me, including my first acquaintance with the legendary 'Mooree Booookchin,' about whom I had heard from my Cuban housemate but never read when I lived in Montreal. He was in fine form, and his speech roused us to go out and overthrow the demon agribusiness—a talk later reprinted as the essay "Market Economy or Moral Economy."[15]

The conference also marked the beginning of a new love relationship, one that arrived in the completely unexpected form of a red-headed, green-eyed, farmer-artist more than eight years my junior. Though I had my doubts, Stewart courted me diligently—a new and pleasant experience in my life. He also offered me the opportunity to live out my dreams at last, to help develop his farming enterprise and build a house together on his mother's thirty-five acres in the town of Barnet, about forty miles south of my cabin. This is the southernmost edge, the banana belt of the Northeast Kingdom, close to the Connecticut River and a full climate zone warmer than West Charleston. The fact that oak trees could grow on this land was the proverbial icing on the cake—the cake itself, rich, crumbly and dark chocolate in color was the stone-free soil.

I moved in with Stewart and his family in the spring of 1984. We were married in the field that summer and started building our house, which was habitable enough to occupy the following spring. We began to make a significant share of our household income as market gardeners, but both of us had other enterprises as well. Stewart made exquisite wooden cooking utensils that he sold primarily at craft fairs; he also did the original illustrations for the first edition of *The Soul of Soil*. I, meanwhile, continued pursuing my teaching, organizing, and writing projects. I was in the thick of organizing educational events and programs for NOFA, as well as participating in the emerging national-level organic scene. This life provided me with a perfect combination of hard work and practical skill-building with educational and advocacy work. Being a grower gave me increased credibility and, more importantly, kept me on the path of walking my own talk—a practice that has remained a cornerstone of what I refer to throughout this story as the "True Organic Vision."

## Encountering Social Ecology

Shaped by my experiences in the organic movement and graduate school, my emerging understanding of the True Organic Vision was further refined by my nearly simultaneous introduction, during this period of the mid- to late-1980s, to the complementary ideas of Social Ecology and

Shambhala Buddhism. Social Ecology was the first to be encountered.

On the strength of the connection I had made with Murray Bookchin, in 1986 I was invited to teach at the Institute for Social Ecology (ISE). Bookchin and Dan Chodorkoff had founded the ISE in 1974 at Goddard College in Plainfield, Vermont. The ISE's relationship with Goddard was a tumultuous one and, though the organization maintained an academic affiliation with that college for more than 25 years, it became an independent entity that for a time ran programs at its own center nearby.

As my involvement with NOFA and organic farming grew in the 1970s, I attended a couple of workshops at Goddard's Cate Farm, then the site of the ISE's campus and experiments in alternative technology. I was excited to learn about their work in Vermont that was similar to that of New Alchemy Institute, including aquaculture research, windmills, and organic gardening. John and Nancy Todd, founders of New Alchemy and early inspirations in my life, had actually been guest lecturers at the ISE. Other organic thought leaders who interacted with the ISE early on were NOFA's founder Samuel Kaymen and Stuart Hill, founder of the Ecological Agriculture Project at MacDonald College, Canada. I had not yet encountered the work of Murray Bookchin, and had only the vaguest notion of what Social Ecology might entail. With Plainfield about a two-hour drive from my home in West Charleston, there was no way that I could afford either the gas money or the time during prime growing season to attend a full summer program.

One day in the spring of 1986 I got a call from Joseph Keifer, one of the co-teachers for the Bioregional Agriculture course in the ISE's four-week summer program. His teaching partner was leaving the area and Murray Bookchin had suggested my name as her replacement. Goddard was then offering both BA and MA degrees in Social Ecology via a low-residency program, a model that the college had pioneered, and I was subsequently hired as a part-time Goddard faculty member. Thus began both my career in progressive higher education and my association with the field of Social Ecology.

Not until I began teaching at the ISE did I begin to absorb—more accurately inhale—the Bookchin experience. Challenged and stimulated, I attended as many of his lectures as possible, along with presentations by other new colleagues and friends. At last I had the opportunity to read his seminal work, *The Ecology of Freedom*, which articulated and substantiated so many intuitive truths gleaned from my own experience. It truly felt, as Stuart Hill has described it, like coming home.

When I was in graduate school in 1980-81, ecology was becoming a respectable scientific discipline, and Thomas Kuhn's The Structure of Scientific Revolutions had anointed 'paradigm shift' as the new buzz phrase. In a paper entitled, "The Emerging Ecological Paradigm—Agriculture as a Case in Point," I began to articulate the case for the importance of organic agriculture as the leading edge of this shift in humanity's relationship to nature, along with its concept of what constitutes credible scientific inquiry. This was probably my first effort to explain the revolutionary potential of the True Organic Vision; more than thirty years later, it still seems to capture the essence of that vision.

## Excerpts from The Emerging Ecological Paradigm:

My premise here is that a new paradigm for conceptualizing reality is emerging in every aspect of human endeavor....The development of agriculture has been hailed as the basic prerequisite to the emergence of civilization as we know it....If civilization can continue to evolve only when more human energy is available than is required to supply the basic necessities of life, agriculture will remain fundamental. Agriculture is, therefore, a fitting arena for investigating the change now taking place.

[It is implicit in ecological thinking] that artificial systems should be designed to enhance living ones, not supercede them. The natural world provides models to be emulated, rather than obstacles to be overcome. Other major precepts of ecological models are:

- Health is the fundamental goal; implicit in health is sustainability (permanence) and harmony (beauty).
- Viability depends on diversity, flexibility, and adaptability (non-specialization).
- Decentralism: Autonomous units are interdependent, and overall health is maximized through cooperation.
- Synergy: The patterns through which individual units are interconnected are important to the health of each, and to the nature of the larger system they comprise.
- Cybernetics: Internal and external changes are incorporated into new strategies for continued evolution.

## The Emerging Ecological Paradigm (Continued)

Ecological principles require the consideration of the broader social context in order to understand the question at hand. Agricultural issues are inextricably related to politics, religion, education, art, and mental health. The built-in biases of our economic system determine the nature and extent of all research conducted in institutions, fables of "objectivity" notwithstanding.

A shift in paradigms means a change in thinking by significant numbers of people—thinking about themselves, their culture, the natural world, and the relationships between them. There is tremendous material and psychological investment, however, in the existing paradigms, and a tangible threat to humanity's survival if the change isn't fast enough. The institutions that shape the thoughts of our culture must, somehow, be restructured to transmit ecological awareness.

Wendell Berry argues that, "If change is to come, then, it will have to come from the outside." Earlier he likens the modern scientific orthodoxy to many another, which "would rather die than change, and may change only by dying," posing the crucial question: "Must we all die with it in order for it to change?"[16]

That question is a challenge, and the challenge has much to do with why I'm writing this. Just as the belief that humanity is outside of nature gave rise to the problems we face, so the belief that change only comes from outside cannot solve them. The institutions that threaten not to change are the very same that produced those who perceive the threat.

Most people credit Rachel Carson and *Silent Spring*, published in 1962, with inspiring the environmental movements of the sixties. But (as noted in Chapter 1) Murray Bookchin had published the largely unnoticed *Our Synthetic Environment* a few months before. While Carson wrote from a scientific perspective and Bookchin from a political and social viewpoint, they converged in raising the alarm about threats to human and non-human health posed by a range of environmental and foodborne toxins. Both also illustrated the links between technologies developed for warfare and the assault on nature waged by the agri-industrial approach to farming. Bookchin, however, identified distorted social relations—not "modern technology" in general—as the root of the ecological crisis. The oppression of nature is an outgrowth of the oppression of one group of humans by another—otherwise known as hierarchy. Although few in the incipient organic movement were aware of the book, *Our Synthetic Environment* outlined the major thematic ideas that shaped its early development.

Bookchin's keynote talk at the 1983 NOFA Conference, "Moral Economy or Market Economy," has also been widely read in organic circles. Inspiring as his message was about the immorality of the market economy which runs on anonymity, his conference talk also criticized "alternative institutions" such as organic farms and food cooperatives for being more entrepreneurial than ethical, where the moral aspects of growing and distributing food are blotted out by considerations of "efficiency" and "success."

The moral economy, in contrast, is based not on antagonism between buyer and seller, but on reciprocity and interdependence. Finally calling for a re-visioning of nature, placing humanity firmly within—not above—it, Bookchin acknowledged the obvious necessity of bringing nature more directly into our lives via eco-technologies such as organic farming, solar energy, and natural building as a means for stimulating our authentic respect for the natural world. Fundamental to that sense of interdependence, he concluded, "is a re-visioning of nature as the moral basis for a new ecological ethics."

## Avoiding the "ism Schism"

The ISE's institutional trajectory has hardly been one of harmony. Any organization professing a radical political agenda is naturally prone to conflict—both internal and external. Substantive political and philosophical clashes undoubtedly contribute to the "ism schism" that Bob Marley

## Key Principles of Social Ecology as Elements of the True Organic Vision

Many of the precepts I identified in "The Emerging Ecological Paradigm" (refer to previous sidebar) are echoed in those articulated by Murray Bookchin and others. Here are a few that resonate most closely with my understanding of the true organic vision:

### Dialectical Naturalism—Humans are not separate from nature

Humanity is as natural as trees or earthworms—we are not separate from nature, and what we do is not "unnatural." Human society, or "second nature," is likewise a natural development. Evolution moves towards ever greater levels of diversity, complexity, and freedom. Humans are unique in possessing the capacity for reason, and have the potential to create great beauty as well as to inflict great damage. Humanity is "nature rendered self-conscious."

### Unity in diversity

Cultural and biological diversity is key to all aspects of ecological and social balance and resilience. Increasing diversity and complexity fosters more synergistic interactions, forming a whole that is larger than the sum of its parts. Increasing diversity produces increased stability in any ecosystem, whether biological or social.

### Reconstructive—utopian vision

It is essential to oppose all forms of domination of one group by another, which is at the root of social hierarchies as well as the oppression of nature. At the same time we must develop and pursue a vision of what is possible. Society can be remade to foster human potential and freedom.

and Peter Tosh complained about so melodically. The social ecology community has had its share of such ideological conflict, but I have long resisted putting people in pigeonholes with labels affixed. Whenever someone asks me if I am an anarchist (or a socialist or perhaps a Buddhist) I respond that I am not any kind of an "ist." Although I appreciate and agree with much of the teaching, analysis, and general perspective

**Local control over basic necessities of life through decentralized, directly democratic politics**

Access to adequate food, clothing, and shelter is a basic human right. Self-reliant, interdependent, and democratically controlled communities are best suited to ensure that these basic needs are met.

**Ecotechnologies designed to mimic nature, based on the precautionary principle**

Murray Bookchin at Goddard College, early 1990's

Eco-technologies are those technologies that are consistent with ecological constraints and decentralized control. Some technologies (e.g., GMO crops, nuclear power/weapons) can be inherently wrong, not because they go against nature, but because they require the concentration of power in an expert class to be applied, and/or clearly violate the precautionary principle. The precautionary principle suggests that even a small chance that horrific consequences may result from deploying a given technology is not worth the risk, especially when a choice exists of a less potentially destructive option.

**Nonviolence**

Any form of coercion is antithetical to establishing a free ecological society. The ends never justify the means.

of these particular "isms," they also all include some ideas and assumptions that I find troubling or incompatible with my own experience. So I do not identify myself by association with any of them—"too much of an anarchist to wear the uniform," I sometimes add. It is perhaps paradoxical that adherents of philosophies that profess the importance of thinking for yourself can sometimes be a bit dogmatic about sticking with the party line. This tendency has certainly been a source of some of the dysfunctionality I have experienced within the ISE. A larger share, from my perspective is due to a lack of emotional maturity and plain old communication skills—most starkly demonstrated by Murray Bookchin himself. An auto-didact genius with incredible philosophical depth and scholarship, he could be cruel to students who voiced politically objectionable positions, and often behaved badly in meetings. Unfortunately, some of his acolytes seem to have emulated this aspect of his character. This tendency to alienate—or even attack—those who should be allies may be a prime reason why the contributions of Bookchin and social ecology are not as widely known as they deserve to be. And yet, the value of what he and other colleagues have taught continues to shine and inspire many around the world.

What drew me into the Bookchin orbit and kept me engaged with the ISE has been the reconstructive vision of a free, ecologically harmonious, and liberatory society, and the recognition that changing how food is produced and distributed is key to creating such a society. My ten years on the Goddard College faculty in Social Ecology gave me a foundation for teaching and learning within a credible academic structure that has sustained me in many ways since then. The opportunity to work with students who find this vision appealing has also contributed to keeping alive my sense of hope for the world.

I was surprised and delighted when I learned, much later, that my old soil ecologist friend from McGill University, Stuart Hill, had migrated to Australia, where he chaired the Department of Social Ecology at the University of Western Syndney.[17] Though this school actually began with no relationship to the Bookchin version of Social Ecology, Stuart introduced that perspective into its curriculum. His version places more emphasis on ecology than on politics, and manages to weave a holistic picture of the necessary interdependence of politics, ecology, health, education, and inner growth that is too often ignored by the more politically focused American and European cadres.

## Social Ecology Meets Buddhism

Bookchin's roots in Marxism and anarchism inevitably made him prone to the prevailing prejudices of the left, including extreme disparagement of anything that smacks of religion. These prejudices are not without justification, but are prejudices nonetheless. My early explorations of Eastern philosophy failed to convince me to renounce worldly engagement or to become a follower of any particular spiritual path. This is possibly due to my tendency to resist authority in any form, or maybe just that I hadn't yet found the right path for me. I nonetheless resonated strongly with the urge toward inner development and self-knowledge gleaned from these teachings, tending towards the "chop wood, carry water" approach to spiritual practice, which I understood as taking care of simple necessities and living close to the land. The importance of this kind of inner work for healthier interpersonal relationships and more effective organizations always seemed obvious to me.

The lessons learned from my organizing work for NOFA convinced me that the greatest obstacles to our cause were an egocentric lack of empathy and compassion, a dash of self-righteous arrogance, and a tendency to demonize the opposition often evidenced in our leaders. It was not until soon after I began working with the ISE and had the opportunity to listen rapt to Bookchin's brilliant polemical teachings that circumstances pulled me into a more serious Buddhist-oriented path.

When I moved to Barnet in 1984 and began farming with Stewart, I knew there was a Tibetan Buddhist meditation center nearby, then called Tail of the Tiger. I also had seen a video that featured its founder, Chögyam Trungpa Rinpoche, and could tell that this guy was the real deal—an authentic enlightened presence. But my life of farming, organizing, and writing, not to mention building a house from recycled materials and tending to my aging parents, did not include time to check it out.

In early 1987 I started working as a freelance reporter for *The Caledonian Record*, the daily newspaper published in nearby St. Johnsbury, Vermont. Although I strongly disagreed with the paper's right-wing editorial position, the work gave me a good grounding in the craft of journalism, as well as the opportunity to become more familiar with local people and community activities. When I learned that March that Chögyam Trungpa had died and that plans were being made to hold his cremation ceremony here in Barnet, I knew that this would be a major event for our tiny town. Timidly approaching the paper's managing editor, I asked if I could report on it even though I was not a regular staff writer. "We weren't planning to cover it," was her offhand reply.

But once she got wind that a crowd of at least 10,000 would be converging on the area, along with representatives of major national media, Buddhist dignitaries, and celebrities from all over the world, I got the assignment. This handed me a rare opportunity to ask a lot of nosy questions and spend a couple of weeks visiting with those in charge of logistics for the ceremony that was to be held on a hillside above the meditation center now called Karme Chöling. Everyone I talked with was gracious and forthcoming about the rather paradoxical reputation of their deceased guru, who was unabashed about his embrace of "crazy wisdom" and known to be a wild partier who also enthusiastically embraced many of his female students. They all treated me with as much respect as might be accorded the reporters from *Newsweek* and *National Geographic* who were also covering the event. I was given reading material and free range to satisfy my curiosity about the place and what it represented.

Following this welcoming encounter, and intrigued by what I had gleaned from reading some of Chögyam Trungpa's prolific writing starting with *Cutting Through Spiritual Materialism*, I decided to try out a couple of weekend meditation programs at Karme Chöling. Over the next five or six years I managed to complete the initial sequence in the Shambhala path—one program a year. The meditation practice taught in these programs, as well as in meetings with local meditation instructors, served as an emotional life raft in the turbulent times that lay ahead of me.

Shambhala Buddhism is the term currently used for this particular sect, based on a mythical Tibetan kingdom that manifested the ideals of an enlightened society. Said to be the source of the Shangri-La story, the kingdom of Shambhala represents a Buddhist version of utopia, employing some colorful imagery to represent various qualities of "spiritual warriorship." A spiritual warrior is one who is brave, open hearted, and compassionate, rather than aggressive; the warrior's rallying cry is "victory over war!"

The foundation of the Shambhala teachings is one of "basic goodness," a simple but profound understanding of human nature that recognizes the potential for any of us to wake up. In contrast to the widely held notion amongst western religions that humans are inherently sinful and must be taught to behave ethically (often via some form of coercion or threat of punishment), this view holds that we are all born with a natural worthiness as human beings. This inherent human dignity is, unfortunately, often buried under a lot of conditioning that teaches us that our happiness depends on gaining power over others, having more stuff, being the best, brightest, prettiest, and so on. Then we are instructed to feel guilty for wanting those things that will make us happy, and so must work to suppress our "natural" tendency towards greed and selfishness.

## Chögyam Trungpa Rinpoche and Shambhala Buddhism

Covering the weeks of preparations for the cremation ceremony, I was able to interview several notable Buddhist leaders. In an interview with Ane Pema Chodron, Buddhist nun and director of Gampo Abbey in Cape Breton, Nova Scotia, she says: "The Shambhala teachings are dedicated to cultivating the goodness of people. The basic view of Buddhism is that people aren't bad—people are good. And the world is good." As with every other  aspect of Buddhism, its focus is on the discipline of meditation, which she says "isn't considered a way of attaining peace—it's a way of letting go of deception."[18]

Reporting on the ceremony itself, my story and photos got front-page space with the headline, "Rainbow Seen at Ceremony."[19] As the smoke from Rinpoche's cremation fire wafted skyward, a faint rainbow appeared around the sun—"a rare event meteorologically, but one that happens regularly, according to Buddhist tradition, whenever a great teacher dies." Among the luminaries present was the poet Allen Ginsberg, a close friend and student of Chögyam Trungpa's, who spoke about his departed friend. "The man himself was a great big sweetheart," he stated, using phrases such as "a tender poet," "full of humor and playfulness," and "kind and gentle" to describe him. "Buddhists practice how to be friendly—starting with friendliness to yourself." Having turned his white painter's cap inside out as he started talking, Ginsberg explained Rinpoche's success and influence by saying that he "turned Buddhism inside out so it would make sense to westerners, whose minds are inside out."

This belief that we are as a species inherently greedy and selfish leads directly to despair when we recognize that the planet is being destroyed by human greed and selfishness. There is no way out, until we begin to accept our own basic goodness—and most importantly, the equivalent basic goodness of every other person in the world.

These teachings offer a non-religious and nontheistic approach to making friends with one's own mind, utterly without requirements to obey a leader, pledge loyalty to a religious scripture, or join an exclusive club. Nobody pressured me to wear the uniform, though the ceremonies can involve lapel pins, ritual objects, and some strange chants. I was impressed with how welcoming this oddly formal institution was to skeptical newcomers. Their egalitarian management approach, which includes a balanced complement of female teachers and administrators, also offers a refreshing difference from other organized Eastern spirituality oriented groups I have encountered. These people, for the most part, appear to walk their own talk.

The kind of inner development offered by meditation practice is common to many spiritual traditions, but this one resonates with me largely because of its egalitarian sensibility that does not call for ascetic denunciation of sensory delights. Anyone can seek more advanced learning, at your own pace and starting wherever you are. The various practices, in which instruction is offered by resident and visiting teachers, provide the opportunity to experience the value of the teachings for oneself; it is not necessary to renounce any other religious or spiritual tradition. Those in this community can freely enjoy the traditions in which they were brought up, and borrow from other Buddhist and non-Buddhist traditions. Zen archery, Taoist Feng Shui, and the indigenous imagery of pre-Buddhist Tibet all enter into the mix at Karme Chöling. There is lots of feasting, celebration, and laughter, and much of the great food served is grown organically in the huge exquisite garden under the supervision of a master farmer.

My devotion to living and teaching the organic vision has remained the focus of my life, with sporadic meditation practice and occasional weekend programs playing a supporting role. Friendships with people who gravitated to the neighborhood to be part of the Karme Chöling orbit have increased my respect for the teachings. My openness about the value of this practice for my work, and my outspoken support for talking about spirituality in the context of Social Ecology, however, branded me as somewhat suspect within the radical establishment. Those students who expressed similar interests and inclinations were routinely assigned to me, unless they were so affronted by the disparagement that greeted them when they broached the subject that they left in disgust.

I have never found any inherent contradiction between what the two disciplines teach, and consider them to be complementary and equally valid schools of thought. The concept of basic goodness in particular points directly to the pursuit of social justice as a fundamental prerequisite for an enlightened society. It also provides an explicit framework for caring for nature as well as other humans. This is comparable to the social ecology world view—that humans are not separate from nature, and that human activities are not inherently destructive or antithetical to an idealized pristine nature.

The social ecology community could most assuredly benefit from greater attention to the dimension of personal growth and inner development, while the Shambhala community would be well served by a stronger level of social and political engagement. I have particularly found the Shambhala concept of spiritual warriorship helpful in confronting the political as well as the personal challenges I have encountered. Courage and compassion are important qualities to have when you are challenging the prevailing paradigm, and working within the system that you hope to replace. When I asked a friend who is a leader in the peace and social justice community whether he thought political engagement was more important than spiritual practice, he quoted our activist friend Dave Dellinger: "That's like asking me whether it is more important to breathe out or to breathe in."

The influence of Buddhist thought on the evolution of the organic movement, as well as its importance to social change movements in general, is clear. Gandhi, while not a Buddhist, derived his nonviolent resistance tactics from the same roots. As I noted in Chapter 1, Gandhi and Indian peasant culture had a direct influence on the early organic theorists and practitioners, as well as on the advocates of rural renaissance and alternative economics. Today internationally known activist and author Vandana Shiva, who promotes organic farming and seed saving in India, consciously emulates Gandhi's *satyagraha*[20] in opposing the use of genetically modified crops by Indian farmers.

The creation of "Enlightened Society" is the current focus for Shambhala Buddhism, now led by Chögyam Trungpa's son, known as The Sakyong (translated as "Earth Protector"). The Sakyong and some senior students actively participated in the massive 2014 climate march in New York City. Students and practitioners are encouraged to find ways to reach out to their community and to help others in any way possible, such as offering programs and meditation instruction for prisoners. This can be viewed as one way to avert or at least minimize the enormous suffering that looms as economies crash and global climate chaos intensifies.

The idea of enlightened society cries out for realization in concert with the nonviolent and reconstructive politics of movements such as Occupy. There is surely some cross-fertilization going on, as engaged Buddhists join forces with the occupiers and social ecologists help train the movement in nonviolent direct action and decentralized democracy.

## Articulating the True Organic Vision

The primary thread connecting Social Ecology and Shambhala Buddhism is the tenet that humans are both part of nature and basically good. This is also an important piece for me of the true organic vision. Bookchin's concept of humanity as nature rendered self conscious is echoed by numerous Buddhist authors, and placed him at odds with some advocates of deep ecology. In a debate that raged in the nineties, Bookchin accused the deep ecologists of being anti-human in asserting that people are no more important than trees or earthworms, and they accused him of being anthropocentric in seeing humans as the center of the universe.

In my ongoing battles over the definition of organic, the widespread presumption that anything that is natural  (meaning untouched by humans) must be good, versus anything synthetic (meaning human-made) must be bad, has led to deep confusion and anger. As the organic label has degenerated into a marketing claim based on this presumption, it is no wonder that consumers are confused by the competing claim by food manufacturers that their products are "all natural." Among my favorite quotes when attempting to unpack this deeply held assumption is attributed to Buckminster Fuller: "If you can do it, it's natural."

A fundamental principle of the true organic vision is that a product can be said to be "organically produced," but not described as possessing any inherent "organic" quality. I certainly believe that organically produced food is better in many ways because I know how it was produced. There is, however, no way to definitively distinguish an organically produced apple from a similar conventional fruit by any kind of quantitative analysis in a laboratory. This, in essence, is why the system of third party certification was developed, as we will see in the next chapter. In a sense, when a consumer purchases an organic product, they are exercising the precautionary principle[21] on an individual level. Given an alternative that has not been treated with possibly harmful substances, it is rational to choose the one that carries less personal risk—however slight the authorities say it may be.

Many who believe in the "nature equals good" and "humans equals bad" dichotomy also believe that natural also means "pure," and they want food and water that is as "pure and natural" as possible. My gut response is that purity, which is about homogeneity, is anathema to the organic process. A good example is distilled water, which is totally pure, but lacking in the minerals that both make it taste good and replenish some of what is lost in perspiration and urine. Ecological harmony and ecosystem resilience demand high levels of diversity, which is the ultimate impurity. Diversity is crucial to health on many levels—genetic, species, cultural and aesthetic, to name a few. And it is health rather than purity that is the ultimate objective of an organic system. As we saw in Chapter 1, the quest for purity has uncomfortable associations with the eco-fascist mindset.

## Soil Is Anything but Pure

There may be no better illustration of the incompatibility of the demand for purity with the true organic vision than its focus on the importance of soil ecology. Various authors have railed against "treating our soil like dirt," meaning considering it to be something unclean with which one is advised to avoid coming into contact. In her recent book, *Farmacology*, physician Daphne Miller convincingly illustrates how literally contact with soil is related to increased health for her patients.[22]

My study of soil science that led me to produce *The Soul of Soil* made this connection crystal clear for me, as did the direct experience of working with my hands in the soil, observing its different qualities, and listening to the voices of its inhabitants. Once the original printing by UVM Extension of 1,000 copies had sold out, the publication became my property and I enlisted my friends Joe Smillie and his wife Susan Boyer, then living out in the boonies of rural Quebec, to help me revise and self-publish it in 1986. Thirty years later the fourth edition is still in print and considered a classic.

We return now to the story of how the organic movement became an industry, and my role in its evolution.

# 3 Big Brother and the Organic Industry

*Our acts as consumers and our acts as citizens can be linked, and one can bear the seeds for the other...consumers who buy organic food as a symbolic gesture may embark on an educational journey which may radicalize them, leading them to demand better policies from their governments or get engaged in building more concrete alternatives.*
— Gunnar Rundgren

Our wedding the summer of 1984 was the event of the season for our community. It had rained the previous few days, but that August morning the clouds dispersed and a glorious rainbow arced over the field where the zinnias and cosmos I had planted in May were in full bloom. Stewart's brother-in-law's contra dance band played a schottische and we came skipping out of the woods separately, both wearing garlands on our heads and carrying bouquets. As we met up we continued down the path to the chuppa where our sisters awaited with our officiating pagan priestess, Olive. The rolling hills of the newly mown field were dense with family and friends old and new, and after the ceremony a local Klezmer band had everyone snake-dancing in a long line through the field and around the flowers. Under a tent in the field was spread a feast from garden and sea. Among the guests were friends of my parents whom I had never met; every so often in the years that followed I would encounter an aged neighbor who would inform me that she had been at my wedding and it was the most fabulous party she had ever attended.

## Building a Life, Becoming a Farmer

Stewart had succeeded in capturing my heart just when my time as a mover and shaker in the world of alternative agriculture seemed to have arrived. Embracing his family and the land he called home gave me the feeling of having it all. All except money, of course—but riches of resourcefulness, community and good soil, coupled with youthful energy and optimism, more than made up for that lack. It was all I had dreamed of, and yet not

Ceremony under the chuppa, August 1984. Left to right: Lee Gershuny, Roxanne Fand, Grace Gershuny, Stewart Hoyt, Olive Ylin, Avis Hoyt-O'Connor, Delsie Hoyt.

as idyllic as the image appears in my rearview mirror. Believing in the dream, I was oblivious to the clues of what was to come. Nevertheless, my whole eight year-plus sojourn as a member of the Hoyt family was breathtakingly happy, filled with new adventures, growth, learning, and love—until it ended in a way that was predictable only in hindsight.

As soon as the last wedding guests were gone and our honeymoon camping trip was over, we set about building our house. The previous winter we had worked out some drawings and models of what we wanted and decided on a good spot, on the edge of the wedding field and hidden by the woods from the main road, with a steep but short driveway that had been the field access drive. Stewart had been collecting recycled building materials for years, adding it to generations of junk dwelling in the family barn. A few miles away lay the mother lode of used construction materials, known as the St. Johnsbury lumber dump, from whence our hardwood floor that was torn out of a demolished school gym was liberated. The best haul was a huge dock that Stewart was hired to dismantle on Cape Cod, where he had spent the winter working on a scallop boat.

We did most of the work together, including digging holes for the concrete piers for our foundation which we poured with the help of a borrowed cement mixer. I taught myself to do the wiring, and still live with

The house, Spring 1985, Barnet, Vermont

my novice mistakes. The design was a six-sided lozenge shape with the long edge facing south, the metal roof sloped at the correct angle for the eventual installation of solar collectors. To the south edge of the roof we attached a recycled glass greenhouse on a steel and cypress framework, salvaged from a family friend's commercial greenhouse business. Inside the greenhouse stood two gigantic fiberglass tanks for use as solar heat storage; they came from the solar greenhouse at Stonyfield Farm where I had interned. The walls of the house were constructed using the ten-inch lumber from the dock as top and bottom plates, held up by a double row of two-by-fours with a dead air space between the rows—giving us a very well-insulated structure and the advantage of being able to use salvaged two-by-fours, almost all of which had one funky edge. We got the roof on just before the first snow, worked on insulation and interior walls during the winter, and pronounced it habitable enough to move out of Stewart's mother Margie's house in the spring.

The gardens were divided between those in the upper fields adjacent to the house, where there was about an acre's worth of flat, well-drained, loamy, and miraculously stone-free ground, and the lower field on the other side of Joe's Brook Road, below the barn that perched right on the edge of the pavement. This bottomland, with its luscious chocolate cake silt loam, offered another couple of acres between the road and the brook that were sufficiently well drained to cultivate. We grew every vegetable you ever heard of and some you haven't. We sold at two weekly farmers markets, we sold to restaurants, and we sold some root crops to Organic Farms, Inc. Later we organized a CSA—a community supported agriculture scheme[23]—which consisted of about 25 shares distributed weekly during the summer, with winter storage crops like cabbage, onions, potatoes, and carrots delivered monthly through the fall. We raised chickens, ducks, and even rabbits for sale, and ate like royalty. We planted a bunch of apple trees in the field, all antique varieties, and a small patch of blueberries just for home consumption. This was my opportunity to put into practice all the theoretical and second-hand knowledge I had been accumulating in the previous years as an organizer and student. I managed the financial end of things, diligently recording everything we bought and sold, and handled the increasing amount of paperwork required for certification. Even then it was getting to be a lot of work to keep track of all the varieties of seeds we bought, record how we dealt with weeds and pest problems, and arrange appropriate soil tests on different pieces of our farming puzzle.

We did a lot of cover cropping and bought very little in the way of inputs; we grew all our own vegetable and flower seedlings in our greenhouse, and mixed our own potting mix using Eliot Coleman's recipes. Eliot was then managing the farm at the Vershire Mountain School in Vermont, and was generous in sharing his vast knowledge and inventive vegetable production techniques with the expanding ranks of professional organic growers. He and Stewart, much alike in their creative ingenuity, hit it off well. I admired Eliot's knowledge and his willingness to mentor the younger generation, but the adulation with which many of my farming friends regarded him, and his obvious relish of that adulation, made me squirm a little.

Eliot and I had some disagreements about the value of certification for helping to expand the ranks of organic farmers and consumers alike. His position was, essentially, that consumers should acquire their produce from someone they know and whose growing methods are explained in written material or through conversations. There is no need for the bureaucracy of certification in such a simple person-to-person transaction. It is hard to argue with this viewpoint; however, even then it was clear that if we wanted high quality organically produced food to be accessible to the majority of consumers in places far removed from our idyllic—some might say remote—rural farms, it was unrealistic to expect them to get to know their farmer directly. This was even more the case for the vast majority of American farmers growing commodity crops like wheat, corn, and soybeans, for whom direct marketing of specialty crops was completely out of the question. I argued that some other way of reliably representing the organic quality of the food was needed if we were to become a major force in US agriculture, rather than an elite niche market serving a small minority of educated consumers.

## Organic Certification Evolves

So why did I devote so much time and effort to the often questionable pursuit of a credible organic certification program? Despite many misgivings and occasional exasperation, I had continued to shepherd NOFA's still dormant organic certification program as a volunteer after getting it started in 1977. Although there was little debate about the standards and the expense and time commitment needed to move the process forward were minimal, there was little marketplace incentive to getting certified and so the program had attracted little interest from growers in either Vermont or New Hampshire. Most everyone was selling their products locally, to people who either were not concerned about their growing methods or were happy to buy direct from a trusted producer. To be sure, there were already concerns about fraudulent organic claims, but with no promotion budget few saw the value of NOFA certification seals for selling what they grew. One of the original growers who declined to renew his certification expressed his lack of enthusiasm for using the certification seal on his products, saying "I'm not selling NOFAs."

NOFA was not alone in this dilemma. A survey conducted in 1980 by the National Center for Appropriate Technology (NCAT) compiled information from 17 organic certification programs in as many states, including a couple of distributors and manufacturers who had "in house" standards and certification programs that they required of producers who wished to sell to them.[24] Three states, California, Oregon and Maine, also had organic labeling laws on the books. The authors interviewed various certification contact people, and identified common themes of a fairly consistent set of organic principles along with a broad range of acceptable practices and divergent verification procedures. "Certification," as depicted by their interviewees, "was seen not only as able to hinder further abuse of that sorry word "organic," but also to encourage good soil husbandry and higher consumer consciousness." Responses to their inquiry about the prospect of legislation and other forms of federal engagement in the process are summed up by saying: "Throughout most, if not all, of the conversations threaded a basic mistrust of anything to do with government involvement in organic certification."

Original NOFA organic seal

In a concluding section the NCAT authors discuss various philosophical approaches taken by their interviewees, boiling down the responses they received into two contrasting viewpoints: the recipe approach vs. the integrated approach. "The recipe approach," as they characterize it, "seems to emphasize substances and techniques (or the avoidance thereof) which are or are not 'organic.'" The integrated approach, in contrast, "emphasizes the wholeness of one agricultural unit (whether a farm or a cow), which cannot validly be analyzed by any one component without taking the whole unit into account." This dichotomy, so aptly summarized by the NCAT authors in 1980, has plagued the world of organic standards and certification since then. The recipe approach is where we're still stuck today—a situation that furthers neither good soil husbandry nor higher consumer consciousness.

## Certification and Its Discontents

The frustrations of trying to organize farmer —like frogs in a wheelbarrow, as one colleague has put it—took their toll. Although I attempted to resign as certification coordinator two years after taking it on, in the absence of another candidate for the position I felt obligated to stick with it. In truth it felt more like it was stuck to me—like gum on the bottom of my shoe.

In the spring of 1979, when I was working as the full-time NOFA state coordinator, the newly organized Vermont Northern Growers Cooperative (VNGC), located in a former potato barn in the hamlet of East Hardwick, Vermont, struck a deal with NOFA to certify its dozen or so members on a group basis. This was intended to give the fledgling growers coop a leg up in marketing its organic root crops and other storage vegetables such as winter squash, onions, and cabbage to urban consumers, and was regarded by both as a mutually supportive arrangement—the growers would get a seal of assurance that they were legitimately organic, and NOFA would get exposure in the marketplace as a credible legitimizer. Nowadays this model is used primarily in the global South (or those countries sometimes referred to as the Third World) as a means of allowing very small producers who are organized under one marketing arrangement—whether as a cooperative or under a contract with a private business—to be certified as a single entity that has multiple subunits. This is often combined with some form of "fair trade" program involving hundreds or even thousands of smallholders who grow a crop such as coffee, cocoa, or cotton in the same region.

The process quickly became contentious. Beyond communication problems, the early growing pains of a marginal movement are evident in the growers' complaints. Difficult decisions had to be made in the spirit of impartiality and avoidance of the appearance of a "buddy system" in our small community. Since the coop sold the products from each member farm under the VNGC label, each member had to qualify for the "Class A" certification category in order to use the NOFA seal. The standard entailed achieving "a steady state organic level in which, besides prohibition of toxic insecticides or herbicides, proper soil balance and biological activity must be achieved." Demonstration of the requisite soil balance and biological activity was required in the form of a soil audit from Woods End Laboratory in Maine, which at the time offered a test for soil humus quality resembling a Rorschach, and similarly subject to interpretation. Although this was a rather subjective yardstick, it represents the attempt to emphasize the achievement of excellent soil quality as a key criterion for organic certification.

I asked the Certification Committee to make a decision about which category to assign to a few growers who had been late in submitting soil test results, and about how to handle the seal use quandary if all the growers could not qualify for Class A. The Committee decided to hold the line on requiring only Class A for use of the seals, but to bend the rules by granting that status to two questionable growers, despite some strong reservations. One thoughtful and heartfelt letter in my file came from Jake Guest, one of the Committee members, in which he agonizes over this decision, saying, "I only hope that in the future all the groundwork you have laid down pans out and becomes the powerful tool that we all hope it will be toward sane food production."

The subsequent meeting with the VNGC group was a difficult one, with numerous complaints lodged against me personally and the NOFA certification program in general. The situation foreshadowed the events that developed during my tenure at the USDA 15 years later, and the issues we grappled with then remain challenges today. First on the list of gripes was a charge of personal bias against one of the borderline growers by the name of George Crane.

George was a handsome slick talker, well versed in organic philosophy and practice, who was actually the very first grower we had certified. His soil tests were not yet up to par, yet he claimed to have devoted considerable care to soil building in the couple of years since he was first certified. The guys at the Coop (and the leadership was all male, though there were a couple of women growers) admired George's ambition and marketing savvy, and apparently felt that his substantial acreage of carrots was important enough to the venture's financial health that he shouldn't be downgraded because of some personal grudge of mine. My suspicions about him had been raised the winter of 1978 after he was first certified for a couple of fields of oats—less than 50 acres total—when I got a call from a company asking if he was a legitimate organic grower. It seems that he was offering them multiple carloads of certified organic oats, and they wanted to check his authenticity. Even projecting bumper yields, which his sandy run-down soil could not have supported, this was beyond the realm of possibility—and this is what I had told them.

Today certification inspections involve a lot of paperwork, central to which is conducting sample audits to make sure that a grower or manufacturer is not selling more organic product than they could have produced. Back then the need for such a complicated exercise was not on our radar—we worked almost entirely on the basis of personal trust and peer review of certification candidates. The postscript to this story is that a major scandal emerged a few years later, after George had withdrawn from VNGC, built his own root crop washing and packing facility, and proceeded to undercut their prices with massive quantities of organic carrots. A delegation from the New England Food Coop Federation (NEFCO) had even been bamboozled when they toured the carrot fields George claimed as his own—except that the fields he showed them actually belonged to VNGC members. It was only after a delegation from VNGC met with the NEFCO management that this deception was uncovered; it turns out that George had been importing carloads of conventional carrots from Canada, washing and packaging them, and claiming that they were organically grown by him. Absent any kind of organic labeling law, of course, this did not rise to the level of being considered a fraudulent claim.

Aside from my suspicions about George that were validated in hindsight, this experience highlighted the question of when and how to allow compromises to our ideal notions of the best organic standards—in this case, the requirement for excellent soil quality—for the sake of practicality and economic feasibility. In an un-mailed tirade I underlined the following statement: "What is emphatically crucial to me is that one be willing to acknowledge just to what extent such compromise has been made." We were groping for some way to introduce flexibility into our standards without violating our principles or misleading consumers. This tension between purist and pragmatist perspectives remains a central source of controversy in the organic world.

Another important lesson learned from this experience is the fact that fraud is very hard to avoid in a system based largely on trust, even—perhaps especially—when the miscreant is a known and credible participant. Fraud is an inevitable temptation for those caught up in the pressure to measure success solely in terms of profit—the hallmark of our market economy. The moral superiority of small organic farmers does not preclude the possibility of falling victim to this temptation.

The remaining issues in my irate missive boil down to the irritation of organizing "frogs in a wheelbarrow," along with some resentment about what might be called male chauvinist arrogance—a corollary of the problem known as "small farmers, big egos." So here I was, a non-farmer and a woman to boot, setting myself up to act as power broker and promulgating bureaucratic hoops through which the oppressed "real farmers" must jump. Implicit in some of the complaints was the accusation that NOFA was becoming an impersonal bureaucracy out to control its members. Yet one of our core principles was democratic control of the organization by its members. The perennial problem—worse with farmers, I suspect than with some other constituencies—was getting them to respond to calls for feedback or input, let alone getting them to attend a meeting. It seems that such over-worked and stressed-out populations as small farmers are difficult to rouse into response without a sense of crisis or an exaggerated threat from an enemy to combat. This kind of "either-or" thinking, with its associated tendency to divide the world into "us" and "them," was a problem I recognized early on as posing the biggest threat to the success of our movement.

Most of the growers' complaints about certification have since been transferred to the federal government and, while there is today considerable justification for the feeling of loss of control over what organic means, farmers remain by and large stubbornly averse to responding to opportunities to engage the process, with some noteworthy exceptions. I also carried some resentment at the farmer superiority argument. This had much

NOFA-VT Board-Staff meeting, Hardwick, Vermont-1985: (l-r) Miranda Smith, Jack Cook, Meredith Leonard, Robert Houriet, Joey Klein, Amy Darly, Stewart Hoyt, Grace Gershuny

to do with my feminist outrage about devaluing the "woman's work" of organizational housekeeping, combined with the frustrations of working for the cause at minimal wages and lacking the resources to realize my own farming dreams. At least the part about devaluing women's contributions has been alleviated in recent years, and myriad programs and projects exist to help young would-be farmers realize their own dreams. To whatever extent my efforts helped bring that about, I give myself a small pat on the back.

## 1984 and the Arrival of Big Brother and the Organic CIA

The year 1984 represents an important punctuation mark in this story, beyond my new life and new home sketched at the start of this chapter. The iconic title of the book by George Orwell about a political dystopia is more broadly symbolic of another cultural shift—1984 also marks the year that the word "industry" was first used in connection with "organic foods." As defined in dictionary.com, this word means "the aggregate of manufacturing or technically productive enterprises in a particular field, often named after its principal product."[25] By this definition, the producers of hand-made craft items could be considered members of an industry. Unfortunately, the connotations of the word are particularly negative when used as an adjective, as in "industrial food." Indeed, from the earliest stirrings of the movement the terms "industrial farming" and "manufactured food" have represented the worst aspects of the prevailing food system that we sought to replace. The move of organic food and farming toward greater credibility and respect among conventional producers and food businesses brought with it the seeds of skepticism on the part of those who had pioneered its principles and methods toward the "suits" who sought to profit from and regulate their work. So it seems apt to call this the year Big Brother and the Organic CIA arrived in Vermont.

Now that I was becoming a farmer I had a perfect way out from under the burden of managing the certification program; because I expected to become a certified grower the following season, I could not also administer the program. But the "gum on my sole" stubbornly persisted. One day in the early spring of 1984 I heard about a growers meeting to be held at the Vermont Northern Growers Coop in East Hardwick, with my good friend Joe Smillie and some guy from Pennsylvania who was looking to set up another certification program.

This meeting was my first experience of Tom Harding, who had hired Joe to work with his farm input and consulting company named Progressive Agri-Systems. Joe and his former partners in Eaton Valley Agricultural Services had branched out a little too far and lost a lot of money through a rather disastrous series of mishaps, including some missteps in their management of the NOFA Bulk Order—the annual cooperative purchase of such organic-friendly soil amendments and fertilizers as rock phosphate and liquid fish and seaweed concoctions, which were hard to find at the time. Joe was now peddling his consulting services solo and working as a stay-at-home dad at the homestead he had built out in the wilds of rural Quebec.

Joe's task was to provide a known and trusted introduction to the growers in northern Vermont and southern Quebec for Tom Harding and his client, a Maryland-based produce distributor called Organic Farms, Inc. Farmers' inherent distrust of middlemen was heightened by the culture clash represented by these straight businessmen from another state. The company's partners were seeking a source of organic root crops and cold-loving crops such as lettuce and broccoli during the summer months, when Mid-Atlantic and Southern suppliers could not readily produce them. They were offering a contract opportunity to a group of growers who consisted mainly of highly educated, authority-defying ex-urbanites who were long on hair and short on cash. Though some of them had already banded together to form this wholesale growers cooperative, they were still uncomfortable with the idea of shipping their products to distant markets, and wary of entanglements with aggressive entrepreneurial types. For their part, Harding and his clients were skeptical of the capacity of this defiantly laid-back bunch to fulfill contracts and meet quality standards. Did they have the know-how to produce the desired quantity at the right time? They would certainly need refrigeration, ice machines, and similar technology in order to keep the vegetables in top condition as they passed through several steps in the supply chain before landing in a consumer's grocery cart.

As the first fresh produce wholesaler to feature only organically grown products, the Organic Farms, Inc. marketing plan called for all suppliers to submit to third party verification of their organic status. This is where Tom Harding's grand scheme came in. Tom is a charismatic natural leader and a brilliant speaker, who dazzled all of us with his understanding of and commitment to the organic vision, and his ability to connect emotionally with our aspirations. He spoke with passion and pride about his commitment to soil health and his desire to extend the benefits of organic farming to as many farmers and eaters as possible. He stood for the importance of good farming and a fair shake for farmers, so long as they were committed to doing it right. Tom's plan was to pilot a national certification program that would feature state-level autonomous chapters, administered locally but adhering to a consistent national set of standards and certification procedures. Each chapter could adjust its requirements to accommodate regional conditions, and certified producers could have access to a nationally recognized logo and promotional program. Modeled on the crop improvement associations that provide certification and information support to conventional seed producers, it was to be called the Organic Crop Improvement Association or OCIA. It quickly became known as the Organic CIA.

I saw immediately that this plan could fit quite neatly into NOFA's decentralized organizational structure, and successfully pitched the idea of hiring me to coordinate the program, rather than setting up a parallel effort in competition with NOFA. Organic Farms, Inc. was to subsidize the program during this initial phase at no cost to the growers, although they were not bound to sell only to that company. It was understood that in subsequent years we would be on our own to support the costs involved. Organic Farms also established a consolidation point at the Vermont Northern Growers Coop's building, springing for a walk-in cooler and an ice machine to keep the produce in top condition.

By June I had drafted a set of standards based on NOFA's and organized a couple of information meetings for growers. Twenty-six signed up to participate that year, ranging in size from one-eighth acre of carrots to over 15 acres of mixed vegetables. This compares with a record of five clients for the NOFA program (not counting the VNGC group) in any previous year, when they had to come up with about 25 dollars to pay travel costs for the inspector but lacked markets that demanded proof of their organic status.

The initial standards were rather vague and general, and since it was already late in the planting season some leeway was granted for use of small amounts of certain highly soluble conventional fertilizers. However, the standards firmly eliminated any land to which synthetic pesticides had been applied for the previous three years. It was during this summer that the defining battles for the soul of organic began crystallizing. Should certification be for a whole farm or field by field? Is the acceptability of specific materials of primary importance, or should the focus be soil health and crop nutritional quality? Should organic standards be determined by market demands and consumer concerns, or by producers' knowledge of what is both important to soil health and practical for them to achieve?

## An Industry Is Born

The OCIA project was conceived in response to a growing need. There was as yet only a handful of food processors who sold their products under an organic label, but they were becoming important markets for larger farms, especially producers of grain and other commodity crops (such as corn, soybeans, peanuts, and the like) who were beginning to convert significant acreage to organic production. The earliest pioneers, like Walnut Acres, had direct personal relationships with ingredient suppliers for their processed products (mostly soups, cereals, and other grocery items), and much of what they processed was grown on their own farm. They did not need independent verification that their ingredients were organically grown. However, by the mid-1980s companies such as Erewhon, Eden Foods, Little Bear Trading Company, and Arrowhead Mills were distributing their organically produced cereals, pasta, soy products, nut butters, corn chips, and similar products nationwide, and even internationally. In Germany, France, and England, where the first organic organizations took root and where small farmers were valued and publicly supported, the organic market was generally better developed. European buyers were offering premium prices for organically produced American grains and courting leading Midwestern producers to supply them.

Some of these companies established their own version of organic standards, and required all their suppliers to be inspected to verify that they were truthfully representing their practices. Others required all their suppliers to be certified by a particular independent program, such as California Certified Organic Farmers (CCOF) or the Minnesota-based Organic Growers & Buyers Association (OGBA). A company based in Connecticut, Mercantile Development Company, set up its own program to certify organic grain for its European customers. Farm Verified Organic (FVO), as it was then known, later became an independent entity and moved its home base to North Dakota, where it continued to focus on certifying Mercantile's suppliers. Problems arose when producers who wished to sell to several of these markets were required to undergo multiple redundant certifications and inspections, often at their own expense, which usually involved similar—but not exactly the same—standards. Moreover, turf battles and marketing wars raged between these companies and programs, fired by accusations of "drive by inspections" as well as the claim of "higher standards." Of course they didn't accept each other's inspection and verification procedures, let alone agree about how high was high enough for their standards.

To illustrate this situation, Mercantile suppliers had to have FVO certification, and if they also wanted to sell to Eden Foods they would need OCIA certification. FVO standards prohibited use of Chilean nitrate (discussed in greater detail further on) in consideration of the demands of the European market, while CCOF and NOFA standards allowed limited use of that material, under the "restricted practices" category. Midwestern grain and bean producers, it should be noted, had no need for a boost of soluble nitrate in cold soils, while it was a very helpful tool for winter vegetable production in California and early spring lettuce and spinach production in the Northeast. FVO, of course, insisted that their prohibition of Chilean nitrate represented a higher standard.

Almost all of these standards and programs only addressed crop production, and rarely livestock products or processing. Many organic consumers were vegetarians, although the integration of livestock into cropping systems has long been a central tenet of organic production. There was a general sense that processed organic products should be "minimally" processed, but no specific guidelines as to what constituted minimal. Certainly ingredients should be "all natural," with no artificial flavors, colors, or preservatives. But what about sugar:  Are raw sugar and honey acceptable, but not refined sugar? How about processing temperatures, which affect nutritional quality? The list of possible issues to consider was daunting. In general, such specifications were addressed by a given company's internal quality control procedures—and its marketing department.

## Consumer Perception: Optics or Metrics?

Consumers, for the most part, had little role in early organic standard set-ting—at least in the Northeast. Although the rationale for involvement in certification included market development and consumer assurance, most of the early programs were initiated and controlled by growers—with occasional representation by someone from a food coop or an aca-demic. The focus was on what made sense ecologically in that region, as well as the practicality of different requirements for working farms. The scientific justification for a given practice was key, and our ultimate goal was to convert skeptical conventional producers to the organic cause, us-ing consumer demand and higher prices as the "carrot" to pull them in. We assumed that consumers would neither understand nor care about the technical details. The promise of "food you can trust" was backed up by a system of farmers watching over each other.

During this period virtually nobody questioned the assumption that the higher the standards the better. Willingness to meet the highest stan-dards was believed to reflect a true commitment on the part of the farmer to the organic world view, as opposed to someone who was only in it for the money. There was less concern for the question of how a given prac-tice would appear to consumers. The focus, however, was about to shift to an increasing emphasis on the optics of a given allowance, rather than the metrics. *How will it look to consumers?* rather than *what credible evi-dence do we have?* started to become a prominent issue as the farmer-led movement began to encounter the marketing profession. The question of what we mean by "higher" organic standards, and the usefulness of this distinction, is a theme that will continue to arise—along with a fair bit of confusion and acrimony—as the newly hatched organic industry begins to enter mainstream markets.

Tom Harding was not the only one looking for a way to resolve the dilemma posed by conflicting organic programs, which was the impetus for developing OCIA. A new international organization had been formed a few years earlier by a group of European organic advocates, under the name of IFOAM (International Federation of Organic Agriculture Movements). A Canadian IFOAM member was organizing an academic conference at Michigan State University in June of 1984, and saw an opportunity to invite representatives of both the non-profit certification groups and the various food processors and traders to a "North American workshop on certification and marketing of organically grown products." I managed to cajole Tom into sending me to the workshop, the first of what was to become an endless meeting parade.

Of the 15 or so people who met in Lansing, less than half represented non-profit consumer cooperatives or organic farmer groups, such as NOFA and Canadian Organic Growers. Most were representatives of food businesses (e.g., Eden Foods, Rainbow Natural Foods, Organic Farms, Inc.) or consultants and input suppliers (e.g., Progressive Agri-Systems, Living Farms). The first two days of informal talks produced the plan to form some kind of North American "organic foods industry" association; some of us reluctantly agreed, for the first time, that such an industry existed. On the third day a more formal meeting was convened and a steering committee was formed, with Tom Harding as chair and me as secretary, to begin establishing an organizational structure for the Organic Foods Production Association. The name was later lengthened to denote its geographical reach to the whole continent, becoming the acronymic mouthful, OFPANA, or Organic Foods Production Association of North America. After the passage in 1990 of the federal organic law, or Organic Foods Production Act, and with increasing organic production of such non-food items as personal care products and fiber, not to mention wine and beer, the organization finally changed its name to the Organic Trade Association.

## Tensions Escalate Back in Vermont

The state of Vermont is a lot like a small town, especially within the organic and alternative-progressive community. A tangle of love relationships connected many of us in the somewhat in-bred organic farming community, and at times made working relationships a bit uneasy. My own life was no exception.

A friend of mine, who was working for the Vermont Northern Growers Coop, was hired in the summer of 1984 to coordinate the produce contracts and orders for Organic Farms, Inc., and we worked closely to-

# Organic Foods

## ORGANIC FOODS PRODUCTION ASSOCIATION OF NORTH AMERICA

*Grace Gershuny and her husband, Stewart Hoyt, display organic produce at the Farmers Market in St. Johnsbury, Vt.*

*Chemical-free pest control is becoming state of the art, as illustrated by this Bug Vac, by Driscoll Strawberry Associates in Watsonville, Calif., which vacuums insects from plants.*

Cover of the first OFPANA newsletter, a slick insert in the Natural Foods Merchandiser, November 1988.

gether to coordinate farm visits and certification questions. At the time this friend was living with Robert Houriet, who was one of the founders of VNGC, at his new farm in Hardwick. Their relationship was a bit rocky and, having had my own clashes with Robert over the certification process, I did not feel that he was good for her. It was through this friend that I was introduced to a young grower by the name of Stewart, whom she had been dating during a period of uncertainty about Robert. Around the same time I was encouraging Miranda, who had recently been divorced, to follow up on her interest in Robert, kindled when she was having conversations with him as part of her job with NCAT in the late 1970s before she came to Vermont. Besides being closer to his age, I saw her as better able to handle his dominating style. Being no fool, Robert recognized what a great asset Miranda and her highly developed farming and financial management skills were to his operation. My friend doubtless carried some resentment over both my romance with Stewart and my support for Miranda to move in with Robert, which probably led to some lapses in communication between us that summer.

Robert and Miranda became key growers for Organic Farms, Inc. and their thinking, both philosophical and practical, figured prominently in shaping how the OCIA pilot project unfolded. Miranda had also introduced me to her good friend Judy Gillan, who was setting up an ambitious demonstration farm and training center in Belchertown, Massachusetts called the New England Small Farms Institute, and who also attended the IFOAM meeting in Lansing. Judy and I soon became collaborators in developing the organizational nuts and bolts of OFPANA.

Once the basic standards and procedures for the OCIA project were established, I began visiting each of the farmers who wanted to participate. My field notes from that time reflect both technical and organizational issues that appear as recurring themes of the growing movement. One aspect of certification that we all saw as a boon to growers was the chance to swap tips with other growers via the field inspector—in this case also the program administrator. A few growers, however, regarded their techniques as proprietary and not for sharing with those less clever growers who might become competitors. Today the rules have evolved to require a strict separation between regulatory and consulting functions, but the best part of the job for me was being able to help the growers learn from each other.

Ambiguities and confusion mixed with distrust, and paranoia proliferated like weeds after a rain in both the certification process and the business arrangements with Organic Farms, Inc. This tension between the grassroots and the "suits" also sparked some interesting confrontations, marked by deliberate provocation, poor communications, and unrealistic expectations all around. A few of the growers were unhappy with the prices they were getting, and there were instances of shipments being rejected for poor quality and orders that were misunderstood or mixed up. My friend who was coordinating the orders and shipments sometimes got blamed, but the middlemen who were thought to be profiting by ripping off the farmers increasingly became the objects of their hostility. To this atmosphere was added an enraging pattern of false promises and unmet obligations—mostly perpetrated by Tom Harding, who left a trail of angry creditors in his wake. My journal of that time includes some entries expressing the fear that we were all being taken for a ride by another charismatic slick talker. I was kept in the dark about a great deal of what he was planning, and disappointed by constant lack of follow-through on verbal commitments.

Many of the growers, in turn, grumbled endlessly about the business relationships, which induced them to drag their feet about completing the bureaucratic formalities of certification, further blurring the lines between technical issues and economic ones. Soil tests were again required, but there was no procedure for sampling or evaluating the results in any consistent way. No longer intended to show that soil quality was up to snuff, the soil-testing requirement became strictly a means for the farmer to demonstrate their attention to fertility needs and an appropriate plan for soil management. However, the marginal value of these tests and the expense of having them done year after year made them hard to justify. For example, Robert was using a do-it-yourself test kit to evaluate his soil every year, testing each of his multiple small fields separately. This was much cheaper than sending samples to a lab, but Tom, who was the arbiter of such technical matters, considered it too unreliable.

The issue of acceptable sources of fertility was also muddy and contentious. Robert and Miranda were both ardent proponents of judicious use of such fertilizers as ordinary (as opposed to triple) super phosphate. Super phosphate is technically a synthetic because it is manufactured from mined rock phosphate by treating it with a strong acid. This rendered it much more soluble than the natural rock version, and engendered much less transportation cost per unit of fertilizer. Their position, which was supported by several other growers, was that while it may not be as beneficial for the soil as the rock powder due to the absence of naturally occurring trace minerals (also lacking the rock powder's small amount of natural radioactivity), super phosphate was more ecologically benign due to low energy expended to transport it, and largely indistinguishable from rock phosphate in its impact on soil chemistry and biology. Its higher solubility could be beneficial in some situations, such as when cold soils cannot release enough phosphate to plants due to reduced biological activity when temperatures are low. On the other hand, excess applications of soluble phosphate—in Vermont, generally coming from good old cow manure—are readily washed into surface water by rain where they contribute to serious pollution problems. Still, the question does not—and as they argued, should not—hinge on whether the substance is left in its "natural" state or manipulated in a manner deemed to be synthetic.

The opposite problem was presented by the widely accepted use of sodium nitrate, called Chilean nitrate because it is mined in an extremely arid region of northern Chile and nowhere else. Though it is a natural mined substance, this material has a number of drawbacks, ecologically speaking. The material is characterized by a high level of solubility as well as high salinity (a result of the sodium ion connected to the nitrate), both of which can harm soil microbes in excessive amounts. Growers who need an extra dose of nitrogen for crops, either for early plantings when soil is cold or as a mid-season boost to demanding crops like corn, generally use such materials sparingly. Beyond recognizing the importance of protecting soil organisms, the stuff is rather pricey. Fertilizer companies who supply products suitable for organic production often depend on Chilean in their high analysis blends— there is nothing else that can bring the nitrate portion of the N-P-K[26] numbers on the bag into double digits.

Chilean nitrate, which up until very recently was still permitted to be used by US organic producers in limited amounts,[27] could be considered the poster child of the problem of fixating on allowed versus prohibited materials and practices in organic standards. This material has been hotly debated in trade negotiations, Europe having resolutely stood against any use of this highly soluble nitrate source, while the US continued to allow its use. The issue remains a problem today with Canada, which otherwise considers the US standards to be equivalent to theirs, requiring that produce coming from the US affirm that no Chilean nitrate was used to fertilize it.

Robert's penchant for melodrama framed the absurdity of having a blanket requirement of a three-year transition period after any use of a prohibited substance. Late in the season, he and Miranda informed me that they had reluctantly resorted to a spot application of Malathion, a broad spectrum conventional insecticide, in order to save a late planting of broccoli from being ravaged by flea beetles. Acknowledging that the broccoli in question could not be sold as organic, he argued that the rest of the crop in that particular field had not been touched by the pesticide, applied carefully to only that single row. But rules are rules, and there was no way to bend them for the sake of one important grower's financial salvation. Painful as the decision was, the entire field must lose eligibility until the requisite three years had elapsed since application of the prohibited substance. Standing in the field, eyes cast down to the beautifully formed broccoli that had been saved from the brink of death, Tom Harding and I sadly delivered the verdict. Clutching his chest, Robert staggered a bit and cried out, "I'm having a heart attack!"

The heart attack was feigned, but Robert's anguish was real. Though we were sympathetic, there was no possibility of making an exception here— it was not a grey area that could be subject to corrective action. Robert was also well aware of the rules before he took the drastic step of applying Malathion. We also understood that there was little likelihood that the pesticide had contaminated the rest of the field, which would nevertheless have to be sold on the conventional market at a substantial loss. What was the lesson in this? How could similar situations be avoided in the future? This incident, along with the George Crane organic fraud episode discussed earlier, highlighted for me the fallacy of putting small producers, even those who are credible and committed, on a pedestal. Whether it was outright fraud or a belief that allowances should be made for the righteous and just, there was no inherent ethical value to being small.

A brief digression may be in order here on the subject of scale because to-day, even more than in 1984, many consumers believe that anything small is good, especially if it is local, and that the converse is also true—anything big is bad and is most likely far away. What is big and what is small, how-ever, is tricky to define. Local can be equally problematic. Vermont, hav-ing very few stretches of flat tillable land, has very few farms that produce vegetables on more than 50 acres. Even the largest dairy farms rarely come close to 1,000 acres, and grow mostly pasture or hay on sloping ground that would be unwise to cultivate. In the Midwest and the Great Plains, however, where land is relatively flat and water rather scarce, a farm that can support a family might need to be hundreds or even thousands of acres, depending on what crops are grown or animals raised there. While there may be few corporate mega-farms within 200 miles of New York, Hartford or Boston, there may be such operations located pretty close to Chicago or San Diego. It is clearly silly to believe that only small farms should or could be organic if one's objective is to convert as much of the farmland and food system as possible to organic management and more healthful food. To complicate things even more, the USDA's Census of Agriculture, conducted every five years, identifies anyone earning at least $1,000 in a given year from agriculture as a farmer. A "small" family farm is one with a gross income of less than $250,000.

## Growing Pains of the New Industry

In 1985 I was no longer NOFA's certification program staff person, but I remained involved as a volunteer review committee member helping to evaluate applicants through our peer review process. This required a few of us to examine all the certification applications and inspection reports and decide on their status, including any conditions that had to be cor-rected. When the application of any member of the review committee was being discussed, that person would leave the room. We also acted as an executive committee and hired part-time administrators and field inspec-

Miranda Smith instructing an apprentice — Hardwick, Vermont, 1985

tors. I still have a letter of application from the highly qualified young woman we hired in 1988, Enid Wonnacott, who went on to become the organization's executive director and has built NOFA into an outstanding organization that continues to lead on the national stage.

After the OCIA pilot year was finished I continued to work with the expanding organization to help set up new chapters in Quebec and New York, which included conducting inspections and organizing informational meetings. I also continued to work as a volunteer on organization-building with OFPANA, scrounging support wherever I could to represent NOFA-Vermont and our growing certification program at meetings in places like Toronto, Philadelphia, and Las Vegas. The Vermont OCIA program, meanwhile, reverted back to NOFA to manage, and at first the group was willing to go along with continuing as a chapter of OCIA. But the confusion and antagonism seemed to escalate as new chapters were formed, and the transparency of the emerging organization left something to be desired. There was, in short, little trust for Tom Harding among the growers. After another year of suspicion and negativity about the scheme, the Vermont chapter voted to drop its increasingly costly OCIA affiliation and become a strictly NOFA-Vermont entity, adopting the name Vermont Organic Farmers for its certification activities. VOF continues to be the NOFA-affiliated USDA-accredited certifier today—boasting over 500 certified farms and processors.

The fact that Tom Harding was a founder of both OFPANA and OCIA, and that meetings were often held conjointly with many of the same participants, was another huge source of suspicion and confusion. My role in the OCIA organization quickly evaporated as chapters proliferated in the

Midwest and Great Plains, and decisions were increasingly made without consulting the membership. Although I had created the original model for its standards and certification procedures, I was eliminated from consideration as a field inspector due to a decision to hold a training session—at a hefty fee—in Colorado, which was decreed to be mandatory for anyone to be considered for these assignments. Although I was allowed to do some inspection work for a handful of OCIA clients, I was never formally accepted due, I  suspect, to the defection of the Vermont group from the organization.

These events set the stage in several ways for the grassroots rebellion against the perceived takeover of the oxymoronic organic industry by "corporate organics." The struggle faced by grassroots organizations to fund attendance at meetings and participation in the work of the organization was a sticking point from the dawn of OFPANA. The "suits" were accustomed to business expense accounts and believed in the importance of maintaining a façade of prosperity. The grassroots people, on the other hand, held meetings in church basements and schools, generally preceded by a potluck supper, and when we ventured far afield would find a place to stay with a friend of a friend. A culture of marketing began to emerge, and discussions about how to entice more dues-paying members to join and support our efforts elicited slogans like "sell the sizzle, not the steak," countered by concerns about selling too much sizzle when there was as yet little meat on the table. For their part, the business people were wary of the perceived anti-business attitude of the "socialist termites" among us, and my complaints about having to find the money to pay for my travel to meetings—let alone compensation for the organizational work I was doing on behalf of the new trade association—sometimes subjected me to their ill-disguised scorn. It was especially tough for me to learn how to "dress for success," and my discomfort with feeling compelled to wear appropriate business attire at these meetings (along with the discomfort of the attire itself) must have been obvious.

The situation was hardly as clear cut or black-and-white as some of my compatriots portrayed it. Despite the damage done to the organization's credibility by Tom Harding, he also contributed a great deal—financially and in time and energy—to making OFPANA work. I just couldn't help liking him and admiring his skill and intelligence at the same time that I knew he was feeding me a line of bull. Some committed grassroots organizers got involved early on as well, including Harlyn Meyer from California, David Yarrow from New York, and representatives from Minnesota,

Ohio, British Columbia, and everywhere in between. In the course of long philosophical discussions with Judy Gillan, Joe Smillie, Miranda, and even Tom Harding, we debated our assumptions, tore apart our motivations, and looked carefully at the legacy we were creating and the precedent we were setting. We believed we were bringing about the organic revolution, and knew that the transformation of this fringe movement into a mainstream idea would not be painless. We also had quite a bit of fun together. Part of the appeal of organics to the conventional farmers and business types, I have long believed, is that we have more fun, and. I count myself a devotee of the Emma Goldman approach to revolution: If I can't dance, I don't want to be part of it.

## Laying the Groundwork for the Industry

With Tom Harding as figurehead and chief promoter, the organizational framework for OFPANA was developed largely through the efforts of Judy Gillan, who established its secretariat at the New England Small Farms Institute (NESFI) headquarters in Belchertown, Massachusetts. Judy was also involved in organizing the Massachusetts chapter of NOFA, and NESFI provided a good central location for quarterly meetings of the region-wide federation of NOFA chapters, which now consisted of Connecticut, Rhode Island, and New York as well as the original Vermont and New Hampshire.

Joe Smillie and I agreed to work together as contractors to develop the document that became the first step in bringing some coherence to the budding organic industry. OFPANA's plan called for developing an endorsement (more properly referred to as accreditation) program that would evaluate the various certification programs operating in North America,[28] and award its seal to those that met its criteria. We set out to create general guidelines to which both the standards and system for verifying that a given operation was in compliance with the standards would have to conform. We also aimed to include some latitude for variation in standards based on regional and local conditions, rather than requiring precise alignment with a one-size-fits-all standard. Our task was to collate information on the standards and certification process from as many programs as we could find, domestic and international, and create a structure that could incorporate their disparate formats. It was a huge undertaking, with various drafts and revisions circulated, discussed, and voted on by the growing OFPANA membership over the course of two or three years.

The final result was a product called the "Guidelines for the Organic Industry," universally referred to as "The Guidelines."

What we noticed as we sifted and sorted through the range of standards and certification processes was that, as had been true when NCAT conducted its survey in 1980, there were very few substantive differences among the standards. Some contained flowery philosophical discussions of why and how to manage soil or care for animals in the best way. Others were more professional or bureaucratic in style, with words like "shall" and policy and procedure specifications arranged in complicated numbering systems. Everyone was clearly still borrowing from each other, and adding their own improvements or adaptations for local consumption. Most included lists of allowed and prohibited materials that were integrated into information about recommended practices, so that a farmer wishing to learn how to go about producing organically could immediately see what to do and what not to do. In most cases there was also a category for "restricted" or "regulated" practices and/or materials—the ambiguous grey area, larger in some and smaller in others.

All the US certifiers also relied heavily on a farm plan requirement that identified what the farmer had done in the previous year and intended to do in the year ahead, and a strategy for avoiding reliance on grey area materials and methods—the plan for continuous improvement. For example, all the US standards identified botanical pesticides such as rotenone and pyrethrum, as well as biological controls such as Bacillus thuringiensis (Bt), as restricted or regulated practices. If a farmer needed to use any of these materials, they had to provide a justification and a plan for reducing or eliminating reliance on this material in years to come. This was the approach we had used in NOFA's program as well as for the OCIA pilot, and the Guidelines were similarly structured.

They did things a bit differently in Europe, where IFOAM had begun working on what it called its "Basic Standards." This was also promoted as a "standard for standards" but, once they began their own accreditation program, no deviation from the specifics of this standard was permitted. Rather than listing materials within the body of the standards, European standards use a system of annexes to list allowed materials and other specific criteria. So a farmer has to flip through the pages to find the appropriate annex when deciding what materials could be used to build soil or control pests. There is also no farm plan tradition in Europe, so much of what is considered a grey area in the US—like Chilean nitrate—is prohibited outright there. On the other hand, European certifiers are allowed to issue what they call "derogations." That is, in certain cases they can allow a producer to use, under specified conditions, something that is generally prohibited. These differences, though seemingly minor, resulted in extreme headaches once government regulations and trade negotiations entered the picture.

The concept of reciprocity was the gold ring to which we aspired—a unified nationwide definition for "organically produced" that was achievable by producers and comprehensible to consumers, with a credible verification system to back it up. Despite the similarities of their standards, every certifier claimed theirs to be the "highest" or "strictest" and the rampant mutual distrust gave everyone a hard time selling their program to a rightly skeptical public. Once an accreditation program was established and a core group of certifiers got on board, we reasoned, they could no longer refuse to accept each other's decisions as equivalent to their own. But this goal receded with each meeting, when the level of internal warfare overwhelmed all attempts to reach agreement. Joe and I tried to drum up support to move ahead with the accreditation (then called endorsement) program, which had been identified as the organization's top priority, but failed to secure enough commitment by any of our deep-pocketed members. Eventually Judy Gillan took the concept to an IFOAM working group, with the result that they initiated their own brand of accreditation program—which, as it turned out, did not require its participants to accept each other's certifications as valid. Back to square one.

## Trying for Reciprocity

Meanwhile, OFPANA hosted several large meetings for the purpose of developing some agreement among the various programs to engage in a voluntary system of reciprocity. At least one of these reciprocity meetings involved hiring a facilitator to help us resolve points of internal dissension and clarify our common goals. Agreements in principle were signed, but ultimately nothing came of it. Despite the clear similarity between the programs and general satisfaction with the Guidelines as a unifying document, the ideological clashes, turf battles, and personal animosity between various program managers and members proved insurmountable. The impetus for these meetings came from the second OFPANA president, Marc Schwartz.

Marc and his then-wife Jennifer had started Little Bear Trading Company in Winona, Minnesota primarily as a grain mill, and then developed a tortilla chip product that later became a huge commercial success. For a couple of years Joe and I worked as a consulting team for Marc who, in the absence of a functioning system of reciprocity among certifiers, devoted considerable resources to his own internal organic verification system. He paid for us to inspect all his grain and bean suppliers, and it was a privilege to be able to tour so many solid Midwestern organic farms—most having previously been managed conventionally—whose owners took such obvious pride in the quality of their crops and the health of their soil.

During the summer of 1988 one of the worst droughts for some time was parching fields in that part of the country, and the difference between these organically managed corn and soybean fields and those of their conventional neighbors was astonishing. The corn in the organic fields was green and, if not lush, was at least producing well, while neighboring nonorganic corn was curled and singed with yellow. Because the organic farmers were building soil organic matter rather than mining it, their soils were better able to hold onto the little water that came their way in these conditions. This is one reason why, back when we started the NOFA program, we considered soil organic content to be a key criterion for organic acceptability. Under the Little Bear standards, however, soil organic matter content was no longer a primary criterion; avoidance of synthetic fertilizers, rather than soil quality, was now the line in the sand.

The inflexibility of this rule gave me pause more than once. One farmer in particular was an enthusiastic and knowledgeable recent convert to organic growing, and had sprayed a water-soluble product on his crop that was touted as a stimulant to biological activity and enhanced nutrient uptake by the plants. Reading the fine print on the label, I noted that the formula contained a tiny amount of urea, a synthetically derived nitrogen source that is identical to the biological molecule commonly excreted in urine. I tried to argue with Marc on this farmer's behalf—the amount of urea actually applied to the crop was really infinitesimal—but he felt that any compromise on this standard would be seen as corner cutting, and he could therefore not purchase grain from this producer.

Marc's certification subsidy to his producers was not sustainable in the end, and Little Bear Trading Company is no more. (The chip business has long since changed hands.) Marc had more affinity for the political and social views of the grassroots activists among us than some of the other business types, and he had actually instituted an ethical practices committee within OFPANA. But when it came down to meeting obligations to his suppliers, his business ethics may have ultimately succumbed to his cash flow problems.

## Two Crucial Debates: Laboratory Testing and Origin of Materials versus Agronomic Responsibility

The first three or four years of the industry's infancy brought a growing consensus about the nature and direction of organic standards. While the denizens of the expanding organic companies gave lip service to the primacy of farm-level production and especially soil quality, even the most conscientious among them were more concerned with how the rules would appear to consumers—the "optics" of the standard—than with allowing farmers to use such "grey area" tools as plastic mulches or medications to treat livestock illness that could mitigate the risks of transitioning "cold turkey" into organic production. The problem of how best to convey what organic practices were all about in a few simple phrases that consumers could quickly comprehend was of utmost importance to them. Two crucial debates, and the decisions about them made by OFPANA's board and membership, gave shape to the question of how organic would henceforth be defined for the public and for the regulatory authorities watching in the wings.

The question of the role of laboratory testing in organic standards was debated at a meeting in California in 1986. On one side were two scientists, including Victor Wegrzyn, an agronomist from Cal Poly Pomona, and chemist Stan Rhodes, owner of a private lab in the San Francisco area. They argued that the most important attribute of organic products, which could readily be analyzed in a laboratory, was the absence of pesticide residues. Stan Rhodes was also promoting his "Nutriclean" program, in which products were tested and given a seal vouching for their freedom from pesticides—a "no detectable residues" claim. The "nutri" piece was an analysis of a product's vitamin content that could be performed in order to make a claim about its nutritional value. Going down this path would shift the discussion of organic standards away from production methods and all their shades of grey to a seemingly more simple focus on product quality. Indeed, the Nutriclean model did not require that food be produced without pesticides, only that there were no residues detectable in the final product.

The opposing scientist was Dr. Maria Linder, a nutritional biochemist at California State University in Fullerton, who has long been aligned with the biodynamic philosophy and anthroposophic medicine. Dr. Linder argued that, inasmuch as the organic vision was a holistic one, the nutritional value of organic food could not be reduced to laboratory analysis of isolated nutrients. This reductionist model of nutrition gives no indication of the vital, living quality of a food product.[29] Moreover, nutrient content can vary considerably due to climate, variety, and other agronomic conditions, in addition to nutrient losses in post-harvest handling.

As a result of this meeting, OFPANA board member Harlyn Meyer, a colorful character who farmed in California, assembled an ad hoc committee on laboratory testing which drafted a position paper entitled, "Laboratory Testing and the Production and Marketing of Certified Organic Foods." OFPANA Position Paper #1 was approved by the board and released in December 1986. The committee looked at three different types of laboratory testing and their potential applications: pesticide residue testing, nutrient testing, and agronomic/environmental testing. The authors concluded that there was value to using pesticide residue testing to identify potential problems from accidental drift or cheating, and that soil testing was useful as a tool to help growers improve their management practices. Concerning nutrient testing, on the other hand, the committee felt that it is "best relegated to the realm of research for the present." The paper's conclusion stands as a foundation for how organic certification and marketing would be approached from then on: "Despite its potential value, all laboratory testing should be seen only as auxiliary to existing forms of direct assessment which include on-site inspection, records of growing practices, etc. It cannot legitimately stand on its own."[30]

This was huge. As a result, nobody in the industry would again advocate for the use of product quality criteria as a requirement for organic certification. The "organically produced" label would thereafter be explained, not as a guarantee of safer, more nutritious food, but as a description of how the product was produced. In effect, the organic label avoids passing judgment on the dangers of conventional agriculture, and instead provides the consumer with information on which to base their own risk assessment. We will return to the question of why this is such a big deal when we explore the task of translating organic standards into federal regulations.

The second debate was much more contentious, and represented a fairly even split among the OFPANA membership. This one also addressed a fundamental precept on which the organic philosophy rests, and dictated the direction that organic standard development has taken since then. The NCAT authors back in 1980 had recognized the seeds of this conflict in describing the distinction between the "integrated" approach and the "recipe" approach to organic standards. The philosophical differences between the sides in this debate continue to divide the movement, and have contributed in no small way to the level of hucksterism and confusion on the one hand and irrational crusading on the other that today characterize too much of the organic discussion. The debate known as "origin of materials" versus "agronomic responsibility" finally and irrevocably moved the emphasis of organic away from the level of soil health, human health, and ecosystem health and into the realm of consumer perceptions.

I have laid the blame for the inelegant, unsexy phrase "agronomic responsibility" at the feet of my good friend Joe Smillie, who used it to describe our approach to writing the OFPANA Guidelines. This idea was highlighted in our introduction to the final draft, where we characterize "traditional" standards as prohibiting most soluble minerals, "especially if they have been chemically treated or synthesized." However, we go on to say, "as technologies for analyzing soil health, crop or product quality, and environmental impact become more sophisticated, both farmers and scientists increasingly advocate changes in criteria which will examine a material's effect on these, rather than focus on its origin. **OFPANA strongly supports this scientifically-based and responsible approach to establishing criteria**" (emphasis in original). Similarly, in the introduction to the section on organic production practices we state: "**The focus is on evaluating practices and materials in light of their effect on soil life, water and environmental quality, nonrenewable resource use, livestock health, and nutritional value and safety of the foods produced**"(emphasis in original).[31]

Soon after the first version of the Guidelines was formally adopted a revisionist movement erupted. The uprising among "traditionalists" was a reaction against the inevitability of judgment calls and grey areas in evaluating candidates for certification under the agronomic responsibility approach. The primary argument for this position rested on the need for a simple explanation that consumers could understand, and that did not violate existing consumer beliefs that organic farmers did not use any "synthetic chemicals," with the associated sales pitch that organic products are cleaner, purer, and safer than conventional ones. Although they acknowledged that such expectations did not reflect the reality of organic production, proponents of using "origin of materials" as the basis for organic standards argued that the flexibility and need for judgment inherent in the "agronomic responsibility" approach could "open the system up to abuse," as opposed to providing clear, bright lines between what was permissible and what was not. Ironically, as was to become clear to many of us only in hindsight, the meaning of synthetic, like that of organic, is based on a process by which something is produced, not a quality that can be measured objectively. You cannot tell whether or not a given substance is synthetic by examining or analyzing it—you have to know how it was produced. Even then there may be "natural" and "synthetic" variants of a substance that are chemically identical but manufactured differently. Hardly a clear, bright line. The story of why Robert and Miranda advocated using "synthetic" super phosphate, while others argued for prohibiting "natural" Chilean nitrate, is but one of many examples of the difficulties created by focusing on origin of materials.

The OFPANA membership was polled by mail on the subject in 1987, and it generated some thoughtful and at times humorous debate. Judy Gillan, Joe Smillie, and I drafted the position paper in favor of agronomic responsibility, while Harlyn Meyer and a few cohorts from California wrote the one advocating the origin of materials position. By a narrow margin the tally resulted in a majority favoring the origin of materials criterion as the basis for organic standards. Following this vote the board decided to change the Guidelines to eliminate all synthetic materials from the "accepted" category, and to establish criteria by which synthetics might be considered acceptable on a case-by-case basis. A couple of years later this approach would be enshrined in the legislation that was to dramatically change the landscape of the organic movement.

# 4 Death and Rebirth on the National Stage

*We have to guarantee our seat at the table and be consistent, articulate, and united in presenting and defending our vision of sustainable agriculture.* — Anthony Pollina and Grace Gershuny

At the peak of our farming activities, our market garden covered two-and-a-half acres of intensively cultivated vegetables. As Dancing Bears Farm we sold at two farmers markets, a few local restaurants, and ran one of the first community supported agriculture projects in our neighborhood. Stewart and I shared all the farm work, from planning and seed ordering through harvest and marketing, with occasional hired help from a local teenager. The Saturday market in St. Johnsbury, held in the middle school parking lot, was better established than the Wednesday market on the green in Danville. In late summer's harvest frenzy we could do most of our picking and packing the day before, loading the truck with boxes of tomatoes, cucumbers, cabbages, onions, leeks, peppers, squash, beets, and carrots. We only had to get up early to pick the more perishable crops, so everything would be in peak condition when the market opened at 9:00 a.m.

In mid-August it would just be getting light as we tumbled out of bed and into the field still filled with fog, to cut, wash, and pack a few cases of broccoli, lettuce, and Swiss chard, gather several bunches of fragrant basil, parsley, and cilantro, and stuff a few grain sacks with fresh picked corn. As we worked the field would emerge from the mist, and as the sun burned the last wisps of fog from view we would hurry to grab a few last bouquets of flowers, the cash box, and the record book for another market day. Some Saturdays we also brought along a couple of local restaurant orders, and one of us would go off to deliver them while the other tended the market stand. Our community supported agriculture shares were distributed on Thursdays; about half of our two dozen or so sharers

Grace as Garden Goddess

picked up at the farm, while the rest we delivered to a more central location ten miles away at a friend's barn on the edge of St. Johnsbury.

The 1989 growing season was especially busy. Between market days I taught Bioregional Agriculture in the Institute for Social Ecology summer program, which lasted four weeks. When that was over I flew out to the Midwest for a couple of weeks to do some organic inspections for Little Bear. Meanwhile, I kept up with fulfilling orders for our self-published version of *The Soul of Soil*, and worked on setting up training sessions and field days for the big grant project that NOFA was administering. Then there was the volunteer work, attending review committee meetings for Vermont Organic Farmers, and helping organize the upcoming national gathering of organic farmers organizations planned for early December in Kansas.

On market days I would come home and take a nap, after a swim in Joe's Brook if it was a hot day, and then get to work on the phone and the computer after dinner. After my second ectopic pregnancy that summer we decided it was time to begin looking into adoption; we registered with a private adoption agency and started the home study process, looking to our parents to help out with the substantial costs involved. I wondered how we would manage caring for an infant while juggling the farm and all our other projects, but we both wanted very much to bring up a child in this version of utopia we were creating.

## Alar Sunday and the Looming Law

Things were beginning to move a bit on a national level in the alternative agriculture world in the late 1980s. The shifts were due in part to devastating droughts throughout the Corn Belt that, coupled with overextended farm debt and depressed prices, brought about a farm crisis marked by a spike in farm foreclosures and farmer suicides. Family farm activists rode their tractors from Iowa and Illinois to Washington, DC, while Willie Nelson, John Mellencamp, and Neil Young organized a benefit concert that drew a crowd of 80,000 and initiated the annual event and farm advocacy organization known as Farm Aid.

While the Reagan-Bush years were not conducive to alternative anything, a modest federal grant program supporting "Low Input Sustainable Agriculture," dubbed LISA, was initiated through the efforts of Senator Leahy. As the precursor to the valuable Sustainable Agriculture Research and Education (SARE) program, LISA provided grants to collaborative projects that helped inform farmers and agricultural professionals about ways to reduce the use of farm inputs such as commercial fertilizers and pesticides and still make a living. Both "low input" and "sustainable" were generally considered to be euphemisms for "organic," a term which was accorded no legitimacy in Washington.

The seven-state NOFA Council, collaborating with Cooperative Extension in each northeastern state, won one of the first LISA grants for an ambitious two-year project. I was hired to organize in-service training programs for agricultural professionals such as Extension agents and researchers from various agriculture schools, and Miranda was hired to edit a compendium of low-input practices gleaned primarily from organic farmers in the region. The grudging respect paid by some of the most skeptical establishment participants with a conventional perspective was encouraging, even though our Extension-dominated steering committee preferred that we avoid using the "O" word.

Northeast Organic & Sustainable Farmers Network Team—A seven state project funded by LISA (precursor to SARE), 1989-1990 Front (l-r): Ed McGlew, Margaret Christie, Enid Wonnacott, Miranda Smith Rear: Grace Gershuny, Vern Grubinger, Judy Green, Karen Idoine

The organic industry was beginning to attract media attention and, at least in some quarters, was beginning to be taken seriously. New companies were getting involved in manufacturing organic products, and certification programs in all corners of the country were increasingly professionalized. Some of the new entrants were larger players in the conventional food business like Smuckers, which began producing organic jams, preserves, and juices. "I have good news and bad news," said Joe Smillie in a presentation at a winter NOFA conference during that time. "The good news is success! Meaning more certified organic products are being made, more farmers are farming organically, and the industry is growing quickly. The bad news? *Success.* The 'big boys' are watching us more carefully and deciding whether to jump into the market or try to shut us down."

All of these shifts in the industry led to the first national conference on organic and sustainable agriculture policies in Washington, DC in early March 1989. The meeting was organized by the Center for Science in the Public Interest and an affiliated non-profit called Americans for Safe Food. As a leader of OFPANA's organic farmers caucus, I had a front row seat. The plenary panel included muckraker Jim Hightower, then Texas Commissioner of Agriculture, who had established one of the first state-run organic certification programs.

The week before the conference the CBS news show *60 Minutes* aired a segment based on information developed by the Natural Resources Defense Council (NRDC) about the dangers of Alar, a chemical (still) widely used on apples to make them hold longer on the trees after ripening. The story, entitled "A is for Apple," raised consumer alarm about this carcinogenic substance that's concentrated in apple juice and therefore consumed by children and infants in much greater quantities in relation to body weight than was accounted for when EPA tolerances were set for the stuff. In other words, the tests to determine the theoretical safe level of exposure to this compound were based on a much bigger person consuming a much lower average amount of apples and apple products than was clearly the case for millions of young children.

In the weeks following Alar Sunday, as it has been known since, apple sales took a nosedive and anxious parents dumped gallon after gallon of apple juice down the drain. Just as quickly the industry responded, trotting out expert assurances of the complete safety of this utterly wholesome, good-for-you product. And lo and behold—several major retailers began hastily promoting displays of gleaming, high-priced organic apples. Hmmm. How could this be? Environmental and consumer groups knew enough about the time lag needed to convert a farm to legitimate organic status (something even more challenging for tree fruit like apples) to understand that this sudden market appearance was bogus through and through. Although this deception was technically illegal in those few states that had organic labeling laws on the books, these laws were poorly (if ever) enforced, and there was no legal definition of organic on the federal level. It could certainly be argued that the relabeled apples met the common scientific definition of organic as "containing carbon atoms."

The perfect storm of public outrage over yet another chemical threat to food safety, juxtaposed with a conference in DC that centered on the growing availability of viable alternatives to these practices, produced a quantum leap in awareness about the fledgling organic industry.

Jim Hightower made sure to emphasize the Alar story in his rousing and witty speech. The time, he assured us, had come to take some serious steps to regulate the organic label and protect all of us from the fake organic hucksters seeking only to prey on consumer fears. A full complement of congressional staff, agency people, and other policy folk mingled and talked with the grassroots activists, organic entrepreneurs, and assorted journalists in the packed hotel conference rooms. Among those who paid close attention was a young protégé of Hightower's named Kathleen Merrigan, who had recently been hired to serve as agricultural staff for Senator Leahy, then Chair of the Senate Agriculture Committee. The sense that we were all present at an historic moment was electrifying.

Our OFPANA organic farmers' caucus huddled up at the conference and hatched a plan to hold a meeting with the grassroots organic farming community sometime later in the fall, after harvest season. We needed to strategize about a united response to potential federal organic legislation. The constituency of our caucus, which functioned as a standing committee that represented the interests of the organic farm community within the industry, ran the gamut from counterculture types from the Northeast and West Coast to Midwestern conservatives. We set about raising funds to organize this meeting, knowing that it would not be easy to get all of the essential organic organizations to participate.

Many important grassroots organic groups were not represented in the OFPANA ranks, mainly because of their concerns about the manufacturers and traders leading the organization. The "suits," principled though they might be, lived in a different world from the farmers, who tended to distrust them. There were plenty of cordial, mutually beneficial relationships, but the distrust was often ideological. Despite understanding that they had to become attuned to business realities in order to survive as farmers, the organic movement vanguard types (myself among them) got a bit queasy around anyone who appeared to be in it mainly for the money. Our rallying cry of "food for people not for profit" sprang from a belief that even the best of intentions would inevitably be corrupted in a system where all decisions must be driven by the bottom line.

However, OFPANA's membership believed that it was important for organic growers to have a seat at the table, and allocated a modest budget to its organic farmers' caucus. OFPANA's democratic structure was key: board members and major decisions were voted on by the membership and members had to be companies or organizations, not individuals. Every member had the same vote regardless of annual revenue. And then there were all the heartfelt proclamations by the captains of the emerging organic industry that it was nothing without its heart and soul—the farmers. "If the farmers would only show up," I would sometimes plead with my grassroots compatriots, "we would have at least as much say in the organization as the suits."

So we put out the call to every organic-minded farm group we could think of to come to an assembly to be held in early December to strategize about possible federal legislation—but we knew we had some work to do to bring out the more recalcitrant anti-corporate types. The invitation to participate in the new OFPANA-sponsored coalition, dubbed OFAC for Organic Farmers Associations Council, was open to any organic group, whether or not they were OFPANA members. There's nothing like fear of federal regulation to rouse the troops.

## A Synergistic Opportunity

Just as this plan was percolating, another unexpected opportunity fell into my lap. Anthony Pollina, a friend who had started an advocacy group called Rural Vermont as a spinoff from NOFA's legislative committee, received some funding to put out a publication. Knowing that I had previously tried to get the various NOFA chapters to cooperate on a region-wide quarterly organic farming newsletter, Anthony asked me if I would be interested in helping develop something more policy-oriented and national in scope. I quickly pitched a proposal to produce a quarterly digest of interesting articles culled from the proliferating grassroots alternative farming newsletters, with a strong focus on state and federal policy developments. Each issue would also have a central theme that explored a subject of concern such as animal agriculture, biotechnology, or women in agriculture. The plan also included a means to cover publication costs through bulk subscriptions from the various organizations whose newsletters provided most of the material. In turn it would provide them with an ongoing voice in national policy discussions, becoming the communications vehicle of the still gestating OFAC organization.

Thus was born *Organic Farmer: The Digest of Sustainable Agriculture*. Our first issue explored "What is organic—and who decides?" and was produced in time for the initial OFAC assembly held in Leavenworth, Kansas in early December 1989. With a tiny staff that included Anthony's wife Deb Wolfe as publisher, and the very capable Chris Wood and Mary Deaett on production and administration, we managed to keep it going for four years (largely thanks to the Wallace Genetic Foundation, originally endowed by Henry Wallace, mentioned in Chapter 2). We never quite succeeded in generating the subscription support we had hoped for, and did not believe that our editorial position would be attractive enough to advertisers to make it viable. While serving a valuable role in the movement, the publication also provided a platform to hone my policy chops and a soapbox for talking to a very receptive national audience—and it was grand.

Premier issue of *Organic Farmer: The Digest of Sustainable Agriculture*. December 1989. Cover art: Stewart Hoyt

The Leavenworth OFAC meeting was a milestone. We had strong representation from all the major certifiers, among them Washington State's Miles McEvoy and several organic cooperatives, including the fledgling Organic Valley. Leading organic advocates converged from across the country, with representatives from organizations based in the Northeast, the Northwest, California, Florida, the Midwest, the Ozarks, and the Great Plains. Most of us had corresponded and collaborated before but had never met. We hired a professional facilitator and in the course of the meeting hammered out consensus documents on our mission and sets of organic principles.

## The Law Takes Shape

In the months leading up to the Leavenworth meeting, Senator Leahy's staffer Kathleen Merrigan had circulated drafts of proposed organic leg-

islation to the grassroots organic community and had also been confer-
ring with Washington-based consumer and environmental groups. In
Kansas she met with us to talk about our concerns and to give us pointers
on the legislative process and the obstacles involved. We had many concerns about the draft legislation, not the least of which was language that
would prohibit any use of synthetic substances by organic producers and
that would allow irradiation of organic foods. The latter allowance was
quickly removed, although no language prohibiting it was inserted, since
irradiation was officially sanctioned by the administration, and prohibiting it, according to Kathleen, would doom the bill.

---

## OFAC Statement of Principles of Organic Agriculture

OFAC participants felt the need for a "preamble" to a legal definition of organic that would form a reference point for all the untidy
ends that are required to be "consistent with the principles of
organic agriculture." This is the February 1990 version:

Organic farming practices are based on a common set of principles that aim to encourage stewardship of the earth. Organic
producers work in harmony with natural ecosystems to develop
stability through diversity, complexity, and the recycling of energy
and nutrients. They:

- Seek to provide food of the highest quality, using practices
  and materials that protect the environment and promote human health.
- Use renewable resources and recycle materials to the greatest extent possible within agricultural systems that are regionally organized.
- Maintain diversity within the farming system and in its surroundings, including the protection of plant and wildlife habitat.
- Replenish and maintain long-term soil fertility by providing
  optimal conditions for soil biological activity.
- Provide livestock and poultry with conditions which meet
  both health and behavioral requirements.
- Seek an adequate return from their labor, while providing a
  safe working environment and maintaining concern for the
  long range social and ecological impact of their work.

Some of us tried to argue for using an approach to organic requirements that was more in keeping with the concept of "agronomic responsibility," even though OFPANA had already voted to shift toward an
"origin of materials" standard. We tried to come up with verbiage that
might avoid the need to base the law on the distinction between natural
and synthetic. I rather liked the term "xenobiotic," meaning "foreign to
living organisms," to refer to substances that organic farmers and food
processors should not use. Using this rationale, a synthesized analog of
a familiar biochemical, such as citric acid, would not be prohibited as a
food additive or fertilizer ingredient since it was not xenobiotic. Similarly, it would be fine to use potassium sulfate (an important soil and plant
nutrient) as a fertilizer, regardless of whether it came from a mine or was
a byproduct of some manufacturing process. Some of us also argued that
the details of allowed and prohibited practices should not be solidified in
a law, but written into regulations that could be more easily amended as
our knowledge evolved. Organic producers, we insisted, should continue
to have an important role in overseeing the new standards, and these
should be based on the ones we had developed for ourselves over nearly
20 years of effort.

Kathleen's consumer-oriented constituency, however, was adamant
about keeping the requirements as strict as possible, and that the synthetic versus natural distinction was essential in order to maintain the
pure image that consumers had come to expect of organic food. The compromise worked out was a system of exceptions that could be made to the
general ban on synthetic substances, allowing certain types of synthetics
on a case-by-case basis, according to a specific set of criteria. Similarly,
natural materials like nicotine could be prohibited if they were known
to be harmful. Thus arose the National List, which became the vehicle
included in the law to allow some synthetic substances, if they met the
criteria outlined, to be used by organic producers. Decisions about which
synthetic substances meet these criteria would be made by a body representative of all the organic stakeholders, called the National Organic
Standards Board.

## A Legislative Miracle

By the end of the first OFAC meeting we had decided to send one of our
own to Washington to help organize our legislative strategy. Tom Forster,
who had worked on the Oregon Tilth organic program and with Gene

OFAC convening board, Leavenworth, Kansas, December 1989. Front (l-r): Faye Jones (MOSES), Kate Havel (CFSA), Judy Gillan (OFPANA), Tom Forster (Oregon Tilth), Patty Laboyteaux (CCOF). Rear (l-r) Fred Kirschenmann (Northern Plains Sustainable Ag Society), Allan Moody (Ozark Organic Growers), Ron Gargasz (Biodynamic Assn.), Marc Ketchel (Florida Organic Growers)]

Kahn at his Cascadian Farm in Washington State, became our "guy with the organic tie." Under Kathleen's tutelage, Tom was able to forge a coalition between OFAC and the big environmental and consumer groups who had helped shape the draft legislation. Groups such as the Sierra Club, Consumers Union, Pesticide Action Network, and Center for Science in the Public Interest all threw their clout and Washington insider connections behind the new bill, now called the Organic Foods Production Act (OFPA).

An unprecedented scenario unfolded in Congress in the spring of 1990. The OFPA was introduced as one of many titles included in the omnibus legislation known as the Farm Bill, which was moving through Congress that year with little fanfare. Introduced by Senator Patrick Leahy, Chair of the Senate Agriculture Committee, it won easy passage there, but the House version, introduced by Representative Peter DeFazio of Oregon, faced undisguised hostility in that chamber.

The OFPA was supported by the coalition pulled together by Tom Forster and a dedicated committee of advisors from the various organic farming, environmental, and consumer groups who had participated in drafting it, but was opposed by the USDA as well as by Representative

Charlie Stenholm (D) of Texas, the powerful Chair of the House Agriculture Committee. Stenholm flat out refused to allow it out of Committee, which would normally mean that it would die there and be omitted from the Farm Bill package voted on by the full House. But this was not a normal situation. A lobbying campaign brought organic farmers and a host of allies to Washington to meet with their Representatives, who were also bombarded with letters and phone calls from members of the Organic Foods Act Working Group (OFAWG), an informal coalition consisting of OFAC's thirty-five member organic producer groups plus 25 environmental and consumer public interest groups. The higher-rolling organic business community, organized as the Organic Foods Alliance, also played a role in the lobbying effort. As a result, the OFPA was introduced on the floor of the House where it narrowly passed, and President Bush (the first) signed it into law—an event that has been called "a legislative miracle." For the first time since the Reagan administration banished it ten years earlier, the "O" word was now grudgingly accorded official credibility.

Our strategy had succeeded against tremendous odds, on largely volunteer efforts and with a minuscule budget. An ironic counterpoint to this story of grassroots triumph is the lobbying strategy employed by the Organic Foods Alliance, consisting of manufacturers and traders who could ante up significant contributions towards hiring a professional lobbying firm called Potomac Partners. By most accounts their services had comparatively little impact on the outcome of the process, but their whopping fee saddled the organization, still lacking a regular paid staff person, with a debt that took years to retire. The grassroots, much more than the suits, were the heroes of the day, but the underlying tension between these industry sectors continued to percolate.

Winning the battle for the law was, we understood, only the beginning. *Organic Farmer* chronicled the painfully slow and often incomprehensible process of finalizing the law through a House-Senate Conference Committee, and then waiting for the USDA to begin work on its implementation. We assembled a stellar cast of editorial advisors, including academics, policy and technical experts, farmers and farmer organizers, and other leaders of the alternative agriculture movement. The complete collection of back issues contains a gold mine of information about the controversies that defined the moment, many of which continue to play out more than 20 years later.

Most of the discussions about organic standards and the direction of the new law chronicled in the pages of *Organic Farmer* (sources for complete back issues can be found in the Annotated Bibliography) revealed a strong level of consensus about the need to resist pandering to consumer misconceptions and base the rules on scientifically sound information. The growers and the scientists of our readership generally seemed to favor the "agronomic responsibility" position, discussed in Chapter 3, that saw the ecological soundness of a given practice as the most important determinant of its "organicness," regardless of the origin of the materials being used. No such consensus could be said to exist about the value of or need for a federal law. Support from most of the reluctant producers who wrote letters and called their representatives was inspired by the fear that if they didn't stay involved the consumer and environmental constituency would make the law untenable for them.

It would be another seven years before the first draft of the regulations to implement the law came out—and the power of the grassroots organic constituency was unleashed to block it, eventually undermining their own interests and the principles of the true organic vision in the process.

## Cycles of Birth, Death, and Rebirth

The situation on the home front, meanwhile, was becoming strained. Late in 1989, after having endured several rounds of fertility testing and treatments followed by two ectopic pregnancies, Stewart and I decided to adopt. We were barely scraping by financially, but with help from both sets of parents were able to come up with the money to cover the fees involved. We were fortunate—less than six months later one of the agencies with whom we had registered called to ask if we would be interested in a seven-month-old African American girl. They sent us some photos of her with her foster parents in Oklahoma City and we agreed. Since Oklahoma is a "closed" state, we could not receive any identifying information about her parents or even her birth name. The only information we had was her birth date and location—Anchorage, Alaska— and a brief medical profile of her mother, who was 18 and already had an older child. We thought carefully about the challenges of raising a brown-skinned child in this predominantly white community, but with the encouragement of friends and family our decision was clear. We would give her Stewart's last name of Hoyt, rather than a hyphenated surname. My father had died peacefully in his sleep just over a month previously, so her middle name became Haia, after Hyman (Chaim in Hebrew) Gershuny. Her first name

Grace and Opal, November 1991, Marshfield, Vermont

came from the book, *The Singing Creek Where the Willows Grow*,[32] about the nature savant Opal Whiteley.

Several weeks later I was on a plane to Oklahoma City. The people from the agency brought Opal to the house where I was staying with the sister of a friend and placed her in my arms. She immediately began to cry so I gave her the bottle I had prepared and sat with her in a rocking chair for a long time, just watching her. She was a long, lean nine-month-old with a powerful voice, and everyone in our community was immediately besotted with her. I spent so much time gazing at her face that I remember being startled when I looked in the mirror one day and noticed that I was white.

That our marriage seemed to have chilled a bit didn't bother me at first—the new parent syndrome was sufficient explanation, and we were cooperating nicely on child care and farm chores. At the height of our farming we were planting as much as two-and-a-half acres of market vegetables, and started all our seedlings in the greenhouse that covered the entire south face of our house. Aside from some tractor work to prepare land in the spring, we did everything with hand tools. Opal could play or nap in the shade while we worked in the garden, and we took turns looking after her to give each other time for other pursuits—Stewart's art and making wooden cooking utensils that he sold at craft fairs, and my writing and organizing work, which increasingly involved travel to meetings far away.

Early in the spring of 1991 we took our first vacation as a family and went to Jamaica to stay with our friend James in a little village up in the hills of the North Coast, about halfway between Montego Bay and Ocho Rios. We thought it would be good for Opal, then a toddler, to form a connection with a culture in which people who looked like her were in the majority, especially since she'd be growing up in Vermont, one of the whitest states in the nation. Neither of us had ever experienced the tropics or the "Third World" before, and the atmosphere was both intoxicating and horrifying. I was inspired by the spirit and ingenuity of the people, the unfamiliar vegetation and, of course, the music. The climate, however, was unbearable, and the violence that permeated the culture was frightening. The stark contrast between the life of the rural poor and the parade of American, Canadian, and European middle class tourists patronizing the fancy resort hotels lining the coast (where the poor, if they were lucky, worked as chambermaids and waiters) inspired my outrage and disgust.

James was still trying to straighten out his wife Shireen's US visa approval a year after they got married, and our small contribution to the family coffers for putting us up was a real boon. During this trip Stewart and I talked deeply about our relationship and, in hindsight, it is easy to see the warning signs that things were awry. During this trip we also met Shireen's cousin Matches, whose little concrete cabin was perched on a rock above the main thoroughfare through the village. Both of us were immediately taken with this beautiful, dignified Rasta. Stewart spent several afternoons hanging out and painting with him. At our farewell send-off Matches and I danced together the whole time, and our attraction was powerful and inescapable.

A little more than a year later, our marriage unraveled and the life we had created together crumbled down around us. When Stewart walked out on me one night to be with a woman he had recently fallen in love with, I was devastated. It felt like the beautiful dream we had shared and were building together had collapsed in a sudden earthquake.

Bentley "Matches" Morgan, Danieltown, Trelawny, Jamaica, April 1991

My only concern at this point was to take care of Opal and keep my life together for her sake. For the time being I decided to stay in the house that Stewart and I had built together so her life would not be too disrupted, but I really wanted to get as far away as possible. In early 1993, I made a plan to move to Jamaica at the end of the year to gain a fresh perspective where I would not be surrounded by reminders of my loss. It would also be good for Opal, I reasoned, to go to "basic school" there with the other four-year-old "pickney" (patois for children). I hoped that the chance to form bonds with Jamaicans would serve her well as she grew in self-awareness. My plan called for renting out the house in Vermont for a couple of years, returning periodically to teach at the Goddard College residencies for a week each semester and continuing to work with students via email (then still a novelty to which only a few of them had access). I was also pursuing a contract with an overseas volunteer agency, a kind of short-term Peace Corps assignment, which would pay my living expenses and costs involved with helping develop an organic certification program in Jamaica.

In the meantime I had been in contact with Matches, and went on a couple of trips to visit him before making the move. I realized that it could not possibly be a satisfying long-term relationship, but was happy to have the adoration and sensuality that he offered and grateful for the refuge of a place where I could simply relax and leave the past behind for a while. It was also valuable for me to immerse myself in his culture as the only white person in the village, and begin to understand both the culture and the feeling of being in the minority—albeit one generally perceived as dominating and exploiting the dark-skinned majority. Opal seemed to thrive as well, with lots of playmates and "aunties" nearby who were always happy to take care of her when we went away for the afternoon, though we took her along on longer excursions to Kingston, three or four hours by bus, or to visit friends farther up the coast. Within a few weeks she was chattering away in patois, helping to translate conversations that I was unable to follow.

I learned to cope with the very primitive living environment, although Matches' sisters looked after the laundry—all by hand in washtubs with their expert technique of forcing the soapy water through the clothing to make a "squipping" sound that indicated that the soap was adequately penetrating the cloth. Matches also did most of the cooking, using a little propane stove we acquired rather than cooking on charcoal outdoors as he was accustomed. We went to the weekly market days in nearby Falmouth, and I learned how to get around and where to get what we needed. I managed to get a little support from the volunteer agency and formed some great connections with the small Jamaican Organic Growers Association group as well as with some sympathetic Ministry of Agriculture folks. We organized a couple of seminars, including one co-sponsored by the Rodale Research Center that included a tour of the island's handful of organic farms.

My time in Jamaica lasted only about six months, and was one of tremendous learning, both joyful and painful. Stewart and I agreed that I would have custody of Opal for the first two years and he would have custody for the next two; after that we would work out a more frequent alternation. I knew that it would be hard for me to stay there for the whole two years, despite my times of respite back in Vermont when Opal got to spend time with her father. But the big problem was that there was no way that Matches could get even a visitor's visa to travel to the US and, though my divorce would soon be final, I really did not want to marry yet again. I had contacted my Congressional delegation, and even called one of Stewart's former Yale classmates in the Foreign Service. All of them advised me that a poor Black Jamaican stood little chance of being admitted to visit, sponsorship by American citizens who would guarantee his living expenses and return home notwithstanding. Having witnessed the visa runaround James and Shireen had endured, even after getting married, the situation looked grim.

## Keeping a Toe in the Organic World

I had given my *Organic Farmer* colleagues almost a year's notice to recruit a new editor and raise more funds to keep it going. Unfortunately, this plan didn't work out as hoped and our final issue was dated winter 1994, completed after my move to Jamaica at the end of 1993. In the years that followed I often wished there was still a publication like it.

When I left for Jamaica I had little sense of where my work life was headed, but figured that I might as well keep up my organic credentials by attending an organic inspectors training session being held in Florida in January of 1994—an easy hop from Montego Bay. There I met my cosmic coyote[33] comrade, disguised as a bald-headed, stuttering, Jewish guy with glasses. Michael Hankin had recently become the second in command at the National Organic Program office at USDA, and as we chatted about how things were progressing there in Washington he informed me that they were starting to hire some new staff and had permission to open one job to applicants from outside the government. He went on to describe the salary, benefits, and work situation in their office. He talked about the job responsibilities, and their search for someone who was both knowledgeable about organic agriculture and respected within the organic community. "Why on earth are you telling me all this?" I stammered. Michael just looked at me and said, "Hey, you're not doing *Organic Farmer* any more, are you?"

I was in shock. I was flattered and aghast at the same time. I wanted to laugh out loud and run away in horror. "Me, move to Washington, DC? You've got to be kidding!" was my immediate reaction. "Think about it," he said. "Talk it over with your friends, call me any time." I told him I had just moved to Jamaica, that I couldn't even get access to a phone very easily, and that the only way I had to call off the island was collect from a pay phone. I told him that I was entering into a relationship with someone who could not even come to the US on a tourist visa because he was too poor and too Black; that I couldn't imagine myself existing in Washington. He mentioned that he had a brother-in-law at the State Department and maybe there was some way to help with the visa situation. That got my attention.

I had a few days left in Florida and I spent them walking around in a daze. This soft-spoken, unassuming man who looked like a stereotypical federal bureaucrat seemed to be genuinely concerned with finding someone who could help them do it right, and he believed that I was that person. I called a couple of people I knew had been following the situation closely for their advice. Joe Smillie confessed to having planted the suggestion in Michael's ear, and posed a nearly irresistible challenge: "You've got to take that job—Bart wants it."

He had me hooked. I understood how much influence that position would have on the whole direction of organic agriculture in the US, and I also understood that the organic farm community deeply distrusted the USDA. Bart, who was Joe's former business colleague, was very knowledgeable but also could be arrogant and insensitive in a way that would surely increase that distrust. In the months that followed we worked out a signal system so I could let Michael know where to call me in Jamaica. This involved a complex process of emailing him from a tailor's shop in the local market town of Falmouth, where I could plug in my laptop and get into the phone line, and then jog over to the local agricultural extension agency where Michael could call me. By this means he kept me informed about the hiring process, and coached me on how to navigate the steps of applying for federal employment. The difficulty of this process was compounded by the damage done to my little laptop's hard drive one day when I was downloading a student packet at the tailor shop. Unbeknownst to me the tailor had call waiting, which in the days of dial-up had to be disabled before going online. When someone tried to call in the midst of downloading, a pulse of energy would come through the phone lines and physically destroy the mechanism. The hard drive fried and I was forced to use small floppy diskettes to compose my job application.

I had applied for the job a couple of months before coming back to Vermont in 1994 for my summer teaching commitments, but interviews had still not been scheduled. I had no idea if I would be moving to Washington soon or returning to my life in Jamaica. Meanwhile, my divorce had been finalized and Michael's brother-in-law at the State Department was distracted by a humanitarian crisis in his country of assignment—

Rwanda. With the help of pro bono advice from an immigration lawyer friend, I decided to apply for a fiancé visa, which she suggested might make it possible for Matches to come to the US much more quickly than if we married in Jamaica.

Job interviews were held by phone in June, and as soon as mine was finished Michael called me back to say it had gone very well and to ask if I had any other questions or concerns. "As a matter of fact I do," I replied after a moment. "Do I have to wear panty hose for this job?" Without missing a beat he replied, "No, but do you shave your legs?" Hallelujah, I thought—this guy was someone I could work with. A couple of days later Hal Ricker, the NOP Program Manager, called to tell me the job was mine. I agreed to start after Labor Day, and went to Washington a couple of weeks later to visit the job site, meet the staff, and look for a place to live.

My plan called for a return to Jamaica in early August, by which time I hoped the visa would come through and Matches could go back with me. The fiancé visa allowed up to 90 days for the marriage to take place—we could get married in Vermont and move to Washington in time for Opal to start kindergarten. Somehow we managed to make this happen, although the ordeal of getting the visa approved in Jamaica was one of mythic proportions. I clearly recall the anxiety and discomfort of scrambling around in the oppressive heat of Kingston to get health exams and police records, then waiting interminably in the frigidly air conditioned US Embassy until it was almost too late, when the desk clerk finally walked over to an absent colleague's desk and fished the notice of approval out of his in-basket. We were barely able to catch the last bus from Kingston to Montego Bay and get home in time to fly out the next day. It felt as if the cosmos was indeed conspiring to put me in a situation that held a great opportunity to make a difference, and for which I felt utterly unprepared.

We landed in a temporary furnished apartment in Takoma Park, Maryland, just over the DC line, the day before school started in late August 1994. I had come down with a nasty flu in Kingston and was still sick, exhausted, and disoriented. I hadn't lived in an urban setting since moving to Vermont in 1973, and was now in an eighth floor apartment surrounded by concrete. No garden and no woodstove to tend. I had no idea what I was supposed to wear and would be working in a building with more inhabitants than my adopted hometown in Vermont. Matches, now going by his "Babylon" name of Bentley, became the perfect house

The newly transplanted family: Bentley Morgan, Opal Hoyt, Grace Gershuny. Washington, DC, December 1994

spouse and step-parent, taking care of Opal and making sure there was a good meal waiting when I came home from work every day. For the first time in more than 15 years I had a regular job and a regular paycheck, health insurance, and even a retirement plan. My little "oreo cookie" family was plopped down in a completely alien environment, each of us faced with a new world to learn to navigate.

# 5 The Real Dirt on the Regulations

*Audit, certification, accreditation…threaten to replace the interpersonal virtues of trust, honesty, integrity, and honor with a far more odious means of holding society together…It would be a world in which the tyranny of the state would be replaced by the tyranny of the market.* — Lawrence Busch

*Those that respect the law and love sausage should watch neither being made.* — attributed to Mark Twain (among others)

On an early September morning in 1994, still recovering from the recent ordeal of transplanting my family in Washington, DC, I got on the Metro in Takoma Park and headed downtown to begin my job with the National Organic Program. The USDA headquarters on the South side of Independence Avenue is a huge building originally designed as a prison, with six wings and fully enclosed courtyards. Striding through the South Building's long tiled halls full of identical doorways gave me a Kafkaesque feeling. When I got to room 2510 I found the door to the office adorned with quotes from Liberty Hyde Bailey, Thomas Jefferson, and Wendell Berry—a clue that someone inside cared deeply about agriculture and the stewards of the soil.

Michael Hankin introduced me to the rest of the staff and showed me to my cubicle—a spot next to a window, overlooking one of the four courtyards. Everyone except Hal Ricker, the Program Manager, worked in one of the other six cubicles, including the two women who served as support staff. As I began filling out the requisite personnel forms, Hal arrived to welcome me and ask if there was anything they could do to make me feel more comfortable. Pointing to the ceiling I asked if there was any way the fluorescent lights could be replaced with full spectrum bulbs. After checking the budget Hal approved my request and had new lighting installed in the whole office, which made a huge difference for everyone's well-being.

The rest of the staff was also very welcoming. Ted Rogers, I learned, was responsible for the doorway declarations, and had a windowsill full of plants that included a huge flowering datura (a psychedelic plant commonly known as jimsonweed). He later put in a worm compost box so we wouldn't have to throw away our lunch scraps. There was a lot of laughter and camaraderie, and I felt respected in spite of my abject ignorance about the world I had entered. As Michael had promised when we met the previous January in Florida, it felt like a family.

## Introduction to the Family

Both Michael Hankin and Ted Rogers, who had only recently been brought in to begin staffing the NOP, had entered government service from experiences living on the land. Michael had managed a goat dairy operation in Wisconsin before becoming a dairy inspector for USDA, and loved to talk about goats. Although he hadn't been involved with organics, his sense of his mission in life was very much one of earth healing. Ted had homesteaded in Virginia and been involved with the origins of the Virginia Association of Biological Farmers before finding work in USDA's poultry division. He was well versed in—and passionate about—the science and philosophy of "organiculture," but with the street smarts of a seasoned fed; his cynicism about the world was thinly veiled. With his Virginia drawl and booming laugh, Ted referred to himself as a redneck, and also had an interracial marriage. Beth Hayden joined the staff soon after I arrived, having previously worked at the Food & Nutrition branch of the USDA. She also had hands-on experience as a conventional dairy farmer in Idaho, and was given charge of the livestock standards. Vivacious and ambitious, Beth became my buddy for a time, though this later changed. We all shared a warped sense of humor and found in each other an appreciative audience for our bad puns.

Michael's gentleness and sensitivity made him seem almost too soft; he cared too much and let things get to him, which would aggravate his stuttering. I have met very few men who radiated as much concern for everyone's personal and spiritual well-being. He also proved to possess a keen intellect and ability to keep a lot of complex information in focus, although his attention to detail sometimes verged on excessive. Despite his high level of compassion and a tendency towards self-deprecation, he did not let himself be pushed around. Michael was officially everyone's immediate supervisor and intermediary with the bigger bureaucracy, and at one time or other counseled us all on career and personal issues. He was the family mediator who wanted everyone to be happy, but was also sometimes resented by those who just wanted someone to tell them what to do.

The rest of the staff, including a couple of new hires on the professional track, were brown-skinned people and I saw the diversity of the USDA's workforce as a big plus. The overwhelming whiteness of the national organic movement, with a few notable exceptions, had always troubled me. Somehow it seemed that this little microcosm presented at least a symbolic opportunity to counter the perception (and reality) of the elitism of the organic movement. Other workers, including a variety of summer interns, came and went; some later went on to stellar careers in the Department.

When the organic law (OFPA) was passed more than four years earlier, the Secretary of Agriculture under the Bush I administration was openly hostile to the whole project. The NOP was foisted off on the Transportation & Marketing Division of USDA's Agricultural Marketing Service (AMS), which was the only place where programs that did not focus on single commodities might fit in. It was also the only division dependent on Congressional appropriations to exist, unlike the user fee-based grading and inspection programs for dairy, poultry, cotton, fresh produce, peanuts, and the like. Within this division were folks who studied things like the availability of rail cars and barges to transport wheat, and some others who worked on marketing assistance, including farmers markets. Among the few managerial-level souls at USDA who had any interest in or sympathy for organic farmers was Dr. Hal Ricker, an agricultural economist in charge of the Federal State Marketing Improvement Program (FSMIP) who had actually helped fund some organic marketing cooperatives. In the absence of funding requested by USDA or appropriated by Congress for staffing or additional expenses, responsibility for fulfilling OFPA's legal mandate was handed to Hal. It was not considered an upward career move.

It was not until the Clinton administration took over in 1992 that federal advisory committee funds were freed up to appoint the initial National Organic Standards Board (NOSB), the citizens' advisory body established by the law. The NOSB was then able to begin work collecting public input about some of the details that were left out of the law. When I arrived in DC the NOSB had been meeting for over two years at different locations around the country. The NOSB is governed by and funded separately under the Federal Advisory Committees Act (FACA), which requires that all meetings be open to the public and include time for comments on any proposed recommendations.

I had attended one of the previous NOSB meetings, held in Maine in 1992, and listened to a number of statements asking that the regulations safeguard the purity of organic foods and not permit any synthetic substances to be used. One such comment, submitted by a lawyer representing an organization of people suffering from chemical sensitivity, suggested that gas ovens should not be permitted for baking organic products because some people had bad reactions to the residues of mercaptan, a chemical added to propane to make it smell. I had not intended to submit a public comment, but found myself asking for a slot at the last minute to counter the escalating misinformation that I was hearing. I commented that the organic label could not be a guarantee of food safety or purity; this would make being an organic producer prohibitive and similarly affect the price of organic foods. People with extreme chemical sensitivities—much as I sympathize with their real problems—could not demand that all organic foods be required to meet their needs. As I spoke I saw that one of the NOP staff members present—whom I later recognized as Ted—was nodding in agreement.

During the two years from formation of the board through the hiring of NOP technical staff in 1994, the NOSB had been forced to fill the role that would ordinarily have been taken up by technical staff at the agency responsible for writing the rules. In short, the advisory board took it upon itself to create draft regulations. Drafts of its recommendations were circulated to interested members of the public, then sent back to the relevant committee and recirculated, discussed at public meetings, and finally ratified by the full Board. It was an exemplary process, and the original 14 NOSB members deserve tremendous credit for their effort. Some of the members who came from the conventional food industry— and were thus considered suspect by the organic community—contributed extensive time and knowledge of food science that proved invaluable. The small staff available at the NOP office at the beginning essentially served as the NOSB's administrative help.

This scenario set the stage for trouble later on, however. Once funding became available for the NOP to hire staff (including me) who were more knowledgeable about organic theory and methods, as well as about legal requirements for regulations and the culture of USDA, differences of opinion became struggles for control over the actual regulation writing. Many in the community also believed that the NOSB is supposed to have the final say on whatever regulatory measures were implemented, and can overrule the USDA authorities if they disagree. This false impression was encouraged by several members of the NOSB and never clearly corrected by the USDA, which only fueled the belief that the agency was acting illegally by contradicting NOSB recommendations in drafting the regulations.

The NOSB itself was divided into two camps: the staunch advocates of protecting organic purity, including Board Chair Michael Sligh, and the realists, including Gene Kahn, CEO of Cascadian Farms (later bought by General Mills), who felt that legitimate organic farmers and manufacturers of organic products could not be held hostage to a misguided public perception about the nature of organic methods. This division closely mirrored the debate about "agronomic responsibility" versus "origin of materials" as the basis for organic standards chronicled in Chapter 3.

Although the OFPA represents a grand compromise of these two perspectives, the purist interpretations were widely publicized as correct, particularly among consumer groups, and proclaimed as evidence that USDA, generally presumed to be corrupted by its coziness with chemical-intensive agribusiness, was hell-bent to weaken, dilute, and otherwise eviscerate organic standards. This fundamentalist mindset, whose proponents the NOP staff referred to as "the Bible-thumpers," set the tone for the massive public outcry that greeted us when we finally succeeded in publishing a regulatory proposal. Even some former colleagues who had previously advocated a more flexible and nuanced agronomic responsibility approach joined the fray. How did such a mental disconnect happen? Though I have some theories to explain it, this question continues to plague me.

## Learning the Regulatory Ropes

I was now ensconced in my own cubicle with the title of Agricultural Marketing Specialist, a designation given to all the professional grade workers in the Agricultural Marketing Service. This is a civil service position in the General Services (GS) system, with a rank and pay grade of 11-12, a step below supervisory level. Although many community members assume that such positions are bestowed based on political connections, this is expressly prohibited in hiring for career as opposed to political appointee slots. No NOP staff members are political appointees, then or now. In this position I was to help develop the regulations to implement the OFPA, specifically the parts dealing with the accreditation of certifying agents by USDA.

Before coming to Washington I assumed that the agency would have staff available to translate my understanding of organic principles and methods into the appropriate regulatory language. Was I ever wrong! Although I had never even read a federal regulation, I was told that it was now my job to write one. The Office of General Counsel (OGC) is the legal staff that is associated with each agency in the federal government. The Agricultural Marketing Service (AMS) has a large legal staff, inasmuch as it churns out more regulations than the rest of USDA put together—possibly more than any other federal agency. Our program was not considered a top priority, however, and OGC made it clear that they would not be able to instruct me in how to write regulations. The best advice they could offer was to write what made sense to me and they would tell me what was wrong with it. I was also given a handbook for generic guidance on regulation drafting which was similarly uninformative.

Loving a challenge, I sat down in my cubicle to study a stack of Code of Federal Regulation volumes containing other regulations issued by our agency. The reason for AMS' huge regulatory output is that its rules are intended to help develop markets, and require more frequent revision than those intended to protect the environment and human health. A major function of the AMS is to facilitate the marketing of various agricultural commodities, almost all of which operate through a system of user fees. That is, all the producers of that commodity are required to contribute a tiny fraction of their sales toward these marketing and promotion programs. The best-known example is the "Got Milk?" campaign initiated through the AMS dairy division. One reason the OFPA was able to garner enough Congressional support to pass was that the operations of the NOP were to be similarly funded through user fees—not at taxpayer expense.

Most of the AMS regulations have to do with setting standards for the various products being promoted, such as grades of apples or butter. These standards are universally about product quality, such as size, color, or insect parts in grain. They rely on objective, measurable criteria that are evaluated for each lot of product that goes to market. AMS also includes the Food Safety Inspection Service (FSIS), which was created before there was a Food & Drug Administration (FDA), specifically for meat, dairy, and poultry products. These are the only standards that address practices required to protect product quality, such as sanitation procedures needed to avoid contamination by pathogens. This also entails frequent—and in the case of slaughter houses, constant—oversight by federal food safety inspectors.

Each marketing program in AMS has its own regulation writers, and each addresses a single commodity, such as cotton, eggs, potatoes, cheese, or avocados. Our closest neighbors down the hall, who focused solely on regulating the peanut market, lent us one of their most experienced regulation writers to help us get started. But the poor guy could not wrap his mind around the problem of how to develop standards that could cover every commodity imaginable, domestic or imported, including how it was grown or raised, processed, and labeled. On top of that, we had to develop a whole regulatory structure for the certification of farms and processing operations, and then accreditation of the hodge-podge of existing and future non-profit, for-profit, state-run, and multinational certifying agents. As far as anyone knew, no such entirely new program had been established at the USDA since the 1940s, and nobody had a clue about how to begin. People in the other divisions of AMS were betting heavily that this program would never happen at all, let alone on time.

## How the Regulatory Process Works

The regulatory process makes sense in theory. After a law is passed it is handed over to the appropriate Executive branch agency to implement. The first step is to draft regulations, which can only include what is authorized by the law and which must address all of its provisions. The draft rule must be published in the Federal Register, along with a preamble that sets forth the legal basis and rationale for each provision it contains, giving anyone interested a chance to submit comments. The agency staff then must respond to each of the comments received, lumping together those that address the same issue, and revise the rules if the comments are justified. A summary of all of the commentary and responses is then published as a preamble to the final regulation. Once a final rule is published, implementation can begin. If the new regulation is deemed "significant" due to its level of impact on the subject constituency, it must first be approved by the White House Office of Management and Budget (OMB) before the draft can be published. The OMB's job is to make sure that it does not contradict other regulations that might exist through a different federal agency, and their mandate is to act as a regulation buster to prevent unnecessary and burdensome new rules from seeing the light of day.

When a new law is passed the agency responsible for its implementation generally has a staff with expertise in whatever it is that the law covers. The staff may even have had a role in reviewing the legislation to make sure it was workable for them. The agency will also have its lawyers review the law to see if there are legal contradictions or typographical errors and, if so, ask Congress to make what are called "technical corrections." None of this held true with the OFPA. Not only did the agency lack the expert staff, the law contained some internal contradictions and at least one piece of nonsensical gibberish. Since the USDA management had vehemently opposed the passage of this law and did not want to implement it, they did not bother to fix either the contradictions or the gibberish.

So it was up to the NOP staff to interpret it and make our rules as workable as possible for organic farmers as well as for the existing organic certifiers. While the NOSB's recommendations were of some help, they were poorly organized and not exactly written in regulatory language. The law itself didn't have a very logical organization or structure and, while it had too many detailed rules in some cases, it also left out some important pieces. For instance, it said nothing about the two big organic no-no's—irradiation and genetically modified organisms (GMOs).

The guy from the peanut program had done what he normally does and created an outline for us based on the structure of our law. The way the law is organized wouldn't make much sense to a reasonable person, nor does it bear much resemblance to the organic rules to which I was accustomed. The whole situation failed to inspire my own confidence that we would have a first draft written in the next four months, as Hal had been promising everyone. After all, the 1990 law set a date of 1993 to be fully implemented, and here it was nearly 1995 and we were just getting started.

I should mention that, since our program had some relationship to just about every other agency within USDA, it would have to be approved by most of those 19 Administrators before arriving at the desk of the Secretary of Agriculture. It also needed to be approved by officials at both EPA and FDA, with the Bureau of Alcohol, Tobacco & Firearms (part of the Federal Trade Commission) thrown in to boot. Inasmuch as our law referenced regulations promulgated by each of these agencies, and we also needed rules about how to put an organic label on an alcoholic beverage, each had to approve our requirements as consistent with theirs. If we anticipated the possibility of organic labels on such things as cosmetics or textiles (there were already organic cotton producers and soap makers), some coordination was required with regulations governing these types of products at FDA and Federal Trade Commission, respectively.

We knew from the start that we would meet major resistance from the Animal & Plant Health Inspection Service or APHIS, which, along with AMS, is part of the USDA's Marketing & Regulatory Programs area and is responsible for keeping foreign plant and animal diseases out of the country. You may have encountered them upon returning from a trip abroad when asked if you have visited a farm or are bringing any fresh produce with you. More to the point, APHIS is the agency responsible for promoting—oops, I mean regulating—the use of genetically modified organisms (GMOs) in agriculture.

I will spare you any further details of how the USDA works, but trust this small taste is enough to illustrate the minefield of bureaucracy we faced. Beyond the challenges of a complex and entrenched "old boys" network, every agency has its own culture just as different corporations have distinctive cultures. Younger start-ups tend to be more flexible and less stuck in old ways of doing things, and the same is true of government agencies. The USDA, the "people's department," is one of the older and larger ones—only the Pentagon is bigger. Just as its headquarters is laid out like a prison, its management culture is modeled after the military—a strict command and control, top down power structure. There is nothing democratic or participatory about it and, though there are all kinds of policies to protect employees from prejudicial treatment by higher-ups, it is virtually impossible for someone in the lower echelons of civil service—such as the position I was in — to challenge authority and remain employed.

## Challenging Authority and Maintaining Sanity

My whole background and, of course, the organic concept itself represented a major challenge to entrenched authority. After experiencing the crushing anonymity of mass higher education in New York City, I had vowed to never again subject myself to such an oppressive bureaucracy. But here I was. It helped that I still had my Vermont home, and had made it clear that my commitment to living in Washington was temporary; in two more years Opal was to return to Stewart's custody, and I was unwilling to stay in DC while she lived in Vermont.

I had a few sanity-maintenance strategies on hand while still living in Washington as well, not the least of which was coming home to a loving family and doing some fun city things together. I would often walk across the street from my office to the National Mall, strolling through the lovely gardens all around the Smithsonian "Castle" on my lunch breaks. If I had time and was feeling ambitious, I would walk to the other end of the Mall to pop into the National Botanical Garden. Strolling through the greenhouse and breathing in the moist, tropical scents helped remind me why I was doing this work.

---

## OFPA Basic Provisions and National List Criteria

The purposes of the Organic Foods Production Act (OFPA) of 1990[34] are the following:

(1) to establish national standards governing the marketing of certain agricultural products as organically produced products;

(2) to assure consumers that organically produced products meet a consistent standard; and

(3) to facilitate interstate commerce in fresh and processed food that is organically produced.

The National Organic Program (NOP) is the agency created by the law, which implements regulations to carry out its purposes.

### Production and Handling Standards

The OFPA establishes broad standards for organic production and handling, including all processing activities. Producers must develop an organic plan that contains provisions to foster soil fertility, along with other methods that will be used to ensure compliance with the regulations. Organic crops must be raised without using most conventional pesticides or petroleum-based fertilizers. Livestock must be fed organically produced feed and cannot be treated with subtherapeutic antibiotics. A processed product may be labeled organic if at least 95% of its ingredients are organic, and the remaining 4.99% are permitted for use in organic handling.

The National List identifies synthetic substances permitted and natural substances prohibited for use in organic production, and nonorganic ingredients permitted to be used as ingredients in organic processed products.

### Production and Handling Standards (continued)

The OFPA calls for the establishment of the fifteen-member National Organic Standards Board (NOSB). The NOSB is appointed by the Secretary of Agriculture and is comprised of four organic farmers/growers, three environmental/resource conservationists, three consumer/public interest representatives, two organic handlers/ processors, one retailer, one scientist (toxicology, ecology or biochemistry), and one USDA-accredited certifying agent.

The NOSB is charged with making recommendations about implementation of the NOP, and with evaluating substances petitioned for inclusion on the National List. The National List must be based on recommendations submitted by the NOSB.

### National List Criteria

Section 2119(m) of the OFPA requires the NOSB to evaluate any substance being considered for inclusion in the National List according to the following criteria:

(1) the potential of such substances for detrimental chemical interactions with other materials used in organic farming systems;

(2) the toxicity and mode of action of the substance and of its breakdown products or any contaminants, and their persistence and areas of concentration in the environment;

(3) the probability of environmental contamination during manufacture, use, misuse or disposal of such substance;

(4) the effect of the substance on human health;

(5) the effects of the substance on biological and chemical interactions in the agroecosystem, including the physiological effects of the substance on soil organisms (including the salt index and solubility of the soil), crops, and livestock;

(6) the alternatives to using the substance in terms of practices or other available materials; and

(7) its compatibility with a system of sustainable agriculture.

We made friends with a Croatian couple in our building whose son was in Opal's kindergarten class, and sometimes shared meals. Bentley found some friends in the Jamaican community and began learning to drive. Weekends often found us heading out to western Maryland, just across the river from West Virginia, to visit the Earhardt's organic farm. Walter and Sylvia Earhardt were knowledgeable retired feds and sympathetic advisers, and their daughter managed their large CSA farm and market garden. Spending a few hours weeding and bringing home some fresh veggies satisfied my need to keep my hands in the soil. We had a worm box in the kitchen, a grow box on our eighth floor balcony, and a small community garden plot, but I was unaccustomed to gardening in such heat and humidity. The weeds grew a lot faster than in Vermont, and I was flummoxed by the unfamiliar and voracious insects that devoured my plants which could only be tended once a week.

All during this time I continued working with students through the Institute for Social Ecology (ISE) and Goddard College. This was another connection to a saner world and my "real" life, and I saved up my comp and vacation time to travel to Vermont for the eight-day Goddard residencies every semester. In the summer, when the climate in DC was particularly unbearable, we would go for longer stays and I would participate in a portion of the ISE's four-week summer program just prior to the Goddard residency.

Challenges to my sanity came from all directions. My time in Washington allowed me to directly experience both the ineffectiveness and the corrosive, soul-crushing impact of this top-heavy bureaucracy. The master-slave relationship lives in the spirit of abused underlings who will, consciously or subconsciously, slow any forward movement to a crawl and sabotage the most well-intentioned programmatic changes. The Peter principle and the Dilbert mind are the reality of this world, where middle managers rise to their level of incompetence and are then shunted sideways to someplace where they can do the least harm. It is a world where all that counts is winning—by any means necessary.

My ability to function within this system had much to do with the fact that Michael Hankin, as second in command, was in charge of the day-to-day operations of our little office and was a remarkable ally in the organic cause. He could not change the hierarchy outside our office, but inside he was able to create a refreshingly egalitarian atmosphere, where each of us was respected and given the opportunity to exercise some control over our own tasks and propose alternatives when we disagreed with him. In our staff meetings, everyone—including the clerical staff—was asked for their opinion about the problem of the day, and everyone's ideas were given thoughtful consideration. Michael did what he could to run interference for me with the system when I made unconventional requests or stepped too far out of line. I have met few people in my life who so fully embodied the holistic understanding and social consciousness implicit in the organic vision, or who had the courage and humility to nurture a cause that could endanger their own career. It was a unique opportunity to make a difference, and we all knew that once we were noticed by the "powers that be" all bets would be off.

The congruence in our philosophical perspectives is best summed up in this ambitious—one might say presumptuous—internal goal statement that I found stuck in one of the many notebooks saved from those years:

> *The real purpose of this program is the conscious creation of an organic field within the USDA, which will represent a model of how administrative, regulatory processes can be designed which are compatible with the principles of organiculture, and reflect the ecological paradigm of the emerging new science.*

## Spinning the Wheels of Bureaucracy

It took more than three years to get the first draft of the National Organic Program regulation published in the Federal Register for public comment. This is remarkable, not for how long it took, but for the fact that it happened at all. The story about what it said and the outrage it provoked in the community has been told and repeated by knowledgeable sources as accepted truth, and cited authoritatively in academic papers. My version of the story contradicts much of this common knowledge.

The process of regulation writing was not without moments of both drama and hilarity in an otherwise plodding, frustrating effort in which almost nobody inside or outside of our agency understood what we needed to do in order to accomplish our task. Added to the internal cluelessness was a community of activists with a long history of opposing the government and distrusting the USDA—a distrust that was, while largely justified, characterized by ignorance about how government actually works. Various groups launched unrelated efforts to derail or at least delay implementation of the program, while some leading advocates appear to have deliberately misinformed their constituencies, for ideological and often self-serving reasons. But the question of motivation is almost beside the point. Humans simply share a common tendency to adjust whatever information we receive to fit our prejudices, a proclivity that was assuredly at work here.

Michael, Ted, and I formed the core team charged with developing the framework for writing the regulations. The first thing they asked me to do was to draft a paper setting down the guiding principles of organic agriculture. After all the years of arguing over definitions, principles, precepts, and standards, after haggling over what should go in the law and what should come out, I burst out laughing. Not again! I thought we did this already! What I put at the top of the page was this: "The only thing I know for sure is not organic is dogmatism." Ted printed that out on a big sign and put it up over the door to the office. The document that eventually emerged from this exercise was discussed by everyone on staff, edited by the higher ups, revised a bit more, and finally approved for official publication as a foundation document. The NOSB also liked our definition (with the possible exception of the seventh principle), and drafted a similar one of its own, just to assert its supremacy as the arbiter of the meaning of "organic."

---

### Definition and Principles Document

#### Prologue: Moving Towards Sustainability[35]

The specific set of rules which delineate organic agricultural systems have evolved out of a wider imperative towards sustainable social, economic, and cultural forms. The definition of organic agriculture which follows acknowledges that the goal of sustainability is elusive. However, the extent to which an organic system moves towards sustainability is highlighted as a critical yardstick of its success. In simpler terms, the long-term durability of an organic system is its most important attribute.

Intangible considerations such as personal satisfaction, social responsibility and respect for cultural traditions are inherent to the concept of sustainability. Although beyond the purview of government regulation, they are implicit in organic production systems. In order for an agricultural system to endure, it must be embedded within a social and economic system which equitably rewards all participants, and protects the capability of future generations to feed themselves.

## Definition

Organic agriculture is a sustainable production management system that promotes and enhances biodiversity, biological cycles, and soil biological activity. It is based on minimal use of off-farm inputs and on management practices that restore, maintain, and enhance ecological harmony.

"Organic" is a labeling term that denotes products produced in accordance with the standards and certification requirements of the National Organic Program. The principal guidelines for organic production are to use materials and practices that enhance the ecological balance of natural systems and that integrate the parts of the farming system into an ecological whole. Organic agriculture practices cannot ensure that products are completely free of residues. However, methods are used to minimize pollution of air, soil, and water. Organic food handlers, processors, and retailers adhere to standards to maintain the integrity of organic agriculture products. The primary goal of organic agriculture is to optimize the health and productivity of interdependent communities of soil life, plants, animals, and people.

## Introduction

The Organic Farm Plan is central to demonstrating progressive improvement of practices and measuring evolution of the management system as a whole towards greater sustainability. In this context, recordkeeping is a key management tool for identifying problems and successful adaptations. Management changes should be evaluated in light of the principles described below.

## Principles

Organic production systems seek to provide food, fiber, and herbal products of the highest quality in sufficient quantities. The following principles are the foundation of organic management methods:

1. Protect the environment, minimize pollution, promote health, and optimize biological productivity.

The primary goal of organic production systems is optimizing environmental health, human health, and biological productivity.

Organic producers, therefore, seek to reduce or eliminate reliance on practices and inputs (natural and synthetic) that may harm soil life, deplete nonrenewable resources, pose a hazard to water and air quality, or threaten the health of farm workers or consumers.

2. Replenish and maintain long-term soil fertility by providing optimal conditions for soil biological activity.

The health of the soil is fundamental to the health of the whole system, and may be evaluated by the extent and vitality of its biological activity. "Feed the soil, not the plant," continues to be a primary tenet of ecologically sound soil management. Fertility improvement practices must balance physical, chemical, and biological considerations to optimize the quantity and diversity of soil organisms. Such practices may include a combination of crop rotations, rotational grazing of livestock, cover crops, intercropping, green manures, recycling of plant and animal wastes, tillage, and judicious application of essential mineral nutrients.

3. Maintain diversity within the farming system and its surroundings and protect and develop plant and wildlife habitat.

Biological diversity is a key ecological precept, essential to stability and therefore to sustainability. Diversity must be enhanced in every aspect of organic production, including the selection of inputs, crop varieties, livestock breeds, rotation cycles, and pest management strategies. The principle of diversity can be similarly applied to personal skills, social interactions, and economic decisions.

4. Recycle materials and resources to the greatest extent possible within the farm and its surrounding community as part of a regionally organized agricultural system.

Organic producers intensively manage the individual farm system and use biologically-based inputs in preference to petroleum-based inputs. Soil and plant nutrients depleted through cropping and natural leaching are replenished by nutrient sources from within the farm and the surrounding community. Livestock and crop production are integrated wherever possible to provide the most effective means of nutrient recycling. Energy expended in transportation, manufacturing, and handling of agricultural inputs and products is minimized to the greatest extent possible.

5. Provide attentive care that meets both health and behavioral requirements of farm animals.

Farm animals are managed to prevent health problems through a focus on diet, housing, handling, and observation. Livestock are bred and selected to enhance stamina and vigor. Organically produced feed, in conjunction with care and living conditions which minimize stress, is the foundation of a health-promoting management system. Attentive care for the healthy animal is a fundamental precept of organic livestock management.

6. Maintain the integrity and nutritional value of organic food and processed products through each step of the process from planting to consumption.

Organically grown food and processed products are processed, manufactured, and handled to preserve their healthful qualities and maintain the principles of the organic management system. Ingredients, additives, and processing aids used in organic processed products must be consistent with the overall principles of organic production. Consumers should be provided with the assurance that products bearing organic labels are certified organic by independent verification from seed through sale.

7. Develop and adopt new technologies with consideration for their long-range social and ecological impact.

New practices, materials, and technologies must be evaluated according to established criteria for organic production. It is assumed that organic production systems will continue to progress toward sustainability over time through technical innovation and social evolution.

So what was the point of this exercise in creating a definition? The law lacked both a succinct definition and any guiding principles of what it means to produce something organically. Without such consensus principles, we believed, the collection of rules that would eventually make up the finished standard would have no coherence or legitimacy—regardless of legal status. The principles we drafted were derived from those developed through various grassroots certification programs over the years, consolidated in the OFPANA guidelines, and refined by the OFAC conveners (refer to Chapter 4). Livestock standards were as yet poorly developed, despite some advice provided by the Humane Society; the law actually mandated that the NOSB hold special hearings on livestock standards to fill in the blanks. This document, entitled "Prologue: Moving Towards Sustainability," eventually became the foundation of our proposed rule after being drastically compressed by our legal team into the definition of "a system of organic farming and handling," which we acronym-happy organicrats referred to as the SOFAH.[36]

From my first week on the job, the question that everyone kept asking was, "When will the rule be out?" I quickly realized that the promised publication date—set for only a few months out—was impossible. This clearly contributed to the frustration and anger in the community as months and years passed with a draft regulation always imminent. I didn't know what to tell people, and didn't know how or when we were going to pull it off. With a confidence born of ignorance, I just set about to try to create a structure that made sense to me, looking to my previous work on the OFPANA Guidelines as a model.

A plan soon emerged to launch the program in a more piecemeal fashion, starting with the accreditation program. The law requires that all operations wishing to use an organic label, or to represent their products as organic, must first become certified by a certifying body that is accredited by the USDA. Until there was an initial set of accredited certifiers, no product could legally carry a USDA-authorized organic label. Our intent was to work with the existing contingent of certifying organizations—non-profit, for-profit, and state programs—who had supported the law and who were already, we hoped, qualified to do the job. We figured that the standards could be released while the accreditation process was under way, and everyone could then start certifying to the national standard at the same time. According to OFPA author Kathleen Merrigan, who was soon to join the NOSB herself, the accreditation portion of the rule was less likely to draw fire from the community than were the actual standards.

Accreditation was my primary job responsibility, and I dove into the guts of arcane programs that accredited laboratories and certifiers of product quality systems. ISO (International Standards Organization) is the international body that oversees all manner of standards, certification, auditing, and accreditation, ad infinitum.[37] As I considered the various models before me, it seemed that this piece of the puzzle could fit pretty neatly into accepted international accreditation procedures—no wheels needed be reinvented. It soon became apparent, however, that the plan to start with accreditation was not workable. There was really no way to begin accrediting certifiers until the standards to which they had to certify their clients were published. The parts of the program were too interdependent, and so it would have to be launched as a whole entity, not piece by piece. We relayed this news to our constituency, again with unrealistic timeframes for releasing the rules. Our focus now shifted back to the standards, and my attention returned to the rules for organic crop production, including my favorite subject, soil and compost.

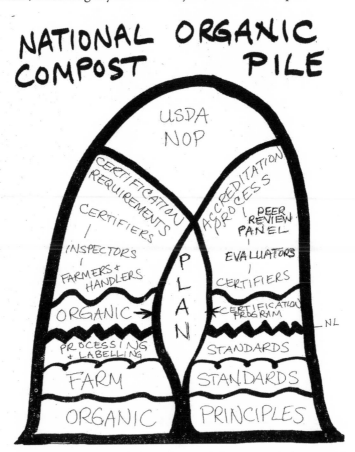

The graphic I drew to explain how the regulations were being organized.

At a meeting in California of the increasingly restive certifier community, my explanation for how this program would fit together took the form of the National Organic Compost Pile. The graphic I put on a transparency in that era before PowerPoint gives a picture of all the pieces that had to fit together.

- The whole thing rests on a bed of principles, which became the SO-FAH.
- The standards for farm production—soil, crops, and livestock—are the next layer.
- On top of this are the rules for processing, which include any handling activities such as packing fresh produce or repackaging a bulk item into retail packages. Important to note: The objective of an organic processing operation is to preserve the organic quality or integrity of the product, which is conferred by virtue of how it was grown or raised.
- Labeling rules apply to what goes on the product when it is sold, whether to a final retail consumer or to a processor who will use the product as an ingredient in something else. The rules governing proper use of the USDA Organic seal are found here.
- The glue, so to speak, that holds the whole pile together is the organic plan, which the organic producer creates to address every aspect of the operation and how it all complies with the standards. The plan includes methods for assessing how well things are going, such as soil tests, crop quality, yield, animal health, and so on. It also identifies changes to be made to improve the outcomes being measured. Processors or handlers also have to have an organic plan that relates to their Standard Operating Procedures used to ensure that the product's organic integrity is maintained.
- The next layer of the pile is the organic certification program, which outlines the rules for applying for certification and how the process generally works. The objective is to verify that the producer or processor is actually doing what is outlined in the respective organic plan. The primary means of doing this is through annual on-site inspections, including review of relevant documentation.
- The accreditation process parallels the certification process, except that here it is the certifier who has to demonstrate to the accrediting body—in this case the USDA—that they are reviewing applications, hiring qualified personnel, and avoiding conflict of interest, among other things, according to the rules. Accredited certifiers then become agents of the USDA, and can grant their clients the right to claim that their products are organically produced and to use the USDA Organic seal.
- The rules also contain an administrative section that deals with rules about things like user fees, appeals, and enforcement.
- The National Organic Program sits on top of the heap, in charge of orchestrating the whole thing.

You will notice that the National Organic Compost Pile does not include a separate layer called the National List. We wanted to minimize the visibility of the National List, and along with it the arguments about whether a particular material should be allowed or prohibited, depending on whether it was deemed to be either synthetic or natural. Rather than try to provide a meaningful definition of "natural," we decided to refer to anything not classified as synthetic as "nonsynthetic." The creative use of definitions is one technique that we found could make up for a lot of the law's defects. Unfortunately, definitions written into the law, such as the meaning of synthetic, could not be changed without amending the law itself—a problem that has thus far proved insoluble.

Our ideal vision of organic standards would minimize the use of purchased inputs such as fertilizers and pesticides, synthetic or not. Our principles included an emphasis on management-intensive practices such as cover cropping and rotations, rather than depending on fertility sources brought in from off farm. Similarly, pest control should rely first and foremost on preventing weed, pest, and disease problems through methods such as providing habitat for predators and good sanitation practices, minimizing the need for *any* substances—allowed or otherwise. Any practices or materials used on a farm would have to be applied in a manner that would not contribute to degradation of soil or water quality. All of this was consistent with the standards that had evolved over the previous 20 years within the organic movement. We deliberately structured the National List as a subset of the standards to keep the focus on good management rather than materials issues.[38]

The way the public thinks about standards, and the general lack of understanding about the different functions of different types of standards, helps explain why our efforts were so easily portrayed as weakening the desirably tough standards that are believed to characterize organic agriculture. In crafting the regulations, we confronted questions about how to design standards that are truly organic in the sense of reflecting a flexible, site-specific, systems-based approach that could also pass muster within the context of federal regulations. I refer to the key insight that has crystallized over the years it has taken me to tell this story as "the myth of higher standards."

## The Myth of Higher Standards

Before we go any further down the standards rabbit hole, let's explore some commonly held assumptions about standards in general, many of which don't really apply to the paradigm-shifting organic sort.

The assumption that our standards must be as high as possible has become very like the tale of the emperor's new clothes in organic circles. Everyone agrees that rigor is essential—the stricter the better—and to be adequately discriminating we must have clear bright lines to separate good from bad. Subjectivity and flexibility are dangerous, and open up the possibility of loopholes through which the unscrupulous will pass with impunity. While grey areas persist, it is only because we have too little information, and our goal should be to collect enough data to eliminate them. On the flip side, anyone who admits to being willing to accept "lower" standards is accused of advocating mediocrity, or worse, collaborating with agribusinesses who wish to take over the organic label and render it meaningless.

Yet, in fact, the push for higher standards has actually made it easier for the large, professional business organizations than for small owner-operators. They are simply better equipped to deal with the increasingly finicky and paperwork-heavy demands of organic certification. So the demand for higher organic standards has helped create the very situation that organic activists feared the most: intensified bureaucratization of organic certification, increased barriers to access to the organic market by small producers, and near elimination of the possibility that organic production systems might become any more than a small niche in American agriculture.

Much of the confusion arises from ignorance of the difference between standards that people, businesses, and organizations set for themselves, and standards that are set—and enforced—by the government to serve some public need. The same kinds of issues that confuse people in the development of organic standards apply to similar process-based standards for products such as shade grown coffee, sustainable fisheries, and fair trade—a category generally called "eco-labels."

Standards that reflect the process of how something is produced (e.g., no sweatshops) and those that address the quality of a product (e.g., grades of lumber) are radically different. This distinction is rarely understood, but its implications are enormous. Evaluating organic standards in terms of product quality standards misses the point. Organic products are not distinguishable from similar conventional ones, whether through sensory evaluation or laboratory analysis. Will higher standards, by which the consumer usually means product quality standards, ensure that organic products are better, safer, or healthier than conventionally produced ones? Will they allow consumers to differentiate between "superior" and "ordinary" organic products? Is there any way of objectively measuring whether an organic product meets the highest organic standards? The answer to each of these questions is an emphatic "no."

Standards whose purpose is to regulate markets, such as meat grading standards, differ significantly from those established to protect public health and safety, such as meat packing plant sanitation standards. This difference is critical for sorting out the confusion surrounding organic standards. Most people—especially environmental activists—are accustomed to thinking of regulations of any kind as serving to protect public health and safety, and that industries want the weakest possible standards to minimize their costs. But standards whose purpose is to regulate markets are generally developed at the behest of the industry being regulated, and serve to protect the industry more than to protect the public.

The purpose of the NOP, as identified in the OFPA, is market regulation. While it does help protect the public from misrepresented products, it is not there for the purpose of protecting public health and safety, but rather to protect the industry being regulated from "substandard" goods entering the market and competing with established producers. Besides driving prices down, poor quality goods serve to endanger public confidence in the product. One major reason that the industry needs federal standards is the fear that a few well-publicized cases of organic fraud will cause the market to shrink for everyone.[39]

Uniformity and standardization are ideas that spring from the requirements of industry for inputs and products that are predictable and interchangeable. This has given us the possibility of mass production and the wonders of cheap consumer goods. Many critics of institutionalizing organic standards argue convincingly that these demands are anathema to organic systems. Complexity, diversity, local adaptation, and evolution do not lend themselves to the cookie cutter concept of standardization. Food from Florida should not be interchangeable with food from Wisconsin, and the appropriate methods for the organic production of artichokes in California do not resemble those for goat cheese in Maine.

However, when we look at standardization from the viewpoint of a process as opposed to a product, we can see that uniform rules do not require uniform methods to comply with the rules. Organic certification represents one of the earliest efforts to standardize a process-based label claim. Because organic systems are dynamic and evolve over time they are fuzzy, context specific, and hard to nail down definitively. In real life, organic standards can and should reflect the reality of organic methods and the philosophical concepts on which they are based (See Chapter 2).

Performance standards, which establish goals for specific outcomes to be achieved by the operation being regulated, can allow for the kind of innovative problem-solving that is a hallmark of organic farmers, and that can quickly be stifled by the need to satisfy prescriptive practice standards. In an organic system, measurable improvements in the health of any factor, such as soil quality or livestock health, can be considered a performance standard. Agroecosystem health can thus be seen as a barometer for the success of the management system, as well as an outcome or goal to be pursued.

While there is little disagreement about these basic concepts, there is also little agreement about where lines should be drawn in practice. For example, organic principles dictate that practices which enhance biological diversity must be a key requirement. However, given the realities of farming and the existing industrial food system, clear lines of acceptable versus unacceptable are hard to identify. Not only is it nearly impossible to decide how much biodiversity is enough, it is very hard to objectively measure how much biological diversity is present in a given farm or field.

Although organic standards are about the process, products can give us information about the process. Product quality may indicate something about how the process is working, but can never absolutely determine whether it passes or fails. An apple can be measured to see if it makes the grade, but worms in the apples can only serve to indicate the level of health in the orchard agroecosystem.

A process is also not static; it is a collection of activities and not a discrete material thing. Although the process cannot itself be measured, its functioning can be monitored at different times by selecting appropriate products—such as the apple example—or outcomes that can be measured. These products or outcomes are called indicators, and changes in indicators over time can be used to figure out if the process is working as intended or needs some adjustment. This creates a positive feedback loop, which ultimately provides a farmer with helpful tools for improving the overall success of the operation.

An organic process involves many kinds of products, only one of which will eventually be sold with a label that reads "organically produced." **If the ultimate goal of organic methods is agroecosystem health, the quality of the product that is sold is but one indicator of the health of that system.** This is why the first proposed rule was intended to orient all production standards towards the SOFAH, with its overarching criterion of agroecosystem health.

People often believe that we need highly prescriptive practice standards, such as those used in food safety rules, in regulating a production process. However, this form of regulation works against both creativity and ecological balance.[40] For instance, one important organic precept is that of integrating crops with livestock, both to encourage greater biodiversity and to recycle nutrients within the farm system. However, if a produce grower can only market meat or eggs as organic by following a strict requirement for 100% organic livestock feed, she may forego raising her own livestock and buy in manure or compost from conventional livestock or food processing operations. Does this farm adhere to higher standards than one that includes animals who are fed some portion of local (mostly nonorganic) food waste?

The insistence on higher organic standards may also come into conflict with the principle of regional food self-reliance. Livestock operations are often the most ecologically sound form of agriculture on hilly, thin upland soils, which may also harbor endemic sheep parasites that resist the most scrupulous preventive health care. Is it really better to prohibit synthetic worming agents for organic sheep production if it means that organic lamb cannot be reliably produced in certain regions? Most tree fruit grown in humid climates is highly susceptible to diseases that are mainly cosmetic problems, such as sooty spot on apples. Is it consistent with organic principles to make it extremely difficult to raise high-quality organic apples in the humid East, where apples are otherwise well adapted?

Ultimately, the integrity of the system is upheld by attention to enforcement, not by setting the standards bar ever higher. Given the imprecision and judgment calls inherent in measuring agroecosystem health, though, at what point would it become clear that the system does not qualify as organic? The answer depends largely on whether a minor infraction is willfully repeated, without effort to correct it. In practice, loss of organic certification is rarely if ever a result of too many minor infractions, but rather evidence of deliberate violation of the most critical rules. Legally, organic certification is considered to be a license granted by the USDA; before the government can take away a license granted to any citizen, a lengthy process with multiple appeal opportunities must be followed.

Consistent standards are a necessary step in the development of a broader organic market, but this is only one step towards the more radical agenda of the organic movement—to transform the way food is produced and distributed in this country. Standards for changing behavior should be attainable by the majority who, by definition, will just be "pretty good." One goal of our education system, for example, is to make sure that every child is able to complete high school and to achieve basic competencies. As my friend Katherine DiMatteo has said, "Do we want organic farmers to only be those who get the A's?"

## Brilliant Ideas and Biotech Collide

Through a long process of trial and error, vision and revision, and lots of arguing with lawyers, we came up with a few brilliant ideas to solve some of the problems of the divergence between the way the law was written and the need for a more organic-friendly regulatory scheme. The "Brilliant Ideas Embedded in the June Draft" on pages 138–139 offers a brief summary of the strategies we used to accomplish the lofty goal of creating an organic field within the USDA. Contrary to the claims of our subsequent attackers, the proposal we developed created the highest standards for organic production, with room for the necessary flexibility and creativity that would allow for justifiable and limited variance from this high bar. It was none other than our chief lawyer, not disposed to handing out compliments, who described our scheme as brilliant.

Our own agency's ignorance about and resistance to the organic concept was the major hurdle to be overcome before our brilliant work could be born as a regulation. In particular, we knew that official positions held by the Clinton administration (and all subsequent ones) supported genetically engineered crops and food irradiation as beneficial—not to mention profitable—technologies. We also knew that organic products could not be portrayed as somehow healthier or safer than the other kind. After all, how could any institution be expected to embrace a process that implied that everything it had been advocating for the past 50 years was detrimental? We did not have much difficulty with internal insistence on allowing irradiation, which was still not approved for use on very many food products. Genetic engineering, however, was another matter.

The issue of genetically engineered food (to which I will refer as GMOs for Genetically Modified Organisms throughout this discussion) was a big one for us. This was one reason we were counseled to keep as low a profile as possible within the Department—the less notice we attracted from higher echelons, the less pressure we would encounter to allow GMOs to wear an organic label. I inadvertently blew our cover soon after my arrival on staff, when Michael handed me a paper outlining the US position on the European Union's "Novel Food" policy. This document was distributed by the FDA, the point agency organizing the meeting of the Codex Alimentarius Food Labeling Subcommittee.[41] FDA's paper opposed the EU's policy requiring that food containing GMOs be labeled, and was actually written by Terry Medley, then Administrator of APHIS, USDA's agency responsible for approving release of GMO crops for commercial use. Medley, part of a long tradition of former Monsanto executives who go on to work for the agency that oversees its activities, had met with us about our position concerning organics and GMOs. My notes from that meeting include the following: "Medley is essentially playing hardball and trying to force biotech on organics under threat of trashing the whole program." In his view, which continues to be that of the biotech industry, the organic community's opposition to GMOs represents a philosophy founded on fear and superstition, not science.

Michael and I attended the Codex meeting on behalf of the NOP and were invited to participate because the same subcommittee also addressed rules for organic labeling. The proposed Codex organic rules clearly prohibited products of genetic engineering as agricultural inputs, a fact that did not seem to matter much to Mr. Medley. There was, however, one bullet point in the FDA/Medley paper that gave me another argument on which to challenge its opposition to labeling GMOs. FDA/Medley's rationale was that such "novel foods" are indistinguishable from non-GMO products, and only differentiated by the process by which they are produced. It included the statement "... *and the US does not label food based on how it was produced.*" "Aha — that's it!" I exclaimed to myself. "Once the NOP is implemented, the USDA will have a regulation that does label food based on how it was produced, not its inherent qualities."

The meeting, held in a conference room up the street at FDA headquarters, was packed with press and protesters. Jeremy Rifkin, an early critic of biotechnology and founder of the Foundation on Economic Trends, had written about the potential problems of allowing GMOs to proliferate in the environment, and was spearheading a campaign to demand that the FDA require that they be labeled.[42] Although I was firmly instructed to keep my mouth shut during this meeting and just listen, I couldn't resist. My comment did not attack the use of GMOs, oppose allowing them to be organic, or contradict the administration's position. Rather, I raised my hand and pointed out that the FDA's paper mistakenly stated that the USDA did not do process standards. The result was a reprimand from the brass in the AMS Administrator's office and, thanks to Michael's intervention, no further repercussions. But now they knew that we existed.

## GMOs and Biotechnology

The World Health Organization defines genetically modified organisms (GMOs) as "organisms in which the genetic material (DNA) has been altered in a way that does not occur naturally."[43]

Typically, genetic engineering involves manipulating an organism's genetic material (genome) in the laboratory by the insertion of one or more new pieces of DNA or by the modification of one or more of the base unit letters of the genetic code. This re-programs the cells of the genetically modified organism to make a new protein or to modify the structure and function of an existing protein.

The central concept of genetic engineering is that by cutting and splicing the DNA of an organism, new functions, characteristics, or traits can be introduced into that organism. The assumption is that the resulting organism will be identical to the non-genetically modified original, except that it will have the new trait that is conferred by the new gene introduced by the genetic engineer.

This is a simple and elegant concept. But the actual practice of genetic engineering is not so simple and elegant. The genetic engineering process is not precise or predictable. Genes do not function as isolated units, but interact with each other and their environment in complex ways that are not well understood or predictable. The genetic engineering process can disrupt the host organism's genome or genetic functioning in unexpected ways, resulting in unpredictable and unintended changes in the function and structure of the genetically modified organism. This, in turn, can result in the presence of unexpected toxins or allergens or altered nutritional value, and the engineered organism can have unexpected and harmful effects on the environment.[44]

Genetic engineering is a technique that falls under the broad category of "biotechnology," a word that is sometimes used to refer to all the bad things organic advocates associate with genetic engineering. However, biological technologies can range from basic plant breeding as practiced by farmers over millennia, to composting, winemaking, and other technological innovations that use living organisms to accomplish a desired human purpose. My first introduction to the concept of biological technologies was at New Alchemy Institute, where John Todd and associates were pioneering the use of "living machines" to purify wastewater. Such techniques

## GMOs and Biotechnology (continued)

are sometimes referred to as "ecotechnologies" to distinguish them from those that involve the manipulation of genetic material.

The first NOP-proposed rule defined "genetic engineering" thus: "Refers only to genetic modification of organisms by recombinant DNA techniques." The "June draft" of 1997 prohibited the use of genetically engineered organisms as seeds or planting stock, but this prohibition did not appear in the version published in December 1998.

In the final rule, the term "excluded methods" was substituted for "genetic engineering" as a way of downplaying the clear prohibition on any use of GMOs in organic farming or handling:

Excluded methods. A variety of methods used to genetically modify organisms or influence their growth and development by means that are not possible under natural conditions or processes and are not considered compatible with organic production. Such methods include cell fusion, microencapsulation and macroencapsulation, and recombinant DNA technology (including gene deletion, gene doubling, introducing a foreign gene, and changing the positions of genes when achieved by recombinant DNA technology). Such methods do not include the use of traditional breeding, conjugation, fermentation, hybridization, in vitro fertilization, or tissue culture.[45]

## Swimming Upstream through Mud

The mounting pressure from the organic community and its allies to get some rules out finally gained us a little higher priority in the Office of General Counsel (OGC). We started having regular meetings with one of the sharpest lawyers in the flock, Cynthia Koch, known for her ruthlessness in slashing verbiage that failed to pass legal muster. A former school teacher, she gave me a priceless education in the use of precise and unambiguous language, insisting on sentences as free from metaphor as humanly possible—a skill that I am today still struggling to unlearn. Each time another piece of the regulation was produced or updated, it was also necessary to explain its intent and rationale in a preamble section. The rationale had to reference a relevant provision of the OFPA, our authorizing statute, and virtually nothing else. No NOSB recommendations, and no previous organic standards or statements of principle. "No philosophizing," was Cynthia's refrain.

The legal team had, if anything, a more demented sense of humor than we did. Someone wandering down the hall in the OGC's wing might occasionally hear lengthy bellows of laughter and all manner of guffaws emanating from the conference room. During one period of peak frustration, someone brought in a 16-inch tall battery operated Godzilla, and we quickly adopted Zilla as our mascot. He rolled around the conference table roaring and raising his plastic arms, red eyes glowing, as we collapsed into tearful convulsions of laughter.

Despite moments when Cynthia brought me to tears by tearing my work apart, we developed a deep mutual respect and even affection. A large woman with multiple health problems, she genuinely believed that our work would ultimately benefit the public. Her goal was to make the program as legally airtight and bulletproof as possible, knowing that legal challenges were already being readied out there. Once she got what we were trying to do, she became one of our most powerful allies. After Cynthia's slashing, our cherished manifesto setting out the principles of organic agriculture[46] was reduced to a single definition of a "system of organic farming and handling," forever after known as the SOFAH. Using verbiage found in the OFPA, this definition served as a solid legal anchor for our regulation. Upon the SOFAH sat all our farm production and processing standards, as well as the all-important decisions about the compatibility of materials being considered for inclusion on the National List.[47] When in doubt as to whether a particular practice or substance was appropriate for use by an organic producer, one had only to ask if it was consistent with the SOFAH.

So we wrote and rewrote and rewrote everything again. Each time we had to wait—for marked up drafts to be returned by OGC, for clearance by superiors at AMS, for opinions from FDA, from EPA, from FSIS, from APHIS. Legal conundrums abounded, and we tried one solution after another to questions of how to set user fees, how to provide for the required accreditation peer review panel, and similar puzzles. Meanwhile we had to start thinking about all the Executive Orders that had to be satisfied, including an Economic Impact Analysis, and begin anticipating the roadblocks that awaited us once the rules arrived at the dreaded Office of Management and Budget (OMB), whose denizens had already let it be known that they did not believe that these regulations were needed. It was explained to me that a long-standing political antagonism between OMB and USDA virtually guaranteed that OMB would do whatever it could to undermine whatever we sent them. Despite these dire warnings of certain doom, onward through the mud we slogged. OGC warned us early on about another legal obstacle that threatened our success. Throughout the drafting process we consulted with everyone who had any knowledge or experience with organic production, processing, certification, or consumption. We attended meetings and trade shows, sent memos with questions, floated trial balloons of provisions we were considering, and conversed with anyone who had facts or an opinion they wished to share. NOSB members in particular were consulted often, both collectively and individually. We were now being told that this process would have to stop once a proposed rule reached the Federal Register.

---

### Brilliant Ideas Embedded in the June Draft

The structure of the first proposed rule was built on a definition distilled from the principles contained in the Prologue document (refer to page 121). The plan was for this definition to become the yardstick by which any practice or substance to be used in organic production or handling should be measured. In other words, any new idea should be assessed in terms of its compatibility with a system of organic farming and handling.

Definition of a System of Organic Farming & Handling (SOFAH):

A system that is designed to produce agricultural products by the use of methods and substances that enhance agroecosystem health within an agricultural operation and that maintain the integrity of organic agricultural products until they reach the consumer. This is accomplished by using, where possible, cultural, biological, and mechanical methods, as opposed to using substances, to fulfill any specific function within the system so as to: maintain long-term soil fertility; increase soil biological activity; recycle wastes to return nutrients to the land; provide attentive care for farm animals; enhance biological diversity within the whole system; and handle the agricultural products without the use of extraneous synthetic additives or processing in accordance with the Act and regulations in this part.

---

Variances to Handle the "Grey Areas"

Each section of the standards identified the "standard practice" as the preferable or ideal organic practice, followed by variances that could be employed if warranted according to a specific set of criteria. There was also a general section that identified the circumstances that would permit use of a variance, and the procedure to be followed when using it. This involved documenting the need to use the variance, and outlining in the Organic Plan steps to be taken to reduce or eliminate the use of the variance in the future. The organic plan would have to identify indicators to be monitored, such as soil quality, to show whether or not the plan was working. In the case of organic processed products, the need for any particular allowed nonorganic additive would have to be justified based on its importance in product quality and the lack of an acceptable organically produced alternative.

For example, a producer could only use antibiotics to treat a documented illness in an animal, and would have to show what she was doing to avoid the need for such treatment in the future. Other examples include the use of nonorganic seed, temporary confinement of an animal, and use of a highly soluble (but non-synthetic) fertilizer material, such as Chilean nitrate. The National List was included as a subset of the standards, and any substance listed, including synthetic micronutrients, animal drugs, and vitamins in processed products, could only be used under a variance.

In all cases, use of a variance had to be justified as supporting agroecosystem health, or at least not likely to do harm to soil, water, or biological diversity.

Orders of Preference

Several of the provisions that included variances also called for an order of preference in choosing which practices should be implemented before resorting to those that are less preferable, or variances. In general, this involved using management practices, such as preventive healthcare for animals, complex crop rotations to provide essential nutrients, and introduction of habitat for predator species to prevent crop pest problems, before

---

### Brilliant Ideas Embedded in the June Draft (continued)

employing any substance—synthetic or nonsynthetic—to address problems that occur. This means that use of any purchased material inputs, including "natural" fertilizers, herbal medicines, or botanical pest controls, would have to be justified in the organic plan, based on information about what preventative methods were being used.

#### Program Manuals as Farm Tools and Certifier Guides

We well understood that even the most adept organic producers would not always be able to meet the bar we set for "standard" practices, and that almost everyone would have to resort to practices identified as "variances" at some point. There was even a variance that allowed for use of otherwise prohibited practices, such as treated seed, for the purpose of limited trials or experimentation. It would thus be possible for a producer to try a new commercial corn variety, for example, to see how well it did in their specific conditions without risking losing certification on an entire field on account of the seed treatment.

This room for flexibility, while leaving a great deal open to interpretation, also made it possible for producers to learn to adapt these methods to their particular regional conditions and develop information on the efficacy of various techniques. We envisioned creating manuals that would serve as tools to teach producers about the best organic practices and how to use them, as well as providing guidance to certifiers concerning what constituted adequate justification for using a variance.

---

The condition known as *ex parte* is intended to prevent any semblance of undue influence on regulators by those subject to the regulations, especially during the time when draft regulations are released for public comment, until a final rule has been published. As it was put to us, this meant there would be no opportunity to respond to criticism or explain what we meant while the public was discussing and commenting on our work. We knew full well that many in the community were predisposed to oppose and misinterpret whatever we wrote. Most others would simply not understand what we were trying to do, couched as it was in legalese and inevitable insider jargon—without benefit of philosophizing. In addition, some self-appointed organic leaders prided themselves on their open hostility to what they fervently believed would amount to the theft of the organic label by "the evil forces of agribusiness as usual." Combined with fear of OMB, the hurdle of *ex parte* added more weight to the gloomy predictions of our inevitable failure. The accuracy of these predictions, viewed in hindsight, begins to answer the question of how the disconnect between what we said and what they heard came about.

## Meeting Resistance

Barely a month after I began working at the NOP, I got an inkling of how much opposition we were about to encounter. As alluded to earlier, widely held misconceptions about the role and authority of the NOSB had already engendered suspicion towards the USDA on the part of the organic community.

The next NOSB meeting was to be held in Rohnert Park, CA in October of 1994. Before my arrival, Ted and Michael had been grappling with some of the materials issues on the agenda and negotiating with various NOSB members about how to resolve them. The consensus plan was to develop a complete initial National List that would be submitted to the NOSB to be voted up or down as a whole. This would allow the standards to be as consistent as possible with existing industry norms from the get-go. Otherwise, once the program started, current organic producers might find themselves prohibited from using materials that had long been accepted under existing organic standards. It could take many months of case-by-case review followed by more formal rulemaking (a rather lengthy process itself) before some crucial materials could legally be used.

A similar problem arose with materials such as baking powder and citric acid. While commonly used in organic processed products, they would most likely fall under the definition of "synthetic" as established by the law.[48] One of the major hurdles to tackling this was a contradiction within the OFPA. One provision of the law prohibited the use of any synthetic ingredients in organic processed products, while another provision contradicted this by allowing nonorganically produced ingredients to be used, provided that they met the criteria outlined in the law (refer to Chapter 4 for criteria), and also *provided that there was "no wholly natural alternative."*[49] Representatives of both the purist and pragmatic

NOSB contingents had worked out an agreement to proceed with a review of synthetic ingredients being proposed for inclusion on the National List, without which many currently certified organic processed products would not be eligible for an organic label. Once the regulations were implemented, however, this agreement fell apart under legal assault—but I'm getting ahead of myself.

## The NOSB vs the NOP — What's The Difference?

| NOSB | NOP |
|---|---|
| Funded by FACA appropriations | Funded by USDA appropriations + user fees |
| Members represent specific constituency sectors, appointed by USDA for five-year terms, unpaid, with potentially substantial workload | Salaried full-time employees with knowledge of organic practices, hired through federal civil service system |
| Responsible for making recommendations concerning substances proposed for the National List and other advice to NOP as needed | Responsible for developing and enforcing regulations and policy concerning all aspects of the NOP, including the National List |
| Must hold open meetings and take public comment on all proposals being considered, but no requirement to respond to comments received | Must follow Federal Register process for any regulatory changes, including responding to all public comments received |
| All recommendations are advisory, not binding | Must consider NOSB recommendations in setting policy |

Ted and Michael's approach to these and other questions of how materials should be reviewed was spelled out in a discussion document entitled "Resolution of Focus," which they had drafted and asked me to evaluate. In it they explained their rationale and legal basis for considering some materials used as ingredients in processed products, even though they met the OFPA definition of "synthetic," to be eligible for inclusion on the National List. I found their reasoning to be, well, reasonable. On the strength of my approval they faxed the document to the NOSB leadership, along with some key players in the industry, to see what kind of buy-in they could get. Katherine DiMatteo, executive director of the Organic Trade Association (OTA—formerly OFPANA), also thought it made sense. The chair of the NOSB, Michael Sligh, not so much. The next day brought a message from Sligh to our higher ups in the chain of command, signed by some of the more purist members of the NOSB, demanding that we withdraw our discussion document—essentially saying "no discussion allowed." The document remains absent from the public record and, alas, not to be found in my personal files.

Appointment to the NOSB is a highly political process. These appointments are technically made by the Secretary of Agriculture, but it is primarily the NOP staff which vets nominees and recommends its choice of candidates; a final decision is generally made by the AMS Administrator. Congressional support was considered crucial, and a key criterion was geographical—which district was the nominee from and whose support was needed in Congress? When the first round of new vacancies for seats on the advisory board was announced in December of 1994, we actively recruited organic leaders we thought would support us on the critically important internal fight about GMOs.

The organic certification community presented another form of intransigence. By now there were a couple of dozen domestic certifiers of varying sizes and structures, including large and small non-profits as well as a couple of for-profit companies that recognized the potential for rapid growth in the organic industry. As was true prior to passage of the law, they seemed to occupy a state of eternal jockeying for dominance, turf battles, and paranoia. The more politically correct non-profit organizations continually conspired against the money-grubbing business-oriented certifiers, of which California-based QAI (Quality Assurance International), which was becoming dominant in the food processing and distribution sector, was the favorite target. My friend Joe Smillie was now working for this company, and was treated like a pariah by the "holier than thou" crowd.[50] But there was nary one amongst them (except the NOFA organizations, of course) who had any claim to superior righteousness.

The hardest part of all this for me was the intense disillusionment of observing the hypocrisy and self-serving dishonesty of people whom I had previously respected and admired. I just could not chalk it all up to ignorance or confusion. In one case, a highly respected academic and organic farmer whom I had helped convince to join the NOSB insisted on making a particular provision mandatory because this is what his European market demanded.

## Curses—FOIA'd Again

The lack of support for our program by USDA is clearly the biggest explanation for how long it took to implement. The first proposed rule was not published until nearly eight years after the law was passed, and the program was not officially implemented for another four years. Delays were not all due to internal obstacles, though. Journalists and public interest groups, among others, would regularly submit requests for a wide range of documents through the Freedom of Information Act. Any time a FOIA, as it was known, was received a great deal of time had to be spent finding the relevant documents, redacting anything deemed "confidential business information," photocopying, and sending them to the requesting party. At one point a photocopy fee was imposed to discourage massive document fishing expeditions, yet even a limited request could gum up the works as support staff were deflected from needed tasks. We suspected that in at least some of these cases the FOIA was a deliberate tactic to slow us down. A similar mechanism was at work when an inquiry from a Congressperson came in, although these were less frequent. A reply had to be drafted and approved up the chain of command. Ironically, at least one such request demanded an explanation as to why it was taking us so long to publish a proposed rule.

The press began pumping out misinformation early on, in some cases acting on "tips" from the organic community. *Mother Jones* magazine, for example, pointed to a memo written by Michael Hankin and addressed to the Deputy Secretary (doubtless obtained through a FOIA) that outlined some of the controversial issues in the draft rule, then wending its way through internal clearance. The memo presented our rationale for not allowing GMOs to be organic, and acknowledged that this was thought to be contrary to administration policy but consistent with all existing organic standards and with international norms. The article twisted what Michael said in the memo beyond recognition, portraying it as evidence that we had acquiesced to industry pressure to allow GMOs to be organic from the start, even though we knew that the organic community would object.[51]

My own experience was even worse. I agreed to talk to a writer for a

Vermont-based journal called *Food & Water*, which took aim at agribusiness wrongdoing from the political left. Having some acquaintance with the publisher, who had on occasion been a guest speaker at the Institute for Social Ecology, I believed talking to them might help my community realize that maybe the government was on the right side of the issues that concerned us. The result was another hatchet job. Everything I said was turned into verbal pretzels and used as more proof that organic's soul had been sold out to the evil corporate overlords, in whose pocket I was now ensconced. A short time later, I was told, the organization's director had actually called Murray Bookchin and demanded that he fire me from the Institute for Social Ecology (refer to Chapter 2).

Of course, some businesses and organizations tried to pressure us as well. The distinction between consultation with industry and movement representatives and lobbying by vested interests can be a fine one. It is important to gather information from many sources and to evaluate the information on its merits, not the power or position of the source. Many assume that corruption in regulatory agencies is widespread, and political influence was clearly a factor in decisions made by our superiors, most of whom were political appointees. However, those of us who were actually writing the rules were career civil servants who had to scrupulously avoid any appearance of conflict of interest with those who were being regulated. We could not even let someone from the organic community buy us lunch.

The NOP staff regularly received phone calls from companies and individuals seeking to influence our decisions. For example, leather meal, a "natural" nitrogen-rich waste product, was sometimes used in formulated "organic friendly" fertilizer blends. In light of information about its high levels of heavy metals from the tanning process, the consensus was to prohibit it for organic production. But the company didn't give up. Every so often I would hear Ted's voice from the next cubicle stretching to maintain composure and civility, and then realize he was on the phone with that leather meal guy again.

By far the most persistent lobbying that I dealt with came from a person at EPA, whom I had chanced to meet in the course of a Takoma Park elementary school sports event. The disposition of industrial waste in sewage sludge, with its myriad non-biodegradable contaminants, continues to be a serious problem for EPA. My acquaintance wanted to make sure that biolosids—the EPA's euphemism for sewage sludge that could be put to "beneficial use" as a fertilizer—would be given a clean bill of health for organic farmers. For a time, she inundated me with literature and phoned regularly. However, my research did not give me faith that biosolids were as beneficial as portrayed by the EPA. Our recommendation to the NOSB was to classify the stuff as "synthetic" due to all the industrial waste mixed in, and not to add it to the National List, thereby prohibiting it for organic production. This is the same regulatory device used to keep leather meal out of organically managed fields, and was retained in the proposed rule that was finally released for public comment.

Unsolicited advice, along with occasional verbal abuse, also came from a handful of the organic true believers. One particularly arrogant and aggressive critic, the editor of a newsletter put out by an Ozark-region organic growers cooperative that was widely circulated among the grassroots organic farmers, believed himself to be an expert on interpretation of the law—the ultimate Bible thumper. At one point we were told not to accept calls from him after Michael was subjected to an offensive verbal tirade that left him visibly shaken. For the most part, though, the agribusiness "big boys" did not pay much attention to us—only Monsanto, which has its fingers everywhere in the USDA, noticed that we existed.

## The June Draft

By late 1996 the end was in sight—or so we thought. OGC was still asking for revisions and revisions to the revisions, but we had nailed down pretty nearly everything that needed resolution. I had by this time moved back home to Vermont through an unusual "flexiplace" arrangement, which was made possible mostly due to the increasing importance attached to getting a rule out, and to Michael's recognition that the regulation writing skill and relationship with OGC I had developed, combined with my organic social capital, made me essential to the project. Meanwhile, Beth Hayden, who was hired soon after I came to the NOP, filed a grievance opposing my preferential treatment. Although she had been given responsibility for some pieces of the regulation writing and had made a strong effort, Beth simply did not have the deep understanding of organic concepts or language skills needed, and also had a hard time dealing with the mounting pressure to produce. Ted, though very well-informed about technical matters, was not all that good at constructing reader friendly sentences. The grievance was

Grace's home in Barnet, late 1990's

unsuccessful; I was able to move back to Vermont in June of 1996, and it fell to me to clean up the regulatory drafts and write virtually all of the preamble language.

I was able to work on my pieces over the Internet (when it worked), with the fax and Fedex as backup. Every couple of months I would be brought down to Washington for a week or two at a time at taxpayers' expense. To compensate, my pay was slightly reduced and my schedule made intermittent, meaning that I could be deactivated or reduced to part-time for any length of time when my services were not needed.

I was grateful to be home again, reconnecting with my amazing community, although my life was now so different than it was when I left. After more than two years in a St. Johnsbury nursing home my mother had died the previous March, while I was off giving a presentation at a conference in New Mexico. I was coming home as an orphan, with a spouse whose native climate did not include winter. Opal was now living full-time with Stewart, who had built a very unconventional solar-powered house elsewhere on his mother's land.

My first project was to have an addition built, which included a half foundation and a small greenhouse, with an oil furnace for back-up heat. The old wood-fired boiler was moved downstairs and linked into the system. Matches and some friends tore off the old greenhouse structure that covered the entire south face of the house to make way for the new addition. My new office space was next to the furnace room, with plenty of windows. It was also becoming necessary to buy the land my house sits on from Stewart's mother, but before that deal was finalized she suddenly died of a chronic heart problem. Stewart and I were able to work it out so that I could own ten acres, the minimum needed to avoid triggering Vermont's household septic system requirement. I have managed to avoid having to install one in all this time, living happily with an approved greywater system and a composting toilet that helps fertilize my fruit trees and ornamentals.

In October of 1996 Hal Ricker, NOP Program Manager and our boss, informed us that he was planning to retire as of January, having postponed retiring until it seemed that the proposed rule would be imminent. As second in command, Michael would have normally just been appointed to the position—this is what we were all counting on as the delicate internal negotiations to produce the draft regulation continued. This was not the plan, however. The decision, made at a higher level, was announced in mid-December: Michael would become Acting Program Manager and the position would be advertised for all sources—meaning that candidates could come from outside of USDA or even the federal government. We were now more visible and under mounting pressure to get the rule out as quickly as possible. It felt like lunacy to consider handing over control of the program to someone who might not be fully conversant with what we had accomplished and the obstacles that still awaited us. It appeared to be a political maneuver—someone had it in for Michael and was possibly grooming their own guy to take over. Hal's explanation was that they did not feel that Michael was the right person to represent the program to the public—his stutter presented some difficulties for public speaking, although he was working on it with a speech therapist and getting it more under control. (Michael has confirmed that this was, however, not a factor in the final decision.) Michael would, of course, be in the running for the job, though we had a few ideas about who else out there could claim to be qualified—and all of them were frightening. Half a page of my notebook for that day just has a scrawled "BLOW-UP." No choice but to keep plowing ahead.

My notes from that period are filled with demands from the office to make revisions and turn them around right away. The connection to the office e-mail system failed almost daily, and I was constantly on the phone to tech support or relying on the fax machine to turn in my work.

In addition to all the actual regulatory and preamble language, I had to develop charts that summarized each part of the docket and how it had to be cross-referenced. The section numbering system used in the Federal Register was not easy to learn, and whenever someone wanted to take out a provision or move it around, the numbers had to be changed. The preamble had to follow the regulation and explain each section in turn, so every change to the regulatory text needed corresponding preamble changes. Provisions that were agreed to at one meeting were crossed out in the next draft that came back to us. Again and again, someone from OGC would inform me that what I sent was not what was wanted.

At one point we got the message that Dan Glickman, the Secretary of Agriculture himself, wanted the proposal ready for departmental review by the beginning of November. It was still not ready in December, when I came down to the office for an extended stay, working late to make revisions to pieces that came back each day. Michael served as the central nervous system that kept track of all the pieces, who was working on which ones, and what details still needed adjustment. He was the one who made sure it all fit together and made sense. He was the one who took the heat when we could not comply with the impossible deadlines handed to us, noting in his quiet philosophical way, "We are being made to suffer for delays created by others."

In February of 1997, and again in April, I was called down for more "emergency" sessions with OGC. APHIS was still trying to force us to allow GMOs to be organic, and my notes for April 11th say "Cert docket returned by OGC—Situation impossible." It was not until early June that the complete docket was approved by OGC and ready for full departmental review and sign off by each of the agencies, including EPA and FDA. In between I was asked to work on informational materials for our AMS superiors to bring across the street to a meeting in the Administration building, where all the big shots worked. The Secretary's office on the second floor was referred to as "the cage" because the reception area was surrounded by glass walls with vertical black support strips. Protocol did not permit Michael to participate because his status was still too low. The announcement for the Program Manager job had still not been issued, and Michael was only "Acting."

My instructions for developing talking points for that meeting with the Secretary were to write down "what we wanted to say in the Preamble but had to take out." What did we have to do to get OGC to understand the program? What were the sticking points and how did we deal with them? What underlying principles guided our thinking? How is this rule different from all other rules? Most importantly, we had to convince the hierarchy that we did not pose a threat to business as usual.

The only way to do this was to emphasize repeatedly that the organic label is not a product quality or safety claim, but rather a matter of consumer choice. Consumers expect that organic products do not contain GMOs, and we had to meet those expectations. This does not, heaven forbid, in any way disparage those technological marvels of modern agriculture, or cast any doubt as to their total safety. Similarly, the organic label does not mean residue-free, but rather represents a system of production that does not rely on agrochemicals to control pests. You can't protect against any possible route of contamination, such as wash water or other forms of "unavoidable residual environmental contamination," short of growing food in a "greenhouse on Pluto," as one friend described it. Neither is there any implied claim of nutritional superiority. Consumers can decide for themselves, based on their own application of the precautionary principle, whether they want to pay the inevitably higher price for products bearing an organic label.

The Department had, by this time, started to become accustomed to process-based regulations issued by AMS. The Food Safety & Inspection Service (FSIS), which oversees all livestock product-related food safety inspections, had recently implemented a new HACCP (Hazard Analysis and Critical Control Points) system for regulating food safety procedures. Cynthia Koch, our lead OGC attorney, had worked on this regulation, which helped her to better understand what we needed to do. This is similar to the approach taken during an organic inspection, particularly for large processing facilities, and is derived from the total quality management model. It entails creating a plan that identifies critical control points in the process where food safety—or in our case organic integrity — could be compromised, and the standard operating procedures to be used to protect against the threat.

As the whole package wended its way through the various agencies that had to approve it, we began preparing for review by OMB—our own critical control point. Meetings with OMB staff were already in process, and their questions had to be answered. A memo from one of our superiors at AMS instructed everyone to "drop everything to satisfy any information requests" from OMB. The rationale for our program had to explain why we needed federal organic standards and certification or accreditation programs at all—an act of Congress was not sufficient justification.

There were a few issues that came up during the internal review process that required more revisions, but they were relatively minor. The Codex Alimentarius organic rules were still being refined, and while Michael had to officially represent the program at international meetings, he delegated to me the task of developing our comments and positions on issues under discussion. Otherwise, we occupied ourselves with thinking about how all this was going to be explained to the organic community, as well as with initial ideas for the program manual.

The program manual was a key piece of our strategy, inasmuch as the rules themselves had to be broad and general. "One-size-fits-all" is often given a derogatory meaning, but in the case of a regulation that was meant to apply to every conceivable form of agricultural product, and some we didn't think of such as algae, it represents the most appropriate approach for organic standards. It is common practice among regulatory agencies to provide detailed guidance about how to interpret their rules in specific situations, and we planned to use this vehicle to make it clear what kinds of justifications were acceptable for practices that would fall under the variances rubric. Keep in mind that, as we constructed our rules, any use of a material that appeared on the National List would have been considered a variance that needed to be justified in the organic plan, whether it was due to commercial unavailability of an organic form of the ingredient, or to weather conditions that caused increased disease pressure. In addition to justification, the plan would have to include a strategy to avoid the need for the material in question in the future. We were also only too aware of how little anyone knew about the most effective organic practices in a full range of environmental conditions—domestic as well as international. Such details would need to be revised and updated as new information and experience on the ground is collected, rather than being subject to a lengthy Federal Register rulemaking process. The program manual would be revised regularly to include such information as appropriate stocking density for different species and breeds of livestock, rates and modes of application of allowed fertilizer and pest control materials, and appropriate sanitation procedures to protect organic integrity during food processing.

This did not sit very well with the certifier community, though. Whenever we tried to explain how it worked, someone would raise the concern that our guidance about recommended practices would not have the force of law; someone could not be decertified for failing to comply with the program manual. This argument later became an accusation that the rules were "full of loopholes," through which corporate agribusiness, who wanted to take over the organic label, would drive their SUVs.

Meanwhile, work on a draft program manual kept getting shunted to the bottom of the task list. We were busy preparing to get the accreditation program up and running as soon as we had a final rule, which involved putting together a training program for certifiers, with some help from another division of AMS. We also had some work to do to get ready for electronic rulemaking: our program was to be the first to offer the option of submitting public comments via the Internet.

By the end of June 1997 we had signoffs from all the appropriate agencies. Dan Glickman himself had approved the prohibition of GMOs in organic products. What became known as the "June draft" was now on its way to OMB. We were under strict orders not to distribute copies to anyone outside our office, and to my knowledge never did. However, several members of the industry were able to acquire them, perhaps from contacts in other agencies who had reviewed the rule. Both Katherine DiMatteo and Joe Smillie, executive director and board chair, respectively, of the Organic Trade Association, thought it was excellent. That, at least, gave me some level of reassurance—even though I knew full well that those out to oppose the program were also reading it and looking for ways to tear it apart.

## OMB Throws Organic under the Bus

Once again, we played the waiting game as the rule was dissected at the White House, and waited again as negotiations were interrupted by summer vacation schedules. I was given a few other assignments to work on while awaiting the outcome of the regulatory digestive system. One was to begin developing criteria for the review of brand-name, mass-produced inputs that wanted to be approved for use by organic farmers or food processors. A private non-profit organization called the Organic Materials Review Institute (OMRI) had recently been organized by Bill Wolf and some other organic materials wonks to provide this service, and the state of California was already developing its own review process. It is a complicated situation because of the need to safeguard manufacturers' trade secret recipes used to make fertilizer products, pest control materials (including the majority of the ingredients, identified only as "inerts," that you see on the label of that benign botanical pesticide), or natural flavoring additives. We believed that this formulated product review function would best be served by the USDA, which was necessarily free from conflict of interest and bound by confidentiality, and would ensure that decisions in keeping with the still in-process regulations were consistently made.

I was also assigned to represent the NOP on the USDA's newly formed Sustainable Development Council, which entailed working with almost all the other agencies in the Department to develop a USDA-wide policy on sustainable agriculture.

Early in September we were asked to respond to a 16-point memo listing OMB's concerns. The rationale behind our variances scheme was put under a microscope, and we had to come up with justifications for including criteria such as biological diversity and agroecosystem health as essential for a system of organic farming and handling. One big issue had to do with the allowance for use of raw livestock manure, which could only be applied to crops for human consumption at least three months prior to harvest, or four months if the edible portion might contact the soil. These rules are meant to ensure that no human pathogens survive to potentially contaminate produce, but the OMB's Office of Risk Assessment was queasy about the public health implications. We reminded them that conventional farmers often use raw manure without any restrictions except the requirement to protect surface water from pollution. Of course the GMO issue came up as well, with a suggestion that we consider establishing two grades of organic—one with and one without GMOs.

A few weeks later a meeting was held at the White House that was attended by the upper echelons of AMS, including one AMS Deputy Administrator who was on detail (meaning on loan for a short time) to the White House. The Secretary of Agriculture was also in attendance, and several key decisions were made at the highest level in the USDA hierarchy. Once again Michael Hankin, still only Acting NOP Program Manager, was not deemed worthy of attending. Although one "friend" in higher places had promised to support our position on GMOs, he had clearly avoided saying anything to contradict the higher-ups. Their message to us was that OMB had rejected our rule, but they were willing to rewrite it "the way it should be." My entry for September 29th is headed "DOOM & DESPAIR," and says only that the administration is rewriting the rule "just to get something published." I was asked to travel to the office to help with the rewrite, once we got the OMB version.

It was a dispirited crew indeed that greeted me when I flew down to Washington in early October 1997. My task was to rewrite the sections that OMB had gutted and attempt to come up with language that they could live with. The Preamble then had to be revised to address the OMB version of the rules. We settled on a desperate "Hail Mary" tactic of using the Preamble to ask for public comment about the questions of irradiation and GMOs, about which the proposed regulation, like the OFPA, was now silent. Once we had the resounding public comment we knew would come, we could then safely put those prohibitions back into the Final Rule.

EPA then saw an opening for their pet issue. As long as we were requesting public comment about standards issues, they thought we should also ask for comments about whether organic farmers should be allowed to use biosolids as a fertilizer. OMB grudgingly allowed us to include these requests. There was no way, however, to solicit public comment about the two concepts that we knew were central to the whole regulatory structure we had created (and to the key principles of organic agriculture we had crafted): *Agroecosystem health* was now missing from the SOFAH definition, and biological diversity was now completely absent from the regulation.

We were able to convince OMB to let us keep the order of preference scheme, which means that a producer or processor would have to first use preventive measures, such as careful variety selection and good sanitation, to avoid the need to use any allowed materials for pest or disease control. Our carefully defined variance scheme, which had limited the permissible rationale for using any practice designated as a variance, was now gone. Without it, the choice was to either make the standards extremely liberal so that almost anything goes or, if we simply deleted any allowance for practices that were previously covered by variances, way too far on the purist side. We were finally able to get permission to use the phrase "if necessary" to identify practices formerly known as variances. For example, if necessary, livestock could be confined and access to outdoors could be limited, as long as living conditions were adequate to maintain their health without resorting to prohibited medications. It was a desperate move which we felt might work, as long as we could use the program manual to spell out what conditions might make using these practices necessary.

## Changes Imposed by OMB

**Provisions Deleted:**

- Prohibition of GMOs as organic products
- Prohibition of irradiation as a means of preserving organic products
- Definitions of Agroecosystem health, Biological diversity

**Changes to the SOFAH:**

All references to 'agroecosystem health' and 'biological diversity in the definition of 'a system of organic farming and handling' were deleted, so that it now read:

A system that is designed to produce agricultural products by the use of methods and ~~substances that enhance agroecosystem health within an agricultural operation and~~ that maintain the integrity of organic agricultural products until they reach the consumer. This is accomplished by using, where possible, cultural, biological and mechanical methods, as opposed to using substances, to fulfill any specific function within the system so as to: maintain long-term soil fertility; increase soil biological activity; recycle wastes to return nutrients to the land; provide attentive care for farm animals; ~~enhance biological diversity within the whole system~~; and handle the agricultural products without the use of extraneous synthetic additives or processing in accordance with the Act and regulations in this part.

Provisions addressing both agroecosystem health and biological diversity were likewise eliminated from the regulation. The general provision requiring that any use of a practice or substance "not result in measurable net degradation of soil or water quality or of any other appropriate indicator of agroecosystem health as demonstrated by monitoring" was reduced to requiring that it "not result in measurable degradation of soil or water quality."

The section entitled "biological diversity and crop rotation" became simply "crop rotation," and the keystone standard practice requiring that "biological diversity be established, maintained and enhanced through the use of practices that are appropriate to the site and type of operation," which included a requirement to introduce diverse

## Changes Imposed by OMB (continued)

species into any field or farm parcel planted with a perennial crop, was eliminated.

### Changes to Variances:

The whole mechanism for using variances, and distinguishing a variance from "standard practice" was deleted. In its place, we were allowed to suggest that practices previously identified as variances might be used "if necessary." There was no regulatory language that spelled out the procedure for identifying conditions that might make a given practice necessary, or requirement for identifying a plan for reducing/eliminating the necessity for such a practice. This vagueness was rightly criticized as likely to invite abuse.

### The Role of OMB in Obstructing Regulations:

The OMB, through its Office of Information and Regulatory Affairs (OIRA), has become better known in the last few years for its role in obstructing regulations. A 2013 editorial in *The New York Times* noted that there were then 136 draft rules under review at OIRA, of which 72 had been held up for longer than the 90-day limit set by executive order, with over half of these having languished for over a year.

"Since OIRA's creation in 1980, the office has been a force for ensuring that regulations reflect presidential priorities. It can advance rules, with or without change; return them to agencies for reconsiderations; or urge agencies to withdraw them. Through most of its history, the office has been used to advance antiregulatory aims, often by emphasizing the burdens rather than the benefits of regulation" [52]

By early November the revisions were completed and ready to go back to OMB. Michael told me they were working on getting it published in the Federal Register before Thanksgiving, but the actual publication date was still uncertain. I was to continue working on an information memo for the Secretary, and question and answer sheets about the rule for the public, all in preparation for the official rollout celebration. I was not in a very celebratory frame of mind. Struggling with my conscience, I was debating the possibility of resigning in protest over OMB's destruction of our work. But I wondered what good it would do. Who would care, except the relatively small network of friends who were concerned about what was happening at the NOP? If I stayed, at least I could help salvage my work of the previous three years; I still had some hope that was possible. And yes, I could continue earning a munificent (by local standards) federal employee's salary while living in my Vermont paradise.

At the same time, Hal had been gone from the NOP for almost a year yet the job announcement for Program Manager had still not been published. There was, however, a new Administrator at AMS who was in charge of that decision; our "friend" from higher up in our agency who had just sold us out to OMB had been the Acting Administrator. Agency Administrators are always political appointees, and this position was now filled by a professor of agricultural economics from Cornell. I had encountered him briefly back when I was organizing training sessions on organic and sustainable agriculture under the old LISA program. It seemed like a possible cause for optimism, inasmuch as this guy at least had some knowledge of and sympathy for the organic community. How mistaken I was.

# 6 We Have Met the Enemy ... or Organic Gone Wrong

*The numerous loopholes and provisions in the rules would open the door for large-scale industrial agribusiness to overwhelm an alternative food system largely composed of small farmers, retailers and processors.* — Ben Lilliston and Ronnie Cummins

In the spring of 1998, the seven professional staff members of the USDA's National Organic Program were meeting with Keith Jones, the recently hired NOP program manager. Our morale was in the toilet after our first proposed rule, released at the end of 1997, was inundated with a record-breaking 280,000 negative public comments. It had taken seven years and nearly superhuman effort after the organic law was passed to produce that regulatory proposal. Michael Hankin, the brains behind the program who by all rights should have been named program manager, was passed over for the job and requested transfer to another division of the agency. Now we were told that we would not be creating a final rule in response to those comments, but rather were to start over with a new proposed rule.

Keith was trying to raise our team spirit by tossing a football around the circle. It wasn't working. Several of us made suggestions about parts of the proposal that we thought should be salvaged, including some important pieces that were deleted by the Office of Management and Budget before it was released. We wanted to at least include the principles of organic agriculture embedded in our definition of "a system of organic farming and handling," known affectionately as the SOFAH, on which our entire regulatory structure rested. "I don't care about organic principles," snapped Keith.

And so it went with other ideas that were vetoed. At one point I recall protesting in frustration, "...but that requirement will make it really hard for small farmers." The rest of the dialogue went something like this:

Keith: "I don't care about small farmers."

Me: "So you don't care about organic principles and you don't care about small farmers—can you tell me what you DO care about?"

Keith: "I like to win."

## The Deluge

Winning had eluded the rest of us. Sure, we had won some battles within the Department, but we had resoundingly lost in our effort to reach the hearts and minds of our organic constituency. We knew we were in for it when the proposed rule was released in mid-December of 1997 with only a 60-day public comment period right in the middle of the holidays. The comment period was extended an additional 60 days after vociferous public protest that this was insufficient time to carefully review and analyze the 458-page document.[53]

The misinformation and action alerts started flowing almost immediately. Some had obviously been readied even before the proposal was published, with the expectation that USDA intended to water down the standards to satisfy its agribusiness patrons. A prime source of misinformation was an organization that called itself the Pure Food Campaign.

Ronnie Cummins took over leadership of the Pure Food Campaign from Jeremy Rifkin, who had started it as a campaign to require the labeling of foods that contain GMOs. Cummins spent some time building his membership base (and credibility with funders) by laboriously copying the names and addresses of people who had submitted public comment, most of them in hard copy. Later changing the name of the organization to the Organic Consumers Association, Cummins became the first of the self-styled "organic watchdogs." He soon joined forces with former NOSB Chair Michael Sligh, who lent credibility to the distorted interpretations offered by Cummins and added the utterly false accusation that we had ignored the National Organic Standards Board's (NOSB) recommendations in creating this proposal.

Whole Foods Market and the food coop network issued bulletins and distributed postcards that people could simply sign and mail. A similar form letter was distributed via the Working Assets long distance phone service, which was popular among the progressive constituency. With growing access to email and Internet capabilities among consumers and grassroots activists, form email submissions also figured into the mix. These postcards and form letters made up the overwhelming majority of the more than a quarter million public comments submitted—a number which broke all records for comments received on a proposed regulation. Because we had also blazed a new trail in creating the procedure by which, for the first time, public comments could be received over the Internet, our staff was given a special award for its ground-breaking work in electronic rulemaking.

The comments were almost universally negative. All of the form letters focused their outrage on the "Big Three" subjects of our requests for public comment—requests made in desperation after our original proposal was gutted by OMB: GMOs, irradiation, and sewage sludge. We expected that many of those who commented would not have actually read the proposal, but I was unprepared for the deliberate misrepresentation by a few organic leaders and activists whom I had previously respected and even considered friends. It was no use trying to tell them that the request for public comment was genuine, that the rules as written would neither have allowed nor prohibited GMOs and irradiation and that, while not explicit, these rules would not have allowed the use of sewage sludge. I remember attending a meeting at which a participant, clearly outraged and disgusted at the idea of organic farmers using a material derived from human excrement, insisted that she knew for a fact that the proposal would allow this practice—even after I explained to her that I had written this particular section and assured her that no such thing was permitted.

Later in 1998 *The Ecologist*, an influential British environmental magazine, published an article co-authored by Ronnie Cummins that repeated some of the worst misinformation about the proposed rule.[54] I drafted a lengthy response that they declined to publish, even after I trimmed it down at their request. I decided to share it with a few organic thought leaders whom I still considered friends; this got me into some hot water with my boss, who threatened me with disciplinary action for insubordination unless I retracted the letter. The letter was based on a draft that Michael Hankin had asked me to write while the public comment period was still open, to debunk some of the misinformation in circulation—a piece that was never cleared for distribution.[55]

It was bad enough to skim through some of the hateful and even threatening comments we received, but lengthier comments from former colleagues left me feeling crushed. A few people with whom I had worked closely during my years in NOFA, people who had shared my preference for a more flexible, agronomic responsibility-oriented approach to organic standard setting, all condemned the proposal as fatally flawed, viciously twisting even the most innocuous language to imply that our goal was to destroy the organic industry. A team of consultants—all former comrades—was enlisted to write comments on behalf of the Organic Trade Association (OTA) and, despite our long-standing relationship and friendly discussions during the previous three years, got it just as wrong as everyone else. There were even some nasty accusations penned by people who knew me and knew I had a hand in it; other old friends, who didn't realize that I had a role in the proposal, would circulate action alerts asking me to help save organic standards. Michael and Ted counseled me not to take it personally, but it felt very personal. "Some of these people I've even slept with," I wailed. It was hard to keep going, or to convey to even my closest friends what I was going through.

Staff were allowed to speak at public meetings and conferences as long as we adhered to strict guidelines which included no private conversations or discussions about "the merits of the proposal"—whatever that meant. It seemed that the *ex parte* rule prevented us from defending our work, or even correcting the misinformation that was flying around.

I was granted permission to attend the annual winter conference put on by NOFA-Vermont and to accept an invitation to keynote a conference sponsored by the Ohio Ecological Food & Farming Association. Both events were disasters. From the stage at the Vermont gathering, surrounded by old friends and people I thought respected me, the hostility was unbearable. One particularly angry farmer who got to the microphone during the question and answer session just kept screaming at me: "Fascist—you're a Fascist."

"Why?" I kept wondering. Why were so many of my old friends willing to assume the worst about the work I had done? Why had nobody even bothered to ask me, in confidence, what I thought? Miranda was probably the one person in my life who truly understood what I was trying to do and totally supported me. A few other close friends stood by me, but were confused by the disconnect between what they were hearing from their own trusted sources and what I tried to explain about why those sources were wrong.

There was one truth-seeker who thought it would be a good idea to find out what I had to say: Donella (Dana) Meadows. A Dartmouth professor who spearheaded the landmark Club of Rome study on *The Limits to Growth* in the 1970s, Dana had started one of the first eco-village co-housing communities in the region and wrote a regular column about food and agriculture for a local weekly. Dana, whom I knew only by reputation and admired tremendously, simply called me up and asked. Her resulting column was one of the few—if not the only—thoughtful treatises on the controversy I encountered. Although we never met, when she died a few years later from a freak attack of meningitis I felt like I'd lost a dear friend.

---

### Some Examples of Public Comments from Former Colleagues and/or Spokespersons for Well-Known NGOs:

*If the USDA's proposed rules are adopted as written, consumers will lose all faith in the "organic" label, and a $3.5 billion industry in organic products will be threatened.*
—Carl Pope of the Sierra Club

*"Organic" should be defined by how the people view organic, i.e., pure and natural, not by how multinational corporations want to rewrite the dictionary.*
— Claire Cummings, California attorney

*The recently proposed rules for organic agriculture are perverse and diabolical.*
— Bill Duesing, Connecticut organic activist

---

I was plagued for a long time by the question of why people with whom I shared a commitment to the bigger picture organic values had launched such an extreme attack on my work. For the most part I wrote it off to a general arrogance, coupled with ignorance about how the government works and a sort of ideological blindness that is common to both left and right. They believed whatever their personal news sources told them, and there was virtually nothing out there to suggest it might be otherwise. One acquaintance summed it up as, "We just assumed you had sold out." Of course, if I thought that the USDA was actually proposing to do what the leading activists claimed, I would have been outraged too.

Some of the individuals who knowingly created misinformation—if not outright lies—subscribe, it seems, to the belief that the end justifies the means. A kind of fundamentalist thinking pervades activists on both the left and the right, mirroring the authoritarian need to divide the world into us and them. Devotees of the old school of leftist confrontation politics don't get the problematic strategy of lying to protect organic integrity, any more than their erstwhile political opponents get the contradiction of killing for peace.

My paranoia about the existence of double agents in the movement, working on behalf of corporations to delay and obstruct the implementation of organic rules, still does not seem so terribly off-base. The tactic of introducing agents provocateurs is a tried and true method of disempowering activist threats to business as usual. This strategy was brilliantly illustrated by the Matt Damon movie *Promised Land* (2012), in which Damon plays an agent of a gas company seeking to buy the right to frack land belonging to cash-strapped Pennsylvania farmers. Damon's character encounters opposition from a firebrand environmental activist who loses the trust of townspeople, and possibly the impending vote, when he is exposed as having misrepresented some facts about the gas company's past misdeeds. The upshot of the story is that the activist was actually sent by the gas company to discredit the opposition (and yes, when he discovers the subterfuge staged by his own bosses, Matt Damon does the right thing). Even the noblest slayer of evil corporate dragons has a certain vested interest in exaggerating the danger against which he (it seems to usually be a he) is stalwartly defending us.

Whether deliberate or not, it seems that the activists who demanded the highest possible organic standards, seeking to defend organic purity against anything deemed synthetic and who condemned our proposal for being so weak as to be meaningless, played right into Monsanto's hands.[56] Monsanto was keenly aware of the opportunity this public outrage over the perceived watering down of organic standards presented. They had lost their battle within USDA to allow the use of GMOs in organic food when the June draft was cleared by the Secretary of Agriculture, but then they had seemingly triumphed by getting OMB to remove our prohibition on GMOs.

But not even Monsanto was prepared for the public firestorm that ensued, and it seems that they quickly reassessed the situation. When their representative, who favored the folksy look of plaid flannel shirts presented the company's public comment he expressed unqualified support for the exclusion of GMOs from organic food. "Consumers deserve a choice" was the mantra that we had used to win the day inside the Department, and Monsanto agreed. Now, rather than exerting pressure to allow GMOs to be organic, their comments suggested that, if a consumer doesn't want these perfectly safe products in their food, products deemed by FDA to be identical to those grown without gene splicing technology, they should be able to buy organic. And to add to this support, the Monsanto guy expressed strong agreement with the prevailing sentiment that organic standards must be kept as strict as possible. Consumers, after all, expect organic to represent a gold standard, and consumer expectations must be met.

This strategy paid off handsomely. The growing movement demanding that GMO foods be labeled as such was squashed, at least in the US, at least for the time being. The strictest possible organic standards would make it less appealing for conventional farmers to convert to organic production and, if organic could be held to less than 5% of the food system, Monsanto would have free reign with the other 95%. This is what has actually come to pass.[57] The only fly in their genetically modified ointment, though, was the tremendous publicity generated by the whole uproar, which created widespread public awareness—and uneasiness—about the stealthy and rapid expansion of genetic engineering in food production. This was the only silver lining I could find in the public response to our draft regulation.

It is important to acknowledge that the proposal that finally came out of the OMB butcher shop really was fatally flawed. It lacked not only the prohibitions on GMOs and irradiation, but a few other key pieces that might have made it more acceptable to those with some insight into the issues involved. Some in the community felt that it was legitimate to interpret the absence of these prohibitions as providing an allowance for the practices; others did not believe that our request for comments reflected a genuine intent to make a change based on the response. Other concerns expressed in the comments, such as the time and expense needed to come into compliance with the rules, were certainly valid. Many did not understand the purpose of the regulatory process that requires public notice and opportunity to comment on any regulatory proposal before it can be finalized.

Some of the biggest complaints received during the public comment period were issues that were a matter of law and could not be changed. One example is the establishment of a single standard for organic and the prohibition of any individual certifier—who would be accredited as an agent of USDA—claiming to require higher standards to use its organic logo. Many existing certifiers had invested considerable effort into their own claims of higher standards, and could not stomach the idea of what they viewed as forced reciprocity (refer to Chapter 3 for a discussion

## Fatal Flaws

Some "fatal flaws" in the proposed rule as published created understandable concerns among organic producers and the industry:

- Substituting the phrase "if necessary" for the well-defined variance structure gave the impression that a producer could do anything they wanted and claim that it was necessary.
- The absence of any reference to the central importance of biodiversity in an organic system, or to the overarching criterion of agroecosystem health, fueled the claim that large-scale organic monocultures would be acceptable.
- The law required that we come up with a proposal for assessing user fees for the program. We knew that no matter what we proposed it would upset virtually everyone, and we were right.
- Although the NOSB narrowly voted against recommending the addition of several controversial substances to the National List, we decided to include them in the proposal and see if public comment came out to support them. For example, piperonyl butoxide (PBO) is sometimes used in pesticide formulations as a synergist, which means that much less of the pesticide (in this case botanicals that were approved for use in organic production) is needed to achieve the desired effect. However, this strategy was widely regarded as a deliberate flouting of the law, which does not, in reality, give the NOSB final authority over the National List.[58]
- The preamble did not include any information explaining the use of a Program Manual to provide detailed instructions to certifiers and organic operators.

of the problem of lack of reciprocity). Another big issue for much of the existing certification community was the process for revoking certification, which could be finalized only by the USDA after the miscreant had ample opportunity for appeal. Such rules are intended to protect the public from abuse of power by the government, but many certifiers perceived it as the government usurping the power that should belong to them. The supposed authority of the NOSB, as an advisory body operating under the rules of the Federal Advisory Committees Act, to overrule the USDA's decisions was another big issue for the public.

## Descent into Purgatory: Managing the Flood of Comments

The NOP office quickly became a flurry of activity, with a squadron of extra staff borrowed from other programs pressed into duty and set up in a basement annex office to help catalog and index the flood of comments. A series of public meetings was planned for February, with top USDA officials who needed talking points about the changes under consideration. Demonstrators greeted them at each session, with one episode of protest theater that entailed an assault with a cream pie.

Once all the public comments on a regulatory proposal are received, the agency is obligated to discuss each discrete comment received in the preamble to the final rule and provide a rationale for either accepting or rejecting it; comments that all say basically the same thing can be lumped together. My assignment, back in the safety of my Vermont home, was to review the substantive comments that were collected and sent to me in a couple of fat ring binders and begin formulating responses. I also had to keep churning out talking points for the upper echelon, who were now the only public spokespersons permitted to talk to the press.

It was early February when we got the news: Michael Hankin would not be the next Program Manager. The winning candidate was Keith Jones, a Texan who had developed one of the first state organic programs as a protégé of Jim Hightower, the iconic agricultural muckraker who had won election as that state's Secretary of Agriculture during the administration of Democratic Governor Anne Richards. I later learned that Kathleen Merrigan had worked with Hightower before joining Senator Leahy's staff, and it was widely known that she and Michael Sligh had recruited Keith and then campaigned for him to be hired.

My only note for that day was an underlined "despair and depression" at the bottom of the page. I clearly remember the feeling of defeat and foreboding deep in my gut the moment I got word of the decision. For the first time I began to doubt that our years of effort would ever come to fruition. Even with the best of qualifications and experience in state government, there was no way that Keith could bring the intimate knowledge of the program we had constructed or the connections within the Department that Michael possessed. He was certainly unlikely to be the egalitarian family mediator that Michael had been. Tall and confident, with a natural political aptitude, Keith projected the image of a strong leader—unlike Michael's soft-spoken bureaucratic persona. He was a guy who would be a real boss and keep his eye on the ball.

Wanting to hope for the best, and willing to put our disappointments aside to get on with the work, we soon learned how much worse it could be. Once Keith came on board in early March, a wall went up. I was not invited to participate by phone in the initial staff meeting, and was then told that I did not have permission to attend the NOSB meeting being held later that month in Washington. When I went over his head to the director of our division and was instructed to come down for the NOSB meeting, Keith did not hide his displeasure. He refused to include me in a meeting with OGC while I was there, and it became apparent that he was taking orders from higher up in the Department.

Within a week of Keith's arrival in early March, Michael requested transfer back to his old office in the Dairy Division. He assured us that he would keep in touch, and confided that there were some serious personnel issues involved. He was later able to extract some concessions from the Department when he obtained a copy of a letter from a congressman that essentially ordered the AMS Administrator to make this hire—a breach of protocol that is definitely against the rules governing civil service hiring.

The public appeared to be mollified by the change of management, and was encouraged to see this move as a sign that the Department meant to give them what they wanted. Keith also carried some of the anti-establishment cachet of his association with Jim Hightower. The belief that they finally had someone in charge who was on their side rankled me no end, and it was all I could do to hide my fury. They had traded the one person in a management position who really was on their side for someone who was a supreme salesman and cared only about winning. Keith prided himself on his persuasive skill, claiming that he could "talk a dog off a meat wagon." His winning strategy now was to give them whatever they wanted, and let them live with the consequences.

I began to understand how this situation was perceived when I was given permission to attend a meeting of the NOFA Interstate Council, the body that connected all seven autonomous state chapters of what is now called the Northeast Organic Farming Association. These quarterly meetings were held at the New England Small Farms Institute (NESFI) in Belchertown, Massachusetts, the brainchild of July Gillan, with whom I had worked closely in drafting the OFPANA Guidelines back in 1987.

I believed Judy could be an important ally with the organic community. But I was quickly discouraged to learn that she was working with Michael Sligh, and that she regarded the advent of Keith Jones as NOP program manager to be a step in the right direction. She recounted to me with glee an earlier meeting at which Michael Hankin had teared up when talking about how much he cared about supporting small organic farmers—implying that this was evidence of his dishonesty. I was aghast and could only sputter, "At least now you have someone who won't cry at meetings."

## Staying Out of Trouble

My next job was to compile a list of key issues that needed to be addressed in the next version of the rule, as going directly to a Final Rule was not an option. So much change was needed that it had to come out as another proposal in order for the public to have an opportunity to comment on all the new material. Simply restoring the key provisions that OMB had slashed from our June draft was also quickly taken off the table. We really had to go back to square one.

At first Keith appeared to make an effort to seek my input and suggestions about what the next iteration of the rule should contain. Before long this pretense was dropped, and Ted confirmed that he was also being stonewalled. With Michael out of the picture, only Ted and I, of those who had been intimately involved in writing the first version, remained. Beth Hayden, my former buddy who had not been able to perform well under pressure and was not so well versed in what we were doing, was now asked to take on major responsibility for crafting the new rule. Ted and I were barred from having any hand in regulation writing, having been given the blame, along with Michael, for the public relations disaster that transpired. My task list was reduced to working on the Executive Orders that were required for the Preamble, such as the Civil Rights piece analyzing the rule's impact on minority populations. It was an exercise in guesswork. Until the regulations were implemented, there would be no way to take an accurate count of organic producers, much less their ethnic composition, nationwide.

Keith made it clear that he really did not care what I did out there in my remote office, as long as I stayed out of trouble. Meanwhile, Ted was able to get detailed (a term meaning a temporary assignment) to a position in the USDA Office of Pest Management, where he felt he could do some good in advancing the cause of alternatives to toxic pest control products.

I did not sit idle, however, and for this I am forever grateful to Adela Backiel, creator and first director of USDA's Office of Sustainable Development. Adela had started as a political appointee, attached to the Office of the Chief Economist, and then established her position as a permanent civil service job. She was charged with implementing the agricultural recommendations of Al Gore's pet project, the President's Council on Sustainable Development (PCSD). Her task was to assemble a working group, drawn from every agency at USDA (of which there are 19), to draft a USDA position and set of guiding principles on the subject of sustainable agriculture. I had been participating in that working group as a representative of the NOP for some time, and we had already created a document that was approved by the Secretary. Our champion in the hierarchy was Deputy Secretary Richard Rominger, whose brother operated an organic farm in California.

Adela was very sympathetic to my plight, and had lots of tasks with which she needed help. She also was a great advisor about how to cope with my situation, and a straight shooter when she thought I was making a mistake. She was able to come up with some money to contribute to my visits to Washington, for which Keith was now unwilling to foot the bill. Although she didn't have the budget to have me work with her full time on a detail, she gave me a big job. My assignment was to pull together the USDA presence—exhibits, information tables, speakers, and the like—for the upcoming Sustainability Summit, billed as a National Town Meeting for Sustainable Agriculture, a culmination of Gore's PCSD project, planned for the following year in Detroit. It was a great opportunity to get to know the leading USDA proponents of sustainability—and there were beginning to be quite a few in rather high places. My old conference organizing skills came in handy, and it seemed that I at least could make some redeeming contribution while I considered my next move. It was a blessing to be able to avoid thinking about the insanity that continued to flow from the public media about the horrors wrought by USDA's looming organic rules.

Back in the NOP office, progress was predictably slow on turning around the new proposed rule. At some point in the late fall of 1998 or early winter of 1999 I went back to Washington for a few days. I had spent some time at the NOP office catching up on the latest developments, and Keith offered to walk me back uptown so we could chat. It was a chilly evening, the wind biting my face on the brisk walk through the National Mall to get to my hotel near Capitol Hill. As we walked Keith filled me in on some of the delays and frustrations he was encountering, and then got right to the point. "Beth has cratered on me," he announced. Admitting that he had treated me badly, and confessing that "sometimes I can be like a bull in a china shop," Keith essentially begged me to step up and go back to work on writing the regulations.

## Getting to the Starting Line at Last

Of course, I agreed. I also genuinely appreciated Keith's willingness to eat some crow. But I could not think fast enough to demand some kind of concession on the content of the regulations. All the key decisions had already been made anyway so, in agreeing to come back, I had little choice but to capitulate to writing rules with which I was far from happy. It was some consolation to know that my assessment of the situation had been accurate, and that someone at least appreciated my hard-won regulation writing skills.

"Give them what they ask for and let them live with it" was the order of the day. A case in point is the prohibition of any antibiotic use for organic livestock, even to treat an infection. Although the OFPA (the organic law) only prohibited routine administration of antibiotics in the absence of disease, the NOSB's recommendation went further, and suggested that no products from an animal that had ever received an antibiotic for any reason should be considered organic. This was the position that was vigorously lobbied for by Mark Retzloff, founder of Horizon Dairy, who was later the subject of activist attack for representing the "corporate-industrial organic" approach. Horizon was already making a "no antibiotics" claim on its label, and wanted this to be the rule for all organic dairy. In Europe, however, antibiotics were (and still are) permitted for organic dairy animals, with extended withdrawal periods to ensure that no trace of the drug would remain in the animal's milk. Public comment at NOSB meetings at which livestock standards were discussed also tended to support such an allowance for treatment of animals when they need it.

Our first proposal had followed the EU approach, but with stricter requirements to justify any use of antibiotics and to outline a plan to eliminate the need for such intervention in the future. This provision got mangled into a cursory "if necessary" as a result of OMB's changes, rather than the specific limitations imposed by our lost variances structure. This, we believed, was more supportive of small organic farmers, who could ill afford to lose an organic animal to a readily treatable infection—unlike Horizon, which operated a parallel conventional dairy and could simply move the cow to its nonorganic barn if she needed to be treated. The law also imposed a mandatory three-year transition period after application of any prohibited substance (including synthetic fertilizers) before farm-land could qualify as organic. This, along with the prohibition on the use of antibiotics, has been cited repeatedly by farmers as a reason for their reluctance to take the risk of conversion to organic management.[59]

Our day-to-day "overseer" at this time was Richard Mathews, a recent transfer from the Fruit & Vegetable Division, who replaced Michael as the NOP's second in command. Rick was even less interested in considering the real needs of small organic farmers, or the industry in general, than was Keith, and he made no bones about it.[60] Besides giving the activists what they wanted, Keith also wanted to make sure that the rest of the De-partment was placated, and had us rework the format of the regulations to be consistent with the "practice standards" model used by the Natural Resource Conservation Service (NRCS). Formerly the Soil & Water Con-servation Service, NRCS rules address practices farmers must implement in order to qualify for various cost-share programs, such as water quality, soil erosion prevention, wetlands conservation, and the like. One sticking point for certain consumer groups concerned with food safety was the allowance for use of raw manure[61] and vagueness about what constitutes compost. Keith's solution was to incorporate the NRCS compost practice standard, which specified that compost made with animal waste must be turned a minimum number of times and reach a specific temperature before it could be considered suitable for organic production. This was not necessarily the best way to make high quality compost, but it would kill most pathogens and weed seeds. Beyond being of dubious value for maintaining and enhancing soil quality, this requirement is among the more labor-intensive options for compost making, and added yet another documentation demand to the growing pile of paperwork to be produced by an organic farmer. The NRCS rules are meant to address commercial composting operations, rather than individual farmers making compost for their own use, with the objective of preventing the nutrients in large concentrations of animal manure from running off into surface water.

The one performance standard that was allowed to stand was the over-arching requirement that any practice used by an organic farmer must "maintain or improve the natural resources of the operation, including soil and water quality."[62] This single provision is one of the redeeming pieces that I can still point to with pride. True, it was not until the end of 2014 that this requirement was elaborated on in any way as we had intended to do with our program manual—now published by the NOP in the form of periodic guidance documents—and so has not been consistently enforced by certifiers. But it still represents a clear rebuttal to accusations that "industrial organic by the rules" is no improvement over conventional monoculture.

Once again Keith asked me to formulate my top ten list of important provisions that should be highlighted in the new proposal. Very few, if any, of my recommendations were included in the new version, and I knew there was little likelihood of that happening. I only managed to come up with nine, and the final one, at least as recorded in my journal, is a reflection of my state of mind:

9. Livestock: Take the bull by the horns, stop playing chicken, and get our ducks lined up. This may sound fishy, but we shouldn't try to teach a pig to sing. Have ewe had enough horsing around? (Seriously, we need strict rules prohibiting confinement of government employees.)

The next proposed rule was finally ready for publication in the spring of 1999, with a great deal less heartburn than the first go-round. The power structure now saw this as a high priority, and Dan Glickman, the Secretary himself, made it known that he wanted it ready to go without delay. Connections in the White House were cultivated, and the necessary approval from OMB was developed simultaneous with the internal USDA clearance process. The interpretation of *ex parte* was now a bit more relaxed, and Keith had considerable leeway to go out and sell NOP.2 to the public. Despite some grumbling, clearer heads were able to accept the previously unacceptable legal mandates, such as the one prohibiting any accredited certifier from making a claim of "higher standards." Once again, as had happened with original passage of the OFPA in 1990, the power of the grassroots activist community had exerted a major influence on US agricultural policy. The voice of alternative agriculture was now being heard loud and clear in the halls of power. Unfortunately, the constituency of small organic farmers had become its own worst enemy.

## The June Draft vs. the Final Rule: How They Differed

| June Draft | Final Rule |
| --- | --- |
| SOFAH definition, including reference to biodiversity and agroecosystem health as criteria for determining appropriate practices and/or materials | No definition of an organic system or reference to biodiversity or agroecosystem health in the rules, although biodiversity is mentioned in the definition of crop rotation |
| Variances mechanism to allow for justified deviation from the 'best' practices | Practices are either compliant or noncompliant. Possibility of variances only when a disaster situation is declared (e.g. drought or flood) |
| Multiple orders of preferences that require use of the best practices first, after which progressively less ideal practices can be used | Order of preference only for weed, pest & disease management remains, and the general order of preference disappeared |
| Outcome-oriented criteria (impact on agroecosystem health, especially soil and water quality) for all practices, whether 'standard practice' or variance | Prescriptive practice standards that must be followed regardless of efficacy or consistency with organic principles (e.g., compost practice standard) |
| Organic plan has to identify efforts to reduce reliance on practices identified as variances | Organic plan is only a description of methods used to comply with the rules |
| National List is a subset of the standards, and does not require listing of processing aids and other 'incidental additives' such as sanitizers and boiler chemicals for use with organic processed products | National List is a subpart of the rules, separate from standards. Anything used as a processing aid, even if not present in the final product (e.g. defoamers) has to be listed if it is not organic |
| Proposal for assessing user fees on all certified operations included | No user fees included, following appropriations by Congress to support the initial costs of program implementation |

Meanwhile, we learned that the AMS Administrator who had made the decision to hire Keith was now being shown the door—not for this misstep, but for various others that were unacceptable to the powers that be. Kathleen Merrigan, now married and expecting her first child, was also in the final stages of her doctoral work at the Kennedy School of Government. But she considered the NOP to be her baby, too, and lined up her considerable political support to secure the position as our new Administrator that fall. She pulled off an amazing triple play as she became the midwife for the birth of the final NOP regulation in December of 1999, gave birth to her own baby boy, and earned her Ph.D., all more or less in the same season. The huge previous uproar about ignoring the NOSB recommendations was calmed with the promise that the NOP would not henceforth attempt to make any changes to their National List decisions, or even take any regulatory action at all, without the NOSB's blessing. But this was a political decision—not even Kathleen could give the advisory board the kind of authority to determine policy that everyone out there believed it had under the law.

## The Personal Front: End of Another Chapter

Now that my mission had been accomplished and I was no longer needed, I knew that my days of USDA employment were numbered. I was dutifully carrying out whatever orders were conveyed, including starting to think about a program manual and helping train certifiers in the procedure they would have to follow to become accredited.

My unconventional remote office arrangement was the pretext for my termination and, in truth, gave all of us an out that did not require recriminations of any kind. Keith was even effusive in his praise of my work. I was given the option of returning to full-time status at headquarters, but this was not an option for me. Opal was now ten years old and was navigating pre-adolescence as a multi-talented star in our local public school. She had a room in Stewart's house, practically next door, and a room in my house, alternating between us on a regular schedule but free to visit as she wished. Even if I had wanted to go back to Washington, I wouldn't dream of disrupting her life and tearing her away from her dad again. And letting her live with him, without being able to be there for her nearby, was simply unthinkable.

As the USDA celebrated the finalization of the National Organic Program regulation at the end of the twentieth century, I received some thanks for the part I played, along with my official USDA brass key ring for five years of service. Because my termination was not considered voluntary I was eligible for unemployment insurance, and came home with little idea of where I was headed next.

I was looking forward to returning to the status of private citizen, and ready to re-engage with the community. Although my disillusionment with some of my former cohort was profound, I believed that the hard lessons I had learned could be of great benefit to the cause to which I was still wholeheartedly committed. My first gift to myself in the early spring of 2000 was to sign up for the Sustainable Agriculture Tour of Cuba, sponsored by Food First,[63] the organization founded by Frances Moore Lappé.

I had heard a bit about the seemingly overnight conversion of Cuban agriculture from Soviet-style industrial and chemical-intensive methods to organic practices, necessitated by the sudden loss of cheap petroleum and spare parts for machinery once the Soviet Union disintegrated. Matches, Opal, and I went back to Jamaica every year to visit friends and family there for a week or two, and it was easy to arrange a hop over to Havana from Kingston. The trip made a big impression on me. Cuba's technical achievements in what we might call "appropriate technology," such as developing ox-powered implements, artisanal community-based compost and biological pest control production, and urban farming, to name a few, were remarkable. The friendliness and warmth of the people was even more remarkable. It was also apparent that, although they were obliged by dire necessity to learn a different route to food security, Cuban agronomists and farmers recognized how much healthier and more equitable this new system was, compared to the previous style of agriculture. This is not to say that Cuba had solved all its agricultural (not to mention political) problems, and I don't pretend to know what the future holds once the US lifts our trade embargo.[64] But the big thing that struck me was how quickly and effectively a previously toxic agricultural system could be transformed once the government got behind it.

There was much to learn about how things had changed in my former world while I toiled inside the Washington bubble. I vaguely saw myself returning as a wise elder to help guide a new generation through the new world of USDA organic rules. I imagined putting together a strong resume as an expert who could provide invaluable consulting services to businesses seeking to enter the organic market. But I was still feeling a bit adrift, reluctant in my wounded bitterness to engage with the community with which I had so recently experienced such rancor. I started to work on finding a way to tell the story of what had really happened with the NOP, and what I learned in the process, in a way that could be heard.

The home front was starting to get rocky as well. After our return to Vermont in 1996, Matches had once again adapted well to a different world and developed an extensive social network in the neighborhood. He was hired by a local craftsperson who made brightly painted household items like candlesticks and switch plates. The work was well suited to his skills, he had friendly company, and the income gave him some degree of independence.

But things started deteriorating after I stopped working for USDA, and Matches seemed to spend more and more time hanging out with his friends after work. In the spring of 2001 he got laid off and was essentially AWOL all summer. It was obvious that he wasn't, as he kept claiming, off fishing—and he never brought home a single fish. We had been married for seven years, and I was as surprised as anyone that it had lasted as long as it did, given our cultural and educational differences. I knew that he would have a hard time making it on his own in this culture, and had a definite sense of guilt about telling him he was going to have to leave if he could not level with me and do more to help out around the homestead. At least he had become a citizen and would not have to worry about deportation.

It was not until Labor Day of 2001 that I learned the truth. A couple of girlfriends sat me down and clued me in about an 18-month-old child, a little boy whose existence had been kept secret even from his best friends. It was, honestly, a relief. Now everything was clear, and there was no uncertainty about needing him to find his own way in the world and do whatever he needed to do to help raise his son—but he could not live with me any longer. A few days later a friend called and suggested I turn on the TV and watch what was happening in New York; it was September 11.

My work and my marriage were not the only parts of my life undergoing a major transition in the now post-911 world. Throughout my time at the USDA I had continued to serve as a faculty member in Social Ecology at Goddard College and work with students in Goddard's low residency program. This connection with radical students and colleagues was part of what helped me keep my sanity, along with my meditation practice, weekends at a friend's farm when we lived in Washington, and my own garden and friends after we came home. Goddard's relationship with the Institute for Social Ecology had long been tumultuous, and the current Goddard president decided it was time to cut some programs. Ours was at the top of the list, along with the school's full-time campus-based undergraduate program.

Despite efforts to establish an independently accredited institution and an attempt to create an academic relationship with another small Vermont college, the ISE was unable to sustain either its regular summer

Opal and her Mom, Barnet School 8th grade graduation, June 2003

programs or its land base in Plainfield, Vermont. By the end of 2002 my
last student was finished, and the Plainfield property was being sold. In
the course of giving a tour to our last group of students, I managed to slip
on a wet wooden foot bridge and break my ankle. Temporarily disabled,
I was confronted with the problem of homestead maintenance and preparing for winter on my own. Thankfully the ISE maintained workmen's
comp insurance, which covered my medical bills (being among the many
uninsured pre-Obamacare) and some of my lost income while I healed.

Now a single parent, the personal challenges began to feel overwhelming. Years of stressful sedentary work had taken their toll on my body, I
was facing the loss of my teaching income, and had an increasingly demanding young teen to support. My daughter grew more beautiful each
day, and each day became more of a sullen, disrespectful teenager who
was certain that parents were a lower form of life; at the age of thirteen
she was six feet tall and stunning.

I looked to my friends in the industry to both help me begin my consulting career and give me an opportunity to engage in discussions with the community and the NOP management about the ongoing process of refining and enforcing the rules I had helped create.

Two years after publication of the NOP final rule, the initial group of accredited certifiers was established in October of 2002. The requirement that anyone wishing to sell, label or represent their products as organic must be certified by a USDA-accredited certifying agent could now be fully implemented and enforced as the law of the land.

# 7 Growing Forward

*Fundamentally, the task is to articulate not just an alternative set of policy proposals but an alternative worldview to rival the one at the heart of the ecological crisis—embedded in interdependence rather than hyperindividualism, reciprocity rather than dominance, and cooperation rather than hierarchy.*
— Naomi Klein

I pull into the visitor's parking spot in an industrial park in Massachusetts. I have been here several times since I started doing organic inspections for QAI, a large California-based certifying agent, a few years after leaving my job at USDA at the end of 1999. I note the time of arrival and mileage, grab a thick file of paper and my laptop, and head for the reception area. Signing in, I give the receptionist the name of the quality assurance manager and take a visitor's badge. The small lobby is decorated with a display of the various products they make, cracker boxes forming a colorful patchwork of familiar labels. A few of the identical-size boxes that carry various supermarket brand names sport a small green and white USDA Organic seal. Photos of the founder and his sons, who now run the company, beam down from the wall.

This is a routine organic processing operation inspection, and we spend most of the day in a windowless conference room, checking off boxes and initialing documents while I fill in the requisite responses to questions in the standard inspection report on my computer. Current organic documents for all ingredient suppliers? Check. Nonorganic ingredient suppliers swear that no GMOs, irradiation, or sewage sludge were used to make their enzymes or leavening agents? Check. The most complicated piece is always the sample audit, but these guys know the drill and are prepared to pull out the shipping docs, batch records, and sanitation logs to trace back a randomly selected outgoing lot of finished product through each step of manufacturing, to the incoming ingredients and their respective documents. Organic product is always run first thing, before the day's conventional production run, after all the equipment has been cleaned and sanitized by the previous shift.

Donning a visitor's smock and hair net, I remove my watch and earrings and ask for a glove to cover the ring that doesn't come off. The QA Manager hands me a plastic wrapped set of earplugs and leads the way through the maze of doorways to show me around the plant, stopping at the hand-washing station before we enter the factory floor. Similarly attired workers, mostly non-white people of various hues, busily tend mixers, extruders, conveyer belts, and other industrial equipment whose names are pointed out to me on the flow chart we are following.

All the organic ingredients are stored in a dedicated area of the warehouse with a big green ORGANIC sign, but I notice a bag of flour with the name of a Kansas grain mill that wasn't on the supplier list we just reviewed. "A new supplier—we're doing some trial batches to see how good it is," says my guide. I write the name down and inform him that he will have to send their organic documentation to QAI. Back in the conference room I add some notes to my report, and a secretary prints out three copies of the twelve-page document for us to sign off. My eyes are tearing from a day under fluorescent lights, and I'm happy to walk out into the sunlight and get on the road home before the traffic gets bad.

On the drive through the White Mountains I reflect on the presentation I am to give in a few days to a class full of young food system activists. How can I use this example of a family-owned industrial food processor, whose products are distributed throughout the US and Canada by huge corporate retailers, to challenge their prejudices about what organic really means?

## Harvey Fractures the Community

Sometime in 2002 I received a letter from an organic blueberry farmer in Maine whom I had met at an organic inspector training session while I was at USDA. The letter, typed on an old manual typewriter, asked my opinion as to whether parts of the organic regulations that are now in effect violate the law, and should be challenged in court. In particular, the letter argued that no synthetic ingredients should be permitted to be used in a processed product with an organic label. It was a familiar complaint.

The law's verbiage was internally contradictory. In one place it appeared to violate the long-standing allowance for certain synthetic ingredients such as baking powder and vitamin fortifications in organic products. In another place it suggested that such ingredients were acceptable in the absence of a "wholly natural alternative," and could thus be included on the National List. Before I arrived at the NOP, the staff had negotiated an agreement with the National Organic Standards Board (NOSB) to develop an initial National List of allowed synthetic ingredients, based on lists of ingredients previously permitted by various state and private certifiers. Similar lists were permitted under international organic standards, including Europe, although the EU made no distinction between synthetic or natural food additives. Most of the grassroots organic community accepted this necessity and agreed that this and other contradictions in the law should be adjusted after the rule was implemented. Others, however, saw this as an unacceptable dilution of organic standards to the benefit of corporate food manufacturers who wished to take over the organic label—the blueberry farmer who wrote that letter among them.

Despite my polite refusal to accord any credibility to his argument, Arthur Harvey proceeded to sue the USDA. The suit, filed without benefit of counsel, was denied by the US District Court for the District of Maine in October 2003. However, the case attracted some interest among the organic activist community. Michael Sligh, now no longer an NOSB member, helped rally the grassroots troops via the newly organized National Campaign for Sustainable Agriculture. The leading consumer advocacy groups, all of whom had opposed the original deal Sligh had struck with the NOP, eagerly signed on to support Harvey's appeal as amici, or friends of the court, and helped hire an attorney. In January 2005, the First Circuit Court of Appeals found in Harvey's favor on three of the original nine counts, and ordered the USDA to revise its regulations accordingly.

## Back in the Trenches

By the time of Harvey's lawsuit I was actively engaged in consulting on policy and standards development work for both the Organic Trade Association (OTA) and QAI, the large San Diego-based for-profit organic certifier. My friends Katherine DiMatteo, executive director of OTA, and Joe Smillie, now senior vice president of QAI, welcomed my perspective, even if I was more or less persona non grata among my former grassroots compatriots. Although these friends had felt powerless to stem the avalanche of outrage and insanity that doomed my work at the NOP, both understood and valued my contributions to making it reflect, to some extent, the true organic vision.

## Regulatory Changes Ordered by the Court

The court order gave the NOP until June of 2006 to revise its regulations to reflect the following changes, and two more years for the industry to change practices or formulations to reach full compliance. My commentary on each one is included:

**1. Remove the allowance for use of nonagricultural substances determined to be "synthetic" in or on any processed product labeled as "organic."**

Commentary: This change would include substances such as baking powder, one form of pectin, ascorbic acid, and carbon dioxide. By some estimates this would remove the organic label from up to 90% of organic processed products (which accounted for 58% of all retail organic food sales in 2004, according to OTA's manufacturer's survey). The ruling would still permit such substances to be used for products labeled as "made with (specified) organic ingredients." However, food companies did not believe that consumers would be willing to pay the organic premium for "made with organic" products which cannot use the USDA Organic seal, and a few suggested that they would eliminate their organic product lines altogether rather than re-label. For instance, bananas, which are often treated with ethylene gas (an allowed synthetic) to promote ripening, might have to display a "made with organic bananas" label. Processing aids such as filtering agents and defoamers, which are not required to be listed on product labels, were also being reviewed by the NOSB for inclusion on the National List, even though this is not a legal requirement. Products manufactured using processing aids that are classified as synthetic would thus no longer qualify as organic, even if they contain only organic ingredients. This is the case for most refined sugar, which uses a synthetic, slaked lime, as a filtering agent. Inasmuch as many organic processed products include significant quantities of sugar, it is possible that these could therefore no longer qualify as organic. Even whole grains, which are commonly treated with carbon dioxide as a fumigant, could lose their organic designation.

**2. Remove the allowance for dairy farms transitioning to organic management to feed their animals up to 20% nonorganic feed until three months before selling milk as organic.**

Commentary: The OFPA (the organic law) says that animals must be fed organic feed, but does not require only organic feed. In the aftermath of the first proposed rule, in which we proposed to allow some nonorganic feed to be used "if necessary," the final regulation was tightened to require that organic animals be fed only 100% organic feed (other than minerals and other nonagricultural ingredients). This means that organic livestock cannot be fed food scraps, even from certified organic products, if those products contain any allowed nonorganic agricultural ingredients (e.g. seasonings that are unavailable in organic form). An allowance for dairy animals being transitioned to organic production was included in the regulations in recognition of the chicken and egg problem that, prior to the implementation of the NOP, there were no dairy animals that were organically managed from the last quarter of gestation (i.e., before they were born). Without this provision, it would have taken about three years before anyone could begin producing organic milk, including the need to feed animals expensive organic feed for a couple of years before they reach milking age. The court order thus made the cost prohibitive for a conventional farmer to transition to organic

**3. Remove the allowance for any nonorganic agricultural ingredient to be used in up to 5% of an organic processed product if the organic form of the ingredient can be demonstrated to be commercially unavailable, unless the specific ingredient appears on the National List.**

Commentary: The task of itemizing which specific nonorganic agricultural ingredients could be used in organic processed products, and the criteria for allowing them, was not something that anyone involved in creating the regulations wanted to attempt. Until the industry had matured and supplies of so-called minor ingredients, such as spices and plant-based thickeners was more predictable, the allowance for any nonorganic agricultural ingredient, if it was commercially unavailable in organic form, made some sense. The number of such ingredients was unknown, and could number in the hundreds if not thousands. This court ruling made it necessary for a manufacturer to petition, and the NOSB to approve, any nonorganic ingredient currently in use in order to continue using it. This process could take a year or more, and then another several months to go through formal notice and comment rule making before the ingredient became legal to use in an organic product. Natural flavors and colors were not affected since they were listed as "nonagricultural ingredients" on the National List. This commercial unavailability criterion was admittedly ill enforced, but could have been strengthened through a regulatory fix.

Katherine was meeting regularly on behalf of OTA with representatives of the 12 amici organizations who had formally supported the Harvey appeal. There had to be some workable compromise that would avoid decimating the heretofore exponentially expanding organic industry. OTA's proposed solution was a surgical amendment to the OFPA that would delete the word "synthetic" in a strategic place, and thus also delete the need to eliminate any substance in that category from organic processed products. This was one of several technical fixes to the OFPA that had been agreed to by a broad coalition of the organic community when the first NOSB meetings were being held, and it was hard to see how many of the same people could now object to making this change.

But object they did. Their position, championed by the consumer lobby (organizations such as Consumers Union, Beyond Pesticides, and the Organic Consumers Association), was that any allowance for synthetic substances would contradict expectations of the purity of organic foods, and so endanger consumer confidence in the label. They also raised concerns that any effort to change the law would open it up to unfriendly amendments intended to weaken the standards, now that the organic unfriendly Republicans controlled the White House. This was the position taken, it should be noted, by the Organic Committee of the National Campaign for Sustainable Agriculture, without any opportunity for its members to weigh in. As a bona fide member of that committee (representing the organization Rural Vermont, on whose board I was serving), it was apparent to me that the leadership of the organization was not interested in practicing the kind of transparency and democratic decision making that it demanded of others.

The alarm within the industry reached a crisis level by early 2005. The threat was felt most urgently by organic processors of all sizes, as well as the larger certifiers such as QAI whose clientele consists primarily of organic processors. Many of the larger organic farmers who had developed relationships with these processors also understood that their markets could evaporate overnight if something wasn't done. OTA's board voted to unilaterally submit to Congress and lobby for the surgical amendment to the OFPA that most members considered to be critical to the continued growth, if not survival, of the organic industry. The law firm of Covington & Burlig was hired to shepherd the amendment through Congress, with Jay Friedman, one of the original NOSB members who previously had tended toward the purist camp, serving as lead attorney.

The amendment that was passed in October of 2005 met with little

Congressional opposition. In addition to the provision that restored the regulatory status quo for synthetic ingredients allowed in organic processed products, a clause was inserted to give some relief to transitioning dairy farmers. Even most of the activists supported this provision, which allowed a dairy farm to provide feed to animals from land that was still in its third year of transition to organic management. This would at least allow the farmer to wait only three years, rather than four, before being able to receive the premium price for milk from cows grazing on their home pastures. The third count won by Harvey and the amici, requiring individual listing of all nonorganic agricultural ingredients in organic processed products (refer to sidebar), was not changed. The NOSB and the industry would just have to figure out how to deal with it.

The reaction from the activist community echoed the intensity of the outrage heaped on the first proposed rule seven years previously. Headlines from the Organic Consumers Association screamed "Another Sneak Attack on Organic Standards," comparing this event to the 1997 proposed rule (in which "USDA tried to allow...."). They also referred to an actual sneak attack that had come out of nowhere a couple of years previously, when a chicken producer from Georgia asked his Congressman to tack on an allowance for up to 20% nonorganic livestock feed to an ag appropriations bill, citing the prohibitive cost of organic grain. The community noticed this only after it became a fait accompli, and OTA led the charge to reverse the damage. Now it was OTA who was being characterized as the sneaky villain.

Once again the engines of hype and misinformation spewed forth, and once again the distortions of fact were as laughable as the cries of alarm and doom were ridiculous. It was painful to observe, especially from my role of consultant to the "bad guys" once again. But the object of the activists' ire this time was my friend Katherine, who was now accused of treachery, even though she had made every effort to keep the community apprised of her board's decision. I was not present at any of these meetings, and am well aware that such situations are never black-and-white. I could certainly empathize with her feelings of anger and betrayal—I knew how it felt to be mercilessly attacked by former allies. At the same time, I couldn't help wishing that she and other allies had had the courage to stand up to them back in 1998.

Publicly vilified and fed up with the stress of having to defend herself against accusations of anti-democratic tactics, Katherine finally decided to resign as OTA's executive director. In the 16 years since she was first hired she had turned a barely viable collection of organic businesses and grassroots advocates into a real trade association, with about 1,600 dues paying members, a national presence, and a professional staff.

The idea that USDA had attempted to allow the so-called "Big Three" in organic food quickly became a widely accepted fact, and repeated—even by respected academics—as common knowledge. The "fact" that OTA was purely a lobbying arm of corporate organics, bent on continuing to weaken the standards, was now becoming a similarly entrenched meme. A few years after the end of the Harvey debacle I attended a meeting with a leader of the National Organic Coalition, which emerged from the previously mentioned National Sustainable Agriculture Coalition's Organic Committee. Alerting those present to the danger of standards dilution, she recounted the tale of how USDA had tried to allow the Big Three to be used in organic production. Of course, I raised my hand and politely reminded her that this was not the case, and asked her to refrain from continuing to repeat this falsehood. Knowing that I had helped write that rule and ought to know what it said, she simply glared at me, saying, "I happen to believe that it's the truth."

## Living in the Material World

The 2005 Harvey decision became my opportunity to get more deeply involved in helping OTA develop its policy positions. Various task forces were formed to address the resulting problems and deliver recommendations. Members represented a wide spectrum of opinions about how best to maintain consumer confidence in the organic brand, and everyone had some level of fear that activists would continue to raise alarms about threats to organic purity. I was happy to become the OTA regulatory expert. There were position papers aplenty to be drafted, and my insider knowledge of the thinking behind the regulations—especially the definitions—proved invaluable in sorting the legitimate concerns from the hype.

By this time the NOSB meeting process was becoming more predictable. Meetings were put on a regular semi-annual spring and fall schedule, with an agenda and subcommittee recommendations on various agenda items published in advance. Public comments on any of these recommendations and discussion documents now have to be submitted far enough in advance of the meeting to be included in the ever-thicker meeting book distributed to NOSB members.

I was also given a chance to put my regulation writing skills to use again. OTA had been working with a group of international, mostly European, certifiers to develop standards for the labeling of organic textiles. Organic cotton, in particular, was becoming an important alternative to the high-input GMO version of cotton that was taking over in places like India, but many environmental and health-minded consumers (again, mostly European) recognized the horrible environmental and social damage of textile processing. What was the point of producing environmentally benign fiber that was then doused in highly toxic and carcinogenic dyes, sizing agents, and other fabric treatments, and spun, woven or knit, assembled, and sewn by a miserably exploited, often underage labor force? The horrors of the conventional textile industry surpass even those of conventional agriculture; just think of the 2013 collapse of the giant garment factory in Bangladesh as one of its more noticeable crimes.

The Global Organic Textile Standard (GOTS) was introduced in 2006, with OTA as one of four owners of the standard. I was sent to Nuremberg, Germany for the annual Biofach trade show for about five years as the OTA representative to the GOTS technical committee, first helping to refine the standard and then evaluating third party certifiers who were interested in auditing companies seeking to make an organic claim for their products. It was a surprisingly interesting assignment for someone who has always stressed out over how to dress, and has no clue about fashion, organic or otherwise.

## The Global Organic Textile Standard (GOTS)

Starting with 27 certified facilities after its launch in 2006, in 2014 there were 3,663 textile processing, manufacturing, and trading facilities in over 60 countries certified to GOTS. The standard covers every aspect of textile manufacturing, including dyes, fabric blends, environmental protection, and social criteria. Certified operations range from small home knitters up to the largest vertically integrated enterprises, selling primarily to the European, North American, and Japanese markets.

By far the most challenging non-food organic standard I worked on was the one that addresses organic cosmetics and personal care products. The factions and rivalries within that group were so combative that I took to calling it the "personal I-don't-care" products task force. Similar to textiles, this is an industry with complicated international supply chains that markets largely to upscale clientele whose concerns center mainly on product purity. One big problem for the point of view that synthetic substances could never be organic is the fact that, under the OFPA (the organic law), soap and its by-products (such as glycerin) are classified as synthetic. This is because soap is produced by means of a chemical reaction between a fatty acid, either as vegetable oil or animal fat, and a strong alkali—either caustic soda (sodium hydroxide) or lye (potassium hydroxide). Your organic coconut oil or shea butter can be as pure as pure can be, but in the end the soap made from it will be a synthetic—at least as it is legally defined under the OFPA. The eventual compromise here was a standard for cosmetic products that "contain organic ingredients." Soap makers could still get their product certified as "made with organic oil," with the remaining ingredient consisting of lye, which appears on the National List as an allowed synthetic (thanks to Newman's Own, who lobbied hard to allow its use for the purpose of making their pretzels turn brown). Knowledgeable foodies may also be aware that these same strong alkalis are used to turn cornmeal into masa harina, whose B vitamins are rendered more bio-available as a result. The "contains organic ingredients" cosmetic standard was soon handed over to a private certifier who developed it further, generating a list of permitted additives to shampoos and face creams that would never pass muster for the National List as food ingredients.

## Esoteric Debates about Materials

The major subject of controversy and alarms raised by activists since the Harvey episode has been, as we feared when drafting the first proposed rule, the question of what substances should be permitted to be used in organic production and handling, and how to definitively decide whether a substance under review should be classified as synthetic or as nonsynthetic. As discussed earlier, the National List identifies not the universe of allowed substances, but only those that are deemed synthetic but are sufficiently benign to be permitted in organic production. There are also sections of the National List that relate to prohibited nonsynthetics, but it is rarely controversial to withdraw a previously allowed substance. Many consumer organizations and other organic watchdog groups hold a firm belief that adding any new nonorganic materials to the National List constitutes a weakening of organic standards, and must be vigorously opposed. They similarly believe that as many currently allowed substances as possible should be removed from the National List following the Sunset Review that must be undertaken by the NOSB of every substance every five years.

## Is It Agricultural or Nonagricultural?

While the classification of synthetic or nonsynthetic is obviously critical for anything used in crop or livestock production, the classification of agricultural versus nonagricultural is also important for substances being considered for use as ingredients or additives in organic processed products. This distinction is needed to differentiate substances that could potentially be produced organically from those that cannot ever become part of the organic ingredients in a product. For example, baking soda is not derived from living organisms and could not be produced organically. Certain ingredients such as enzymes, bacterial cultures, and most notably yeast were designated as nonagricultural, even though their production involves agricultural feedstocks such as grain or sugar. Other products originally listed as nonagricultural, such as natural flavors and colors (many of which have since become available in organic form[65]), certain plant-derived gums, and even multi-syllabic (and therefore suspect) ingredients such as fructooligosaccharides, may come from agricultural products but were deemed nonagricultural because they are unrecognizable, manufactured fractions of the original material.

The rules also allow certification of wild harvested crops, which are not managed agriculturally. It is fairly common to find organically labeled seaweed, medicinal herbs, mushrooms, and other uncultivated products that are certified as having been harvested in accordance with the NOP requirements for wild crops. The designation of agricultural or nonagricultural is at least as fuzzy as that of synthetic.

This has raised a number of problems, such as the eventual availability of organic baking yeast, without the requirement that the organic form of yeast be used in an organic product, as long as it is commercially available. Despite several attempts by the distributor of the organic yeast product to have it reclassified as agricultural, it remains in the nonagricultural column. A major stumbling block for the yeast problem has been the requirement that livestock feed consist of strictly 100% organic agricultural ingredients. Were yeast to be reclassified, livestock producers who feed nutritional yeast to their animals as a good source of B vitamins would not be able to find enough of the organic kind, and there is no exception in cases of commercial unavailability when it comes to livestock feed—anything agricultural fed to an organic animal must be 100% organic. The animals' nutrition would consequently suffer, or else the conscientious organic farmer would be forced to add synthetic (but nonagricultural) B vitamins to their rations. A compromise was finally reached to include an annotation accompanying the listing of yeast as an allowed nonagricultural ingredient that requires a certified organic form to be used if it is commercially available, thus allowing livestock producers to feed nonorganic yeast if that is all they can find.

All of these and more tangled issues have occupied endless hours of meetings and proposals for how to sort it all out in a way that would be fair and consistent—discussions that have been likened to theological questions about the number of dancing angels that could be accommodated on a pinhead. The controversy over a material known as Corn Steep Liquor (CSL) illustrates the absurd extent of concern for "organic purity" engendered by these discussions.

In 2010 the NOSB Crops Committee voted to recommend classifying CSL, a byproduct of the wet milling of corn, as synthetic. CSL is widely used as an ingredient in commercial organic-approved fertilizer formulations, due to its high nitrogen content, and classifying it as synthetic would make it prohibited as a fertilizer ingredient. A minority opinion of the Crops Committee opposed this determination, based on the technical reviews of the CSL production process, the OFPA definition of synthetic, and the secondary definition of chemical change. The discussion involved fine distinctions about different types of chemical reactions, and whether the addition of sulfur dioxide, resulting in release of tiny amounts of lactic acid to balance pH during the milling process, constitutes a chemical change. The full NOSB did not vote on the recommendation at its fall 2010 meeting, and in 2011 the NOP issued a memorandum stating that CSL would continue to be classified as nonsynthetic and therefore acceptable for use as an organic fertilizer ingredient until such time as the NOSB were to vote that it should be classified as synthetic. As of June, 2013 the NOSB had not yet voted on this, and the NOP issued a request for public comment about how to classify CSL, along with a list of other widely used organic waste products that are subject to some kind of chemical treatment. While there was some public gnashing of teeth over the NOP's action to try to remedy the problem, as of early 2015 there has still been no move by the NOSB to resolve it. The question remains: What difference does this distinction make with respect to the principles and values of organic agriculture?

## A Modest Proposal to Simplify the Materials Conundrum

From my perspective, it is no exaggeration to say that many of the problems to which the organic industry has fallen prey can be attributed to the decision to base the definition of "organic" on the distinction between "natural" and "synthetic" (discussed at length in previous chapters). This distinction does not amount to the "clear bright line" that can be used to determine whether a given practice or product is "really" organic, as many people believe it to be. If the organic model is full of grey areas and is all about process rather than product, so is the meaning of synthetic. You can take two chemically identical substances to a laboratory and never be able to determine which is synthetic and which is not synthetic without knowing how each was manufactured, what was used as a raw material, and what other additives were used to process it. Neither has the NOSB been unanimous in its votes concerning how to categorize various substances—citric acid, a common food additive produced by fermentation of a corn-based medium, for example, was deemed synthetic by a slim majority of NOSB members.[66]

Prior to the OFPA, various attempts were made to get around this problem by using a more precise word in place of synthetic. One that I rather liked was "xenobiotic," as suggested by a respected agronomist during the original OFAC meeting in Leavenworth, Kansas (see Chapter 4). This term means "foreign to biology," and would apply to those substances that did not evolve within a biological system, and are thus not readily metabolized by living cells. Although "xenobiotic" was dismissed by consumer representatives as a made-up word in 1989, today it is an accepted term in scientific circles.

In 2010, ten years after the final regulation was published, the idea of changing the law to do away with the synthetic versus natural distinction was outside the realm of possibility. At least we had managed to get rid of using natural as the opposite of synthetic in the regulations.[67] Then one day in Germany, as I was listening to a presentation about textile processing, a light went on. The presenter explained that she was able to produce her garments without synthetic dyes, since she could combine her plant-derived colors with proprietary fixatives that prevented them from running or fading. I was a bit puzzled, since the resulting dyes would certainly be considered synthetic under the US organic law, plant derived or not. Then it hit me—in Europe, where the organic rules did not mention the word synthetic, the public understood that term to mean "substances derived from petrochemicals."[68] I realized in a flash that this is probably also what comes to mind for most US consumers when they hear that something is synthetic. In a word, plastic. It makes perfect sense to prohibit such petrochemical substances from being used as preservatives, colors, or flavors in organic products; this, I was convinced, was the original intent of the "no synthetics in organic" language of the OFPA.

This really got me thinking. If only the legal definition of synthetic could be changed to reflect what most consumers understood it to mean, most of the acrimony of the previous few years might go away. There would be no need for OTA's surgical word change. It meant that fertilizers like potassium sulfate, which is a useful soil amendment for certain mineral imbalances, would be allowed to be used even if it was obtained as an industrial byproduct and not dug out of the ground, inasmuch as the law banned all synthetic fertilizers without exception. It would sure cut down on the National List, which many complained was too long and lax. Any materials that might be rendered nonsynthetic but should not be allowed in organic production could be added to the Prohibited Nonsynthetics section of the National List. This is essentially the line of reasoning laid out in a comment I made to the NOSB on my own behalf, taking pains to emphasize that I was not speaking for OTA. In it I suggested starting a public discussion about the question, with lots of opportunities to debate the pros and cons of this idea, before approaching Congress to request another technical correction to the law.

A few of my OTA colleagues thought my idea was worth discussing, but it was met with polite thanks and a smirk or two by the NOSB. Later I read a report about this meeting in NOFA's quarterly newsletter, warning darkly about a proposal brought up by an unnamed industry flak to possibly amend the OFPA again. No mention of the substance of the proposal, of course. This was yet another stinging affront by people I had, in my previous life, considered friends.

"Optics" has become the buzzword used both by the activists and the industry for what was wrong with any suggestion that might be perceived by consumers as weakening the standards, whether or not this perception was accurate. We can't risk the appearance that the industry is trying to create loopholes that allow more synthetics in organic food. It doesn't matter how common or harmless the material is—all consumers care about is how it looks.

## The Industry Blasts Off

With the change in administration in Washington at the end of 2008, the NOP evolved from a minor program in a small division of USDA's Agricultural Marketing Service (AMS) to its own division, with its budget and staff doubling in a single year. Miles McEvoy, former director of the Washington State organic program, became deputy AMS administrator in charge of the NOP in 2009. Kathleen Merrigan, author of the OFPA and AMS administrator during the last months of finalizing the NOP regulation, was appointed Deputy Secretary of Agriculture that same year, serving until May of 2013, and created the high level position of organic program coordinator to better integrate organic into every aspect of USDA. Hopes were running high that organic food and agriculture was finally getting some respect. To many in the activist community, all the previous problems with lax enforcement of threats to organic integrity by the NOP could be chalked up to corrupt political appointees from the wrong party.

As expected, the organic industry took off once the imprimatur of USDA could be affixed to organic products. Growth rates continued in the high teens and low twenties until the 2008 recession hit, and even then outpaced the flat-lined grocery business. New organic certifiers sprang up overnight, needing only a couple of knowledgeable people with laptops and a few contract inspectors to set up shop. The initial accreditation of certifiers did not require a USDA site visit, or the fees associated with it. Rather, the prospective certifying agent had only to undergo a desk audit by submitting its documentation for review by USDA to determine that the organiza-

tion had appropriate procedures in place and sufficient qualified personnel. As of 2015 there were 84 NOP-accredited certifiers, 48 of which are based in the US, and almost 30,000 certified operations in 133 countries.

Foreign certifiers can also be accredited, and any foreign producer or processor who wants to export organic products to the US market must be certified by an accredited certifying agent that they meet the NOP standards. Meanwhile, bilateral equivalency agreements have been negotiated between the US and Canada, the EU, Japan, South Korea and, most recently, Switzerland. Increasing numbers of countries have their own organic regulations, which are generally modeled on either the EU or the US. Inasmuch as organic food constitutes close to 5% of US retail sales, but the amount of US farmland under organic management has not yet reached the 1% level, it is safe to assume that a large share of the ingredients used in the various types of organic processed products, as well as some of the fresh produce, is imported. This has become yet another concern among some consumer groups, especially as large retailers like WalMart and Costco account for an ever-larger share of organic sales. How, they wonder, can Chinese organic products be trusted in light of well-publicized food safety scandals? Among the biggest organic imports, ironically enough, are corn and soybeans needed for feed in the rapidly expanding organic livestock sector. The organic industry has unquestionably engaged with the globalized food chain as enthusiastically as its conventional counterpart.

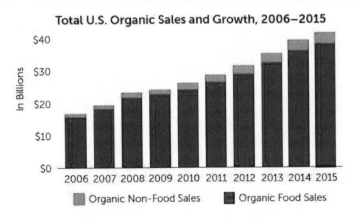

Source: Organic Trade Association

The organic industry has also been subject to mergers and buyouts as venture capital has played an increasing role in the expansion of small organic companies. This trend is nicely documented and updated regularly by Professor Phillip Howard of Michigan State University in a graphic depicting who owns whom in the organic world.[69] Many giant agribusiness players own some kind of organic company, including some formerly small family-owned enterprises. Cargill, General Mills, Dean Foods, the Danone Group, and Kraft all have their organic brands. The Hain Celestial Group has gobbled up many of these pioneering organic companies, including the original organic processor, Walnut Acres. Most recently, the largest fresh organic produce brand, Earthbound Farms, was acquired by White Wave, the soy products manufacturer formerly owned by Dean Foods. Numerous conventional supermarkets, such as Kroger, Safeway, and Shaws, in addition to Whole Foods and Trader Joe's, have developed their own private label organic brands. A single large distributor, UNFI (United Natural Foods), now controls virtually every wholesale territory for organic and natural products.

The growth of the organic industry has been paralleled by the growth of the organic watchdog industry. The Organic Consumers Association, from its modest beginnings as Ronnie Cummins' one-man show, has become a well-staffed non-profit advocacy organization with a multi-million-dollar budget, claiming a combined network of 850,000 individuals.[70] The Wisconsin-based Cornucopia Institute bills itself as an educational and investigative organization "supporting the ecological principles and economic wisdom underlying sustainable and organic agriculture." They got into the watchdog business with a lawsuit that alleged abuse by large "factory" organic dairies—specifically the Colorado-based Horizon—of the allowance in the regulations for animals to be confined without access to outdoors or pasture. In addition to filing lawsuits, their tactics include threatening companies and organizations that they accuse of representing "industrial organic" with a barrage of negative publicity.[71]

Many grassroots organic organizations, including some of the NOFA chapters and CCOF, have created staff positions devoted to policy and regulatory matters, charged with closely following the NOSB meetings and NOP policy memos and developing public comment. Any time OCA or Cornucopia issues an alert about another "sneak attack" on organic standards, these organizations' public relations machinery gears up to issue alerts and generate irate press releases, form letters to Congress, public comments on proposals and recommendations, and endless chatter in social media.

The former Organic Caucus of the National Campaign for Sustainable Agriculture (now called the National Sustainable Agriculture Coalition), meanwhile, launched its own organization dubbed the National Organic Coalition (NOC). Its fifteen member organizations currently include consumer and public interest groups (such as Beyond Pesticides and Consumers Union), organic farm organizations (such as NOFA and the Midwest-based Midwest Organic & Sustainable Education Service [MO-SES]), and a few organic businesses (such as Equal Exchange and Organically Grown Company) that are "dedicated to organic integrity."[72] This organization espouses the purist cause, and has taken the position through its public comments that anything deemed synthetic must be eliminated from use in, on, or for the production of organic products. Their most recent campaign raised a huge outcry over a minor rule change that the NOP instituted in the NOSB's process for voting on Sunset Review recommendations. Each substance on the National List must be reviewed by the NOSB every five years, and a vote taken as to whether to remove it from the list. The revised process makes it slightly more difficult to remove a substance, and institutes a two-step process that offers the public more opportunity to weigh in on the need for the substance under review.[73] Once again, exaggerated charges of corruption and weakening of the standards instilled doubt and confusion about the trustworthiness of the USDA Organic label. One colleague who works for a major certifier mentioned observing several members of the NOC leadership sitting together at an NOSB meeting. "Yeah," he quipped, "I wonder what the Organic Taliban is cooking up today."

## Moving On, Boots on the Ground

QAI was meanwhile sold by its founding entrepreneur in 2004 to the large Michigan-based certification company called NSF, which is primarily a food safety certification body. Subsequently, my work for QAI devolved from a regulatory policy, new standards development, and internal review role to one of swimming in the pool of contract organic inspectors. Ironically, though NSF is technically a non-profit, QAI's culture became much more corporate. I was sent out to inspect various manufacturers and distributors, including an occasional maple producer, primarily throughout the Northeast US and Eastern Canada. Like most of the other large certifiers, such as Oregon Tilth and OCIA, QAI depends on independent inspectors to cover its geographically dispersed clientele. Doing this work has given me great insight into the workings of the industrial organic—or simply the industrial—food system, and a more boots on the ground understanding of how the regulations are playing out in the real world.

During this same time, my consulting relationship with OTA, which began during Katherine DiMatteo's tenure and continued under her successor, Caren Wilcox, was steady and supportive. A politically connected former USDA Under-Secretary for Food Safety, Caren and I got along well—especially in light of the fact that she was one of the USDA officials who had to sign off on the first proposed rule. She knew what I had accomplished and understood how it had been undermined. She fiercely defended her staff and knew how to handle conflict, but internal politics got the better of her and she only lasted a couple of years before being forced to resign. I was sorry to see her leave.

The management changes at OTA were probably inevitable. As the grassroots organic groups deserted the trade association over the Harvey uproar, the organization was forced to more closely resemble the caricature of the corporate-controlled entity previously depicted by some of the activists. I continued on in my policy consulting role for a couple more years after Caren left, but saw my scope of assignments steadily narrowed until I was left with only the GOTS project. I did not see eye-to-eye with my new boss, and she made it clear that she had no use for a consultant who disagreed with her. I was considered to be insufficiently business oriented and unapologetically insubordinate. Several long-term staff found other jobs and resigned, often with hard feelings. The organization moved its headquarters from Greenfield, Massachusetts to Brattleboro, Vermont and stripped it down significantly, while a second office was opened in Washington, DC, where any serious trade association has to have a presence. The DC office was subsequently designated as the official headquarters. While in Nuremberg, Germany on my final GOTS assignment I learned that a new management position had been created that included responsibility for all the work I had previously been doing—and it was not being offered to me.

A feeling of relief and a bit of sadness accompanied my exit from the organic industry. I was a founding member of OTA, but never had a business interest in the industry. I still had a regular writing gig with the international newsletter, *The Organic Standard*, to keep me somewhat informed about what was going on with the NOP, and also needed to stay current with the regulations for my inspection work. In truth, it felt like a huge weight was lifted from my psyche, and I no longer dreaded sitting down at the computer to check the day's messages. More than ten years after I began to write this book, I could finally go back to it without being confronted daily by the increasingly absurd arguments over what constitutes a real threat to organic integrity.

Home, community, and garden became more of a haven. Opal was now a Columbia University grad living independently (and practically debt-free) in Brooklyn, along with several members of her former cohort from rural Vermont. After a few years of adventures in online dating, I finally met Pete, the best companion and life partner I could want, one who completely understands what I'm all about.

## Finding Hope

Did the uproar over the initial NOP proposed rule help spark the good food revolution of the early 21$^{st}$ century? Does it really matter that the public has been misinformed about what transpired in bringing the organic vision to the USDA? Although he was guilty of perpetuating some rather inaccurate and lopsided stories denigrating "industrial organic" in *The Omnivore's Dilemma*, Michael Pollan deserves considerable credit for galvanizing widespread awareness about the benefits of a more ecologically sound food system. A new generation of food system activists has flocked to organizations like NOFA, eagerly soaking up practical knowledge and embarking on new ventures to produce ecologically grown food, including every kind of processed product imaginable, generally for local and regional markets. Many of them are even proud to call their operations organic. Profiles of these new farmers and food producers appear regularly in the press, and they are aided in their efforts by access to capital, advice, and markets at levels that were unheard of a generation ago. My great dream has come to pass: No longer are organic farmers greeted by laughter or hostility when they walk into a USDA-affiliated agricultural research or extension office.

It is safe to say that very few members of the public were even aware of the existence of GMOs in the food supply until 1998. The demand that genetically engineered foods be labeled as such, forestalled at the time by the furor over the organic rule, has now acquired considerable momentum as various states introduce—and pass—GMO labeling bills.[74]

In a small bit of irony, a recent *Los Angeles Times* article co-written by Kathleen Merrigan, now a private consultant, and Dan Glickman, secretary of Agriculture when the rule was released and eventually finalized, argues against the rising demand for mandatory labeling of GMO foods. Their position is that consumers have a choice if they want to avoid such products. Just as Monsanto understood when commenting on the first proposed rule—those wishing to avoid GMOs can buy organic.[75] The tag lines about this article from various activist blogs include the phrases "Kathleen Merrigan sells out organic" and "ex-USDA officials want to co-opt the GE labeling movement." There is also a non-GMO certification scheme that is among the fastest growing food labels in the market. Non-GMO project logos now appear on organic products as well as many that are labeled "all natural."[76]

The organic label has also spawned a wild profusion of other kinds of kinder, greener labeling claims—for food as well as clothing, personal care, household cleaners, and most every kind of consumer product. You have no doubt seen many of these labels—fair trade, dolphin-safe, grass-fed, animal welfare and its variants (cage-free, free range, humane, etc.), and have scratched your head over the question of what they really mean and why you should pay more—sometimes a lot more—for the products to which they are affixed. Many are quite legitimate; others not so much. Some are, like organic, about the production process (e.g., fair trade) and others are about the product (e.g., non-GMO). It takes a fair amount of effort on the part of a committed conscious consumer to sort them all out.

Along with the profusion of eco-labels has come increased confusion about the meaning and value of the organic label itself, thanks in no small part to the regular alarms raised by those organic watchdog groups about yet another imminent threat to organic integrity. Many manufacturers have gone in the direction of the "all natural" claim, which you must know by now is utterly meaningless (except perhaps for meats, which are allowed to make a "natural" claim by the USDA if no artificial ingredients or preservatives are added during processing). Still, it is understandable that many consumers don't recognize the difference—except price, of course—between the organic label and one claiming "all natural."

Perhaps one of the biggest sources of confusion is the suggestion that all that really matters is how far the food has traveled to get to the eater. "Local is the new organic," proclaim some locavore enthusiasts and, having read this far, you may be excused for heaving a long sigh. Of course, support for local farmers and the encouragement of bioregionally based food production of all kinds are central to the true organic vision. It would not make sense, however, for a local label to replace organic as a coveted marketing claim; it would be virtually impossible to come up with a definition of local that is accurate everywhere, and rather absurd to employ a third party agency to verify that a product was indeed local. After all, the worst affronts to ecology and equity in food production are all local to somewhere. The concept that eating close to home is somehow important does, however, belong in the tool kit of a much broader social goal that is now permeating every sphere of life—that is, sustainability.

Sustainability is an idea that recognizes the interconnectedness of the many concerns about food, environment, right livelihood, social well-being, and community-based control over the necessities of life that are bubbling up at this time. It includes recognition of one giant problem that was hardly on the radar when organic standards were being debated in the seventies and eighties: climate change—or climate chaos, as it is more accurately described. In a real sense, the quest for sustainability—that is, the long-term viability and continued evolution of human civilization—has been a key motivator of the organic movement. But a sustainable label on a consumer end product, whether it is a box of organic crackers or a package of 100% recycled toilet paper, is no more likely to solve the problems created by the market-driven imperative toward increased consumption than is the organic label.

So my feelings have been rather mixed about my involvement in a project to create a unified standard for sustainable agriculture, initiated in 2008, known as the LEO-4000 Sustainable Agriculture Standard. In October 2015 the initial standard, having gone through two rounds of public comment and revision, was formally adopted by ANSI (American National Standards Institute).[77] Work on this project has crawled along toward actual trial by real producers, breaking the NOP's record for length of time taken to implement it. Now that it has arrived at the starting line, its usefulness for any purpose other than as an educational exercise for students of sustainable agriculture has yet to be demonstrated.

The LEO-4000 experience has been an interesting ride, and has given me an up-close encounter with the proponents of agribusiness as usual, who have lately been attempting to portray themselves as advocates of science-based sustainability (as opposed to the anti-science organic ideologues). Folks from groups such as the American Farm Bureau, corn, cotton and soybean commodity groups, and Crop Life America were initially represented on the LEO-4000 Standard Committee. Most of them resigned en mass when it became apparent that they could be outvoted by those of us who organized ourselves as the "earthworm coalition."

Unlike the NOP, this new standard is derived from a voluntary, non-government process. So far, the standard is not oriented towards consumer end products, but rather toward what is called B2B or business-to-business recognition. If Walmart, for example, wants to promote itself as striving for greater sustainability, it may demand that its suppliers demonstrate that they comply with some kind of sustainability standard (and there are many to choose from). The problematic nature of that arrangement should be obvious. The structure of the LEO-4000 Standard draws heavily on the approach used for the first NOP proposed rule, particularly in its focus on a site-specific Producer Sustainability Plan and its emphasis on measurable outcomes and evidence of improvement toward producer-defined goals rather than rigidly prescribed practice standards. This is not a coincidence; my experience with the NOP has had a large influence on the structure of this new standard. This approach is in turn based in large part on the methods advocated by Allan Savory and others under the rubric of Holistic Management.[78]

Sustainability, meanwhile, has also become a hot topic in the academic world. Although I continue working on the fringes of the organic industry, my (organic, gluten-free) bread and (pasture-raised) butter has shifted to an emphasis on teaching. Thanks to one of the first Masters programs in Sustainable Food Systems (Green Mountain College, Poultney, Vermont), I have regained a connection with a diverse contingent of (mostly) young food system activists who look to me to help shepherd them through the confusion. Green Mountain College's online program offers less opportunity to form relationships with the students than does the Goddard model, but it is satisfying in a different way. The students are knowledgeable, motivated, and delightful, and my colleagues are supportive and inspiring. This work is now my greatest source of learning and hope for the future.

In this time of becoming one of the wise elders, I can savor both long-standing and more recent friendships and connections to a vibrant community—local as well as international. I'm traveling less and working closer to home, yet the planet has never seemed smaller. More important than the still tiny minority of food system revolutionaries in the privileged developed world, I see hope in the savvy of the small holder peasantry of the so-called Third World. These are the indigenous farmers whose intimate understanding of their own ecosystems and the plants and animals that nurture their communities inspired organic pioneers like Sir Albert Howard. These farmers—often women—are the best hope for the world to feed itself, and to do so sustainably, village by village, region by region. This understanding was articulated in a report by an international body of agricultural scientists that came out in 2009.[79] Even in this time when the ranks of climate refugees grows daily, it is possible to "become native to this place" in the words of Wes Jackson. There is ever more work to be done, and lessons to be learned.

## Conclusion: Can the "O" Word Be reclaimed?

It is hard to disagree with those who bemoan the loss of the True Organic Vision in the consumer-driven labeling claim, given the story of what has occurred in the course of bringing organic food and agriculture into the mainstream. I would contend, however, that the organic watchdogs and their activist followers are at least as much to blame for this loss as the corporations they love to hate. The focus on optics rather than substance has turned the "O" word into a narrow concept that perpetuates consumer ignorance to the detriment of understanding human-soil-ecosystem health as the source of "organic integrity." In the years since I started writing this story, I have to admit that I've lost hope that this situation can be redeemed.

So why bother? This year a new Pope has brought the world's attention to the intertwined threats of global poverty and global ecological collapse. Naomi Klein has convincingly informed us that *This Changes Everything.*[80] The ecological disasters now facing us came about as a result of the capitalist imperative to extract energy and wealth from the earth, and to continually expand as a cancer that must grow or die. Climate chaos—and the social chaos it engenders—is already under way. This crisis urgently demands a larger cultural shift than we have previously thought necessary if human civilization, or even humanity itself, is to survive this century.

A shift to organic production methods, as demonstrated on a small scale in Cuba, could be implemented relatively quickly.[81] Even absent significant carbon sequestration, a massive transition to organic methods would have an immediate impact on greenhouse gas emissions from agriculture by eliminating the production and dispersal of millions of tons of synthetic nitrate fertilizer. Market incentives have been an essential strategy for launching the organic approach into the mainstream and stimulating widespread public demand and awareness within the limitations of our capitalist system. But market incentives alone cannot bring about the revolutionary social, political, and economic changes needed to avert certain worldwide catastrophe. As I tell my students, you can't dismantle capitalism with a marketing plan.

There is huge potential to create a better society in the seeds sown by the "good food" movement, whether you resonate with Murray Bookchin's vision of a free society or with the Shambhala vision of enlightened society or some combination of the two. There are also huge obstacles and powerful opponents to this vision, and an unthinkable price to the planet for failure to overcome them. In the end, it really doesn't matter if the "O" word has been corrupted by the marketplace and the consumer-driven fantasy of purity. What matters is the increasing knowledge of better—healthier, saner, more equitable—ways of feeding ourselves and our communities. What matters is that more and more planetary citizens are waking up to the peril faced by human civilization, perhaps even the human species itself, should we fail to change course quickly enough.

The organic revolution appears to be picking up momentum day by day. Examples and inspiration turn up everywhere on the planet, including Vandana Shiva's championing of organic cotton production and seed saving in India, Zimbabwean pastoralists using Allan Savory's system of planned grazing to arrest desertification and build soil organic matter, and Asian peasants using simple techniques of rice intensification to increase yields. Not to mention nations such as Ecuador and Bolivia that have included constitutional protections for the Rights of Mother Earth. Here in the US people of color are increasingly learning to grow food for the community in urban as well as rural settings, organizing to support low-wage workers throughout the food system, and leading the demand for healthy, planet-friendly food for all.

The challenge that remains is largely one of how to avoid making the same mistakes and derailing the increasing momentum of this multifaceted revolution—playing right into the hands of the tiny minority that profits from the runaway environmental and social costs of our bad case of "affluenza." That challenge is reason enough to persist in telling my story.

The bumper sticker on my filing cabinet reads: "There's no hope—but maybe I'm wrong." Right or wrong, the only choice is to work as hard as we can, in whatever way we can, to create that free, enlightened society, united in diversity and joyful in working together for the benefit of all beings and the health of the planet. ⵌ

# Epilogue — Advice to a Young Food System Activist

On a cold January morning, 15 years after first sitting down to write my story of the organic revolution, I awoke uncharacteristically early with an urgent need to write down what was buzzing through my mind. It felt like a sudden bolt of clarity about the connections between everything that is critically important right at this moment in history. What came out could possibly be the seed of another book, entitled *Breath of Gaia: Planetary metabolism, food, and politics*. Here goes.

Carbon is literally the stuff of life; the dance between carbon, oxygen, and hydrogen forms the basis of all living organisms. Most of this stuff is derived from the atmosphere, and all of the requisite energy transformations are fueled by the sun. Green plants evolved an amazing ability to store energy from the sun with biochemistry. Carbon, oxygen, hydrogen plus other key elements (e.g., phosphorus) made it possible to pass that ability on to the future—encode it in a system of reproduction. Energy transformation is mediated by specific "minor" elements like magnesium (in plants) and iron (in animals). Let's not get lost in the wonder of evolutionary biology, except to note that complex organisms can be seen as colonies of formerly single-celled creatures that, over millenia, organized themselves in cooperative, communal bodies of mutual support.

This train of thought started with the realization of how profoundly the way we breathe affects our biochemistry, and the role of carbon dioxide in our body systems. Homeostasis mechanisms indicated by blood $CO_2$ levels are critical for health by keeping blood pH in the proper range. This of course ties in to the food we eat and the habits of mind we cultivate. All very applicable to this personal body of mine, including the tendency to try to hoard energy in the form of fat—the most energy dense biochemical fuel.

What kept me awake that morning was the insight of the intimate relationship (obvious to the ancients and indigenous peoples everywhere) between our bodies and the earth. At this moment our minds are preoccupied by the disastrous imbalance of excess $CO_2$ in earth's metabolism, a result of profligate worldwide expenditure of that precious biochemical energy that was captured by plants from ancient sunlight. The biochemistry of our oceans has many parallels with that of our blood and our soil, with so much transformation mediated by changes in pH. Today our planetary fever is alerting us to the need to restore a healthier balance before it is too late.

My life has been devoted to healing the earth, and simultaneously human bodies (individual and collective), assaulted by toxic pollutants in the 20$^{th}$ century. The same strategy that can remove the toxins from air, water, soil, and food can also help restore the critical metabolic balance of $CO_2$ levels in our planetary respiration pathways. This virtuous cycle is known as organic agriculture.

And so once again, as I finish telling the story of my own journey along this path, I rededicate what remains of my own life to promoting the widest and fastest possible adoption of organic methods, as they may be adapted to work within the particular human culture and ecology where they are practiced.

This means political, economic, and social revolution, by the way.

To the young farmers and food system activists who must carry this work forward on the ground, I hope the lessons embedded in my story will prove beneficial. In case my message has been too subtle, here are a few important points to keep in mind:

Basic goodness means there is no "us and them"—we're all in this together, and have to unlearn habits of thought that see any human being (not to mention any other species) as "alien" or "other" that is assumed to be a threat. That our Western capitalist political economy is predicated on such beliefs is the dirty secret that is now, with the resurgence of movements such as Black Lives Matter, being exposed repeatedly. The enemy is not other people; the enemy is racism and all its related "isms" that allow any fellow human to be brutalized for the sake of our own need for security and comfort.

I have long campaigned against the demand for purity in the context of organic food and farming. This is related to my gut reaction to the demand for purity advocated by the openly racist segments of society, most especially the Nazis who were the evil bogeypersons of my childhood. My feminist and sexual liberation impulses are similarly repulsed by the repression of women in the name of virginal purity and, beyond that, its connotations of whiteness (pure as the driven snow) and refinement. Which brings us to the connection between food and racism.

The story of sugar in a way encapsulates the horrific consequences of the quest for purity in the food system. A similar story could be told about the fate of our major cereal grains, especially corn, wheat and rice, in which whiteness and purity have been valued to the detriment of health and nutrition. Not to mention cotton, the foundation of industrialization of the West, built on slave labor that was justified in the minds of its perpetrators by relegating its victims to less than human status.

As impurities have been refined out, the social status of foods such as white sugar, white flour, and white rice has been elevated, while at the same time their life-giving qualities have been diminished. The addictive qualities of both refined carbohydrates and refined hydrocarbons is not a coincidence. That the production, processing, and manufacture of foods and textiles from these now lifelessly pure products is predicated on an exceptionally vicious dehumanization of brown and black people by those of Caucasian descent is a shameful and sordid chapter of our history that lives on at the very core of our so-called civilization.

So the demand for purity is antithetical to the need for health. Purity requires monoculture. Purity rejects our symbiotic relationship with the teeming microbiome that contributes the huge majority of our metabolic well-being, but instead strives for an illusory sense of germ-free safety. But some purity can be good and beautiful—the rare and exquisite product of well-crafted artifice. That's a different aspect that we should not forget any more than we should turn the tables on racists by making them into the enemy, any more than we should seek to eliminate $CO_2$, a waste product and pollutant in excessive levels, from our atmosphere or our bloodstream.

Much of the damage to the true organic vision, as I have tried to elucidate it, has been done by those who earnestly believe that organic food must be pure, and that ideological purity must trump political compromise. To overcome this belief, we need compassion for our own inner fascist. At this moment, it is critical to the health of our Gaian respiratory metabolism that we freely share this vision with everyone—even with those whose political views or position of extreme wealth and power we may despise.

The hour is late; do as much as you can, but learn to be patient. Be kind but be persistent.

# Endnotes

## Chapter 1

1. Extension Agronomist, University of Vermont from 1954 through 1986. Win Way, a prolific generator of helpful information for farmers, was considered a maverick among his peers. He advocated for small farms, local food, and organic farming at a time when it was considered cultish, and wrote a regular column for the NOFA newsletter for years. University of Vermont Extension. http://www.uvm.edu/extension/about/history/?Page=audio_list.php&SM=audio_sm.html&name=winston%20arthur_way. Accessed November 27, 2015.
2. USDA Agricultural Marketing Service. http://www.ams.usda.gov/AMSv1.0/Farmers-Markets. Accessed November 27, 2015.
3. The contrast between Von Liebig and Goethe exemplifies the tension between reductionist and holistic approaches to science, discussed more thoroughly in the following chapter.
4. Steiner's instructions have been found to create effective microbial inoculants by combining just the right materials that are allowed to ferment under the right conditions. Animal organs may be combined with specific flowers that concentrate certain trace minerals needed by microbes that help improve compost.
5. Anthroposophy is the name of the spiritual philosophy taught by Steiner; it's also the foundation for the well-known Waldorf school movement.
6. See for example, Jared Diamond, *Guns, Germs and Steel*, (New York: W.W.Norton,1999) and Charles Mann, *1491: New Revelations of the Americas Before Columbus*, (New York: Knopf, 2005).
7. http://www.rodaleinc.com/content/about-us
8. See Peter Staudenmaier's discussion of Anthroposophy and Ecofascism at: http://www.social-ecology.org/2009/01/anthroposophy-and-ecofascism-2/. Accessed November 28, 2015
9. See the next chapter for a discussion of organic principles and the contradiction of the desire for purity.
10. Upton Sinclair, *The Jungle*, (New York: Doubleday, 1906).
11. What has come to be called 'progressive' farming today is, ironically, at odds with populist impulses and associated with faith in technological progress as the solution to agricultural problems.
12. http://www.acresusa.com/history/ accessed November 28, 2015
13. Now available online at: http://www.nal.usda.gov/afsic/pubs/USDAOrgFarmRpt.pdf
14. Bob S. Bergland and Susan E. Sechler, *A Time to Choose: Summary Report on the Structure of Agriculture*, (Washington, DC: USDA, 1981).https://archive.org/details/timetochoosesumm00unit Accessed December 3, 2015.

## Chapter 2

15. Murray Bookchin, *The Modern Crisis*. (Montreal: Black Rose Books, 1998).
16. Wendel Berry, *The Unsettling of America: Culture and Agriculture*, (San Francisco: Sierra Club Books, 1977), pp.173-174.
17. See Stuart Hill's explanation of social ecology here: http://www.zulenet.com/see/chair.html#seis Accessed December 3, 2015.
18. Gershuny, Grace. "Buddhism Becomes Majority religion in Barnet as Special Day Approaches," *Caledonian Record*, May 23, 1987.

19. Gershuny, Grace. *Caledonian Record*, May 27, 1987.
20. Loosely translated as "insistence on truth" (*satya* "truth"; *agraha* "insistence") or soul force or truth force, is a particular philosophy and practice within the broader overall category generally known as nonviolent resistance or civil resistance. The theory of satyagraha sees means and ends as inseparable. The means used to obtain an end are wrapped up in and attached to that end. Therefore, it is contradictory to try to use unjust means to obtain justice or to try to use violence to obtain peace. From http://en.wikipedia.org/wiki/Satyagraha
21. The most widely quoted definition of the precautionary principle comes from a conference known as Wingspread, held in Wisconsin in 1998: "When an activity raises threats of harm to human health or the environment, precautionary measures should be taken even if some cause and effect relationships are not fully established scientifically. In this context the proponent of an activity, rather than the public, should bear the burden of proof. The process of applying the Precautionary Principle must be open, informed and democratic and must include potentially affected parties. It must also involve an examination of the full range of alternatives, including no action." http://www.sehn.org/state.html#w accessed December 3, 2015.
22. The author has credited discovering a copy of *The Soul of Soil* in a used book bin in Berkeley with inspiring her to pursue a study of this connection. See the Annotated Bibliography.

## Chapter 3

23. Community Supported Agriculture consists of a community of individuals who pledge support to a farm operation so that the farmland becomes, either legally or spiritually, the community's farm, with the growers and consumers providing mutual support and sharing the risks and benefits of food production. http://afsic.nal.usda.gov/community-supported-agriculture-3 accessed December 3, 2015.
24. Keith Kemble and Susana Merriam. "Report on organic certification programs in the US: Networking, goals and various reactions." National Center for Appropriate Technology, Butte, MT, June 1, 1980. Note: Although her name is not listed as an author, Miranda Smith is credited with suggesting that this project be included in NCAT's work plan; she had by this time left Butte to settle in Vermont.
25. http://dictionary.reference.com/browse/industry?s=t accessed January 8, 2016.
26. The three numbers on fertilizer bags stand for the percentage of Nitrrogen (N), Phosphorus (P), and Potassium (K), three of the major plant nutrients. Conventional fertilizers that use synthetic nitrate may contain 20% or more of this nutrient in soluble form.
27. Actually still technically allowed, due to a bureaucratic error in placing it in the prohibited category.
28. At the time, there were over a dozen such programs operating in North America, including a couple of state-run programs in Texas and Washington.
29. Note the recent, highly publicized Stanford Study, a meta analysis that purported to show that organic foods do not offer any health or nutrition benefits as a case in point of the pitfalls of relying on reductionism to support the case for organic. See Mark Bittman, "That Flawed Stanford Study," New YorkTimes, October 2, 2012. http://opinionator.blogs.nytimes.com/2012/10/02/that-flawed-stanford-study/?_r=0 accessed December 3, 2015.
30. Harlyn Meyer, editor, "Laboratory Testing and the Production and Marketing of Certified Organic Foods." OFPANA Position Paper #1, December 1986.
31. Grace Gershuny and Joseph Smillie, *Guidelines for the Organic Foods Industry*, Organic Foods Production Association of North America, January 1986.

# Chapter 4

32. Opal Whitely and Benajamin Hoff, *The Singing Creek Where the Willows Grow: The Rediscovered Diary of Opal Whiteley*. (New York: Warner Books, 1988).
33. 'Coyote' in the sense of the trickster legends, a mischievous spirit who uses cunning to undermine the oppressor, such as Bre'r Rabbit in the African-American tradition.

# Chapter 5

34. 7 USC 6501 Title 21, Organic Foods Production Act of 1990.
35. National Organic Program Staff, 1995.
36. The first six principles were ultimately compressed into this definition (discussed at length later in the chapter): A system that is designed to produce agricultural products by the use of methods and substances that enhance agroecosystem health within an agricultural operation and that maintain the integrity of organic agricultural products until they reach the consumer. This is accomplished by using, where possible, cultural, biological, and mechanical methods, as opposed to using substances, to fulfill any specific function within the system so as to: maintain long-term soil fertility; increase soil biological activity; recycle wastes to return nutrients to the land; provide attentive care for farm animals; enhance biological diversity within the whole system; and handle the agricultural products without the use of extraneous synthetic additives or processing in accordance with the Act and regulations in this part.
37. This system has evolved to become a bureaucratic hall of mirrors, with watchers endlessly watching the watchers. Refer to Lawrence Busch, *Standards: Recipes for Reality*, in the Annotated Bibliography.
38. In response to a draft of this chapter, Michael sent me this comment: "I personally would like to see more discussion about our approach to the National List and how we tried to protect organic integrity by working the list into the standards instead of going the shaky route of approving substance by substance. Remember, there is nothing in the OFPA that really sets criteria for approving substances. We did this also because we did not trust the USDA in the future to appoint members to the NOSB who wouldn't try to sabotage the National List." (e-mail correspondence dated July 11, 2014).
39. In a recent interview Bob Scowcroft, former executive director of CCOF, describes the California 'carrot caper' that paralleled the George Crane episode discussed in Chapter 3. This incident helped drive home the need for enforceable organic regulations that made California growers willing to get behind the OFPA. Refer to Brian Barth, "Organics Aren't Just for Hippies Anymore: A Q&A with Bob Scowcroft." *Modern Farmer*, October 12, 2015. http://modernfarmer.com/2015/10/bob-scowcroft-interview, accessed December 4, 2015.
40. Organic advocates have more recently come to recognize the problematic nature of highly prescriptive practice standards for food safety, with promulgation of new regulations implementing the Food Safety Modernization Act.
41. Codex Alimentarius is the international body that seeks to harmonize all food-related standards on behalf of the WTO (World Trade Organization).
42. Twenty years later, with GMO corn and soybeans accounting for upwards of 90% of those crops, the demand for labeling of GMO foods may finally be unstoppable.
43. http://www.who.int/topics/food_genetically_modified/en/ accessed December 4, 2015
44. Adapted from John Fagan, Michael Antoniou and Claire Robinson, *GMO Myths and Truths*, 2nd ed. 2014. www.earthopensource.org, pp. 22-23
45. NOP Regulations: 7 CFR Part 205 §205.2
46. See "Prologue: Moving Towards Sustainability" sidebar.
47. Refer to Chapter 4 sidebar with criteria for evaluating substances for the National List.
48. OFPA definition of Synthetic: A substance that is formulated or manufactured by a chemical process or by a process that chemically changes a substance extracted from naturally occurring plant, animal, or mineral sources, except that such term shall not apply to substances created by naturally occurring biological processes.

49. 7 USC 6517 Sec. 2118 (c)(1)(A)(ii)

50. Subsequent to leaving the NOP staff I did a lot of consulting for QAI, and continue to serve as a contract inspector for them.

51. Leona Broydo, "Organic Engineering," *Mother Jones*, May/June 1998 issue. http://www.motherjones.com/politics/1998/05/organic-engineering accessed December 4, 2015.

52. New York Times Editorial Board, *Stuck in Purgatory*, published June 30, 2013. http://www.nytimes.com/2013/07/01/opinion/stuck-in-purgatory.html?_r=0 accessed December 4, 2015.

## Chapter 6

53. The actual regulation began on page 349. The first 348 pages were devoted to various Executive Order analyses, such as impact on small businesses, as well as the Preamble.

54. Ben Lilliston & Ronnie Cummins. "Organic Vs. "Organic": The Corruption of a Label." *The Ecologist*, July/August 1998.

55. My original letter to the editors, based on that draft memo, is reproduced in the Appendix.

56. I reference Monsanto not only as a well-known symbol of the 'evil corporate dragon,' but as one of the few, if not the only, such players who had actually tried to manipulate the process up to this point.

57. Well over 90% of corn, soybeans, sugar beets, canola and cotton grown in the US is now GMO's, most designed to resist the herbicide glyphosate (and now older, more toxic herbicides), and some engineered to express the pesticidal toxin derived from *Bacillus thuringiensis* in all their tissues.

58. OFPA (7 USC 6517) Section 2118(d) outlines the procedure whereby the Secretary establishes the National List, which must be based on a proposed National List or proposed amendments to the National List recommended by the NOSB. It then goes on to describe the standard requirements for notice and comment rulemaking, in which a formal proposal is published in the Federal Register and the public has the opportunity to comment on the proposal. *The Secretary must identify any changes made to the proposal developed by the NOSB, and cannot add exemptions for use of synthetic substances that were not contained in the proposal published in the Federal Register.* The language is confusing, but the intent is clear, underscored by the presumption that the Secretary has ultimate authority over the contents of the National List. However, the Secretary cannot make changes to the NOSB's recommendations (especially with respect to whether to approve an exemption for a given synthetic substance) without first giving the public an opportunity to object. In the case of the NOP and the NOSB, any such attempt would surely be met with huge public objections.

59. Michael Hankin commented that, "I still believe it is inhumane and a huge financial burden to small farmers to prohibit its use and I strongly suspect that they are quietly being used with extended withholding times and their (illegal) use in organic milk production will someday be exposed." (personal email July 11, 2014)

60. 60 In 2008, then serving as Program Manager, Rick Matthews was responsible for proposing outrageously strict standards for access to pasture as the ultimate 'give them what they want and see how they like it' strategy. It worked nicely, and the community was forced to request that the final rules be made a tad less draconian.

61. The regulations follow the law and mandate at least 120 days after raw manure is applied before a crop for human consumption that may contact soil can be harvested. This is plenty of time to eliminate any pathogens that may be present.

62. NOP §205.200 states:...Production practices implemented in accordance with this subpart must maintain or improve the natural resources of the operation, including soil and water quality.

63. Now called the Institute for Food & Development Policy

64. Not likely any time soon, despite recent diplomatic openings, given the makeup of Congress

# Chapter 7

65. The NOSB voted at its October 2015 meeting to add an annotation to the listing of natural flavors and colors that will require use of a commercially available organic form of these ingredients.

66. See the OFPA definition of synthetic, endnote 47. The term 'synthetic' is not found in the EU organic regulations, and is generally equated with substances that are derived from petrochemicals.

67. Although the OFPA used the term 'natural' in contrast to 'synthetic,' the regulations were written to avoid the use of this indefinable and meaningless term.

68. This insight was confirmed by asking several European colleagues if this was the case. Restrictions on the use of synthetic fibers under the GOTS rules clearly relate to polyester, spandex, and similar petroleum-derived materials.

69. Professor Philip Howard of Michigan State University has maintained a widely reproduced graphic that shows "who owns organic," available at https://www.msu.edu/~howardp/organicindustry.html accessed December 8, 2015.

70. https://www.organicconsumers.org/about-oca accessed December 8, 2015

71. Unlike OCA, Cornucopia does not publish financial information or membership numbers. See http://www.cornucopia.org/about-us accessed December 8, 2015.

72. http://www.nationalorganiccoalition.org/about accessed December 8, 2015

73. OFPA (7 USC 6517) Section 2118(d) is pretty clear about needingan NOSB recommendation with notice and comment rulemaking any time the National List is changed. This makes sense if you think about the need to give people who are following the rules a chance to object if a material they are currently using may no longer be allowed.

74. Vermont passed the first mandatory GMO labeling law in 2014,slated to take effect in July 2016. Two or three other states have passed labeling laws that do not take effect until a minimum number of neighboring states trigger it. Popular referenda to require GMO labeling attempted in Colorado, Oregon & California have been defeated by an extremely expensive campaign by the conventional food industry. Vermont's law has survived at least one legal challenge, and a Congressional effort to pass a bill preempting such laws appears to be dead at the end of 2015.

75. http://articles.latimes.com/2013/dec/19/opinion/la-oe-glickman-organic-gmo-foods-20131219 accessed December 8, 2015

76. See http://www.nongmoproject.org/ accessed December 8, 2015.

77. http://www.leonardoacademy.org/newsandevents/press-release/577-ansi-approves-leo-4000-american-national-standard-for-sustainable-agriculture-.html accessed December 8, 2015

78. See the Annotated Bibliography for information on Holistic Management and work by Allan Savory. I was grateful to be able to participate in a training program in Holistic Management taught by Savory and others that took place from 2002 through 2004.

79. McIntyre, et al., eds. Agriculture at a Crossroads: IAASTD Synthesis Report. Island Press, 2009 at http://www.unep.org/dewa/agassessment/reports/IAASTD/EN/Agriculture%20at%20a%20Crossroads_Synthesis%20Report%20(English).pdf.

80. See Annotated Bibliography

81. See, for example, this recent article in *Slate* magazine by Raj Patel:http://www.slate.com/articles/health_and_science/future_tense/2012/04/agro_ecology_lessons_from_cuba_on_agriculture_food_and_climate_change_.html

# Annotated Bibliography and Information Resources

Key authors and publications that have influenced me are listed here. Some of the classics are available in full text on the web. Organizations and web-based information sources are simply listed.

## Publications Applicable to the Introduction

Naomi Klein, *This Changes Everything: Capitalism vs The Climate*, (New York: Simon & Shuster, 2014).
Naomi Klein tackles the most profound threat humanity has ever faced: the war our economic model is waging against life on earth. The market can't save us, and the addiction to profit and growth is digging us in deeper every day. We are part of the solution.

Frances Moore Lappé, & Joseph Collins, *World Hunger: 10 Myths*, (New York: Grove Press, 2015).
In this updated version of a classic, Lappé and Collins dispel the myths that prevent us from finding solutions to hunger across the globe. The authors argue that sustainable agriculture can feed the world, and that most in the Global North have more in common with the world's hungry people than they thought.

Joanna Macy, & Chris Johnstone. *Active Hope: How to Face the Mess We're in without Going Crazy*, (Novato, CA: New World Library, 2012).
Buddhist and deep ecologist Joanna Macy describes Active Hope as something we do rather than have. The authors offer practical wisdom for those seeking to participate in the Great Turning and act for the healing of our world.

Gunnar Rundgren, *Global Eating Disorder*, (Uppsala, Sweden: Regeneration, 2014).
A former IFOAM World Board Chair, Gunnar Rundgren explains how our food and farm system developed into the system we have today, and how interdependent our food system and society are. Loaded with factual information, data about the global food system, and references.

## Publications Applicable to Chapter 1

Wendell Berry, *The Unsettling of America: Culture and Agriculture*, (San Francisco: Sierra Club Books, 1977).
This collection of essays was a huge influence on this author and my compatriots. In it, Wendell Berry uses his elegant prose to argue that good farming is a cultural development and spiritual discipline.

Ralph Borsodi, *Flight from the City: an experiment in creative living on the land*, (New York: Harper & Bros, 1933).
ONLINE AT: http://soilandhealth.org/wp-content/uploads/0302hsted030204borsodi/030204borsoditoc.html
Borsodi is credited with introducing J.I. Rodale to organic gardening and the Nearings to simple living, as well as with coining the term 'appropriate technology' and developing the ideas of the community land trust and local currencies. In this book Borsodi comments on decentralization, of both industry and population, of moving away from the city and ultimately back to the farm and family enterprise to produce the food and goods needed by local societies. His concept of a "School of Living" is carried on by present day utopian community builders.

Rachel Carson, *Silent Spring*, (Greenwich, CT: Fawcett, 1962).
  ONLINE AT: https://archive.org/stream/fp_Silent_Spring-Rachel_Carson-1962/Silent_Spring-Rachel_Carson-1962#page/n5/mode/2up
  Published in 1962, Silent Spring exposed the hazards of the pesticide DDT, eloquently questioned humanity's faith in technological progress and helped set the stage for the environmental movement.

Philip Conford, *The Origins of the Organic Movement*. (Edinburgh, UK: Floris Books, 2001).
  Philip Conford chronicles the surprising origins of the organic movement in Britain and America and reveals that the early exponents of the organic movement actually belonged more to extreme right-wing conservative groups.

Ben Hewitt, *The Town that Food Saved: How One Community Found Vitality in Local Food*, (Emmaus, PA: Rodale Books, 2010).
  Ben Hewitt explores the contradictions inherent to producing high-end "artisanal" food products in a working class community. His portraits of local agripreneurs and small farmers include a number of the people who have played important roles in this story.

Robert Houriet, *Getting Back Together*, (New York: Coward, McCann & Geoghegan, 1971).
  Robert Houriet chronicles his exploration of communes throughout the nation in the late sixties, concluding with his depiction of Frog Run Farm in East Charleston, VT, where I first met him. In it he says, "Our friends in the cities, still fighting the good fight within the system, regard us as escapists. To them we are repeating the American error; doing what our parents did in fleeing to the suburbs, turning our backs on the real problems and issues."

Sir Albert Howard, *The Soil & Health: A Study of Organic Agriculture*, (London: Faber & Faber, 1945).
  ONLINE AT: http://journeytoforever.org/farm_library/howardSH/SHtoc.html
  This is the book that inspired me to make a more in depth study of soil and why soil health is central to producing nutritious food. Howard introduced the idea that disease, whether in plants, animals or humans, was caused by unhealthy soil and that organic farming techniques would make the soil and those living on it, healthy.

F.H. King, *Farmers of Forty Centuries or Permanent Agriculture in China, Korea and Japan*, (Mineola, NY: Dover, 1911).
  AVAILABLE ONLINE: http://soilandhealth.org/book/farmers-of-forty-centuries-or-permanent-agriculture-in-china-korea-and-japan/
  This classic of ecological agriculture describes the voyage agronomist and former US Department of Agriculture official Franklin Hiram King made to China, Korea and Japan in the early 1900s, in order to learn how the extremely dense populations of the Far East could feed themselves century after century without depleting their soils. His observations reveal highly sophisticated systems of water management, crop rotation, and ecological relationships.

Al Krebs, *The Corporate Reapers: The Book of Agribusiness*, (Washington, DC: Essential Books, 1992).
  A veritable almanac of information, this book details how multinational agribusiness has worked to destroy the family farm.

Peter Kropotkin, The Conquest of Bread, (New York: G.P. Putnam's Sons, 1906).
  ONLINE AT: http://dwardmac.pitzer.edu/Anarchist_Archives/kropotkin/conquest/toc.html
  Kropotkin points out what he considers to be the fallacies of the economic systems of feudalism and capitalism, and how he believes they create poverty and scarcity while promoting privilege. He proposes a decentralized economic system based on mutual aid and voluntary cooperation.

Frances Moore Lappé and Joseph Collins with Cary Fowler, *Food First: Beyond the Myth of Scarcity*, (Boston: Houghton Mifflin, 1977).
Lappé's first book, Diet for a Small Planet, inspired my short-lived experiment in vegetarian eating. In it, she showed that human practices, not natural disasters, cause worldwide hunger. Food First opened my eyes to the real causes of starvation that include the economic pressures to produce cash crops rather than basic food products and other consequences of colonization.

Stephanie Mills, *On Gandhi's Path: Bob Swann's Work for Peace and Community Economics*, (Gabriola Island, BC, Canada: New Society Publishers, 2010).
Swann spent his life (1918–2002) working for strong communities and peace, and worked with Ralph Borsodi to develop the concepts of community land trusts and local currencies, among others. Mills traces the history of Swann's thinking, risk-taking and sacrifice, while painting a portrait of a fulfilled life.

Helen Nearing and Scott Nearing, *Living the Good Life: How to Live Sanely and Simply in a Troubled World*, (New York: Schocken, 1970).
First published in 1954, this book inspired a new generation of twentieth century back-to-the-landers. The Nearings chronicle their transition from urban radicals to hard-scrabble homesteaders, refusing to compromise by using technology or even cooking their food. The austerity of their lifestyle, coupled with the absence of children to raise and the presence of multitudes of visitors to help with the manual labor of stone house construction, represents an ideal which few could emulate.

J.I. Rodale, Editor, Encyclopedia of Organic Gardening. (Emmaus, PA: Rodale Press, 1971).
A hefty volume, consulted often as I set out to become a homesteader in the seventies. It covers the gamut of organic gardening wisdom from A to Z, including general gardening techniques, vegetable growing, small fruits, nuts and orchards, herbs and flowers, pest control and much more.

E.F. Schumacher, *Small is Beautiful: Economics as if People Mattered*, (London: Blond & Briggs, 1975).
ONLINE AT: http://www.ditext.com/schumacher/small/small.html
Schumacher's statement on sustainability has become more relevant and vital with each year. The pursuit of profit and progress, which promotes giant organizations and increased specialization, is a cause of economic, environmental and social degradation. He proposes a system of Intermediate Technology, based on smaller regional working units, using local labor and resources.

Wolf D. Storl, *Culture & Horticulture: A Philosophy of Gardening*, (Milwaukee, WI: Bio-Dynamic Farming & Gardening, 1979).
The most readable and comprehensible explanation of Steiner's philosophy and bio-dynamic agriculture I have encountered. In addition to practical guidance on gardening methods, it provides sound historical information about the evolution of alternative agriculture.

## Publications Applicable to Chapter 2

Stephen Batchelor, *Buddhism without Beliefs: A Contemporary Guide to Awakening*, (New York: Riverhead, 1997).
Stephen Batchelor explains that the concepts and practices of Buddhism are not something to believe in but something to do. This is a practice that anyone can engage in, regardless of background or beliefs.

Murray Bookchin, *The Ecology of Freedom: The Emergence and Dissolution of Hierarchy*, (Palo Alto: Cheshire Books, 1982).
"The very notion of the domination of nature by man stems from the very real domination of human by human." This is the central idea in Bookchin's most ambitious work, a book of breathtaking scope. Bookchin's synthesis of ecology, anthropology and political theory traces our conflicting legacies of hierarchy and freedom from the first emergence of human culture to globalized capitalism, and sets out his vision of communalism as the path to a sane, sustainable ecological future.

Murray Bookchin, *Our Synthetic Environment*, (New York: Knopf, 1962) (published under the pseudonymn "Lewis Herber").
ONLINE AT: http://dwardmac.pitzer.edu/Anarchist_Archives/bookchin/syntheticenviron/osetoc.html
In his introduction to the 1975 edition Rene Dubos declares this to have been "the most comprehensive and enlightened book on the environmental crisis." Addressing agriculture in chapter two, Bookchin paints some eloquent portraits of life in the soil: "… It is not within the realm of fantasy to suggest that if the breakdown of the soil cosmos continues unabated, if plant and animal health continue to deteriorate, if insect infestations multiply, and if chemical controls become increasingly lethal, many of the preconditions for advanced life will be irreparably damaged and the earth will prove to be incapable of supporting a viable, healthy human species."

Thomas S. Kuhn, *The Structure of Scientific Revolutions*, (Chicago: University of Chicago Press, 1962),
ONLINE AT: http://projektintegracija.pravo.hr/_download/repository/Kuhn_Structure_of_Scientific_Revolutions.pdf
Thomas Kuhn was one of the most influential philosophers of science of the twentieth century, and The Structure of Scientific Revolutions is one of the most cited academic books of all time. His account of the development of science held that science enjoys periods of stable growth punctuated by revisionary revolutions. We can thank Kuhn for coining the phrase "paradigm shift" to describe such revolutions.

James Lovelock, *Gaia: A New Look at Life on Earth*, (Oxford: Oxford University Press, 1979).
The Gaia hypothesis, formulated by the chemist James Lovelock and co-developed by the microbiologist Lynn Margulis, has had a radical effect on scientific views of evolution and the environment and has been fiercely debated by biologists, chemists, and cyberneticists. According to the Gaia hypothesis, the environment does not coincidentally support life on earth; rather the two form a complex system which can be seen as a single organism.

Richard Merrill, Editor, *Radical Agriculture*, (New York: New York University Press, 1976).
With an Introduction by Murray Bookchin, this collection of essays includes several gems that remain relevant today.

Daphne Miller, M.D., *Farmacology: What Innovative Family Farming Can Teach Us About Health and Healing*, (New York: William Morrow/Harper Collins, 2013).
Daphne Miller says she was inspired to write this book after finding a copy of The Soul of Soil in a free book bin in Berkeley. In *Farmacology* she brings us beyond the simple concept of "food as medicine" and introduces us to the critical idea that it's the farm where that food is grown that offers us the real medicine.

Sakyong Mipham, *The Shambhala Principle: Discovering Humanity's Hidden Treasure*, (New York: Harmony Books/Crown Publishing, 2013).
The Sakyong is well positioned to refresh the message his father brought to the West from Tibet, and speak to a new generation. Here he conveys the urgency of our situation, saying "We humans have come to a crossroads in our history: we can either destroy the world or create a good future. The Shambhala Principle offers the principle of basic goodness as a way of addressing the personal and social challenges that we face."

Bill Mollison and David Holmgren, *Permaculture One: A Perennial Agricultural System for Human Settlements*, (Tasmania: Tagari Publications, 1978).
ONLINE AT: http://library.uniteddiversity.coop/Permaculture/Bill_Mollison-Permaculture_Two-Practical_Design_for_Town_and_Country_in_Permanent_Agriculture.pdf
Permaculture is an integrated system of design which Bill Mollison co-developed with David Holmgren, encompassing not only agriculture, horticulture, architecture, and ecology, but also economic systems, land access strategies, and legal systems for businesses and communities. After collaborating on Permaculture One, Mollison and Holmgren went their separate ways and spawned a worldwide movement of designers and educators as well as numerous books that elaborate on the theme. Mollison published Permaculture Two on his own in 1979.

Theodore Roszak, *Person/Planet: The Creative Disintegration of Industrial Society*, (New York: Doubleday, 1978).
This is one of the books that helped me understand my mission in life. As bleak as the fate of the Earth may seem, Roszak offers the hopeful hypothesis that that the Earth itself speaks through us, and that the needs of the planet are the needs of the person.

Miranda Smith, *Greenhouse Gardening*, (Emmaus, PA: Rodale Press, 1985).
Miranda's first published work, one of the first to address organic methods for working with vegetables as well as ornamentals in a greenhouse environment. The best of her many excellent gardening books can be found at http://www.amazon.com/Miranda-Smith/e/B001H6SZHQ/ref=dp_byline_cont_book_1

Nancy Jack Todd, *The Book of the New Alchemists*, (New York: E.P. Dutton, 1977).
The Book of the New Alchemists is a document of a living experiment begun in 1969 by a group of people concerned with what they saw as an approaching ecological crisis. This book documents the optimistic early experiments in self-reliance that so inspired my own journey.

Chögyam Trungpa, *Cutting through Spiritual Materialism*, (Boston: Shambhala Publications, 1973).
ONLINE AT: https://archive.org/stream/pdfy-WB1Fzh_m8Ljplk16/Cutting%20Through%20Spiritual%20Materialism#page/n3/mode/2up
In this spiritual classic Chögyam Trungpa highlights the most common stumbling block on the path to enlightenment. Spiritual materialism is a universal tendency to see spirituality as a process of self-improvement, which is just another form of egotism. Recognizing this tendency, we can work with it and aspire to a wider form of human liberation.

## Publications Applicable to Chapters 3–7

Natasha Bowens, *The Color of Food: Stories of Race, Resilience and Farming*, (Gabriola Island, BC: New Society Publishers, 2015).
One of the first of the new African American farmers to highlight the issue of agriculture as birthright and a route to reclaiming power, dignity, and self reliance through food sovereignty. Bowens beautifully tells the stories of diverse farmers of color through interviews and photographs.

Lawrence Busch, *Standards: Recipes for Reality*, (Cambridge: MIT Press, 2011).
I first encountered Larry Busch when I gave a presentation to some of his Michigan State University students as a staff member of the NOP. This book sheds needed light on how the edifice of agricultural standards has been erected to confuse the public and serve the corporate agenda.

John Fagan, Michael Antoniou, and Claire Robinson, *GMO Myths and Truths: An evidence-based examination of the claims made for the safety and efficacy of genetically*

*modified crops and foods* (2nd edition), (London: Earth Open Source, 2014).
ONLINE AT: http://gmomythsandtruths.earthopensource.org/
The GMO debate is often characterized by tirades about evil corporate agribusiness, on the one hand, and anti-science zealots on the other. Co-authored by two former genetic engineers, *GMO Myths & Truths* analyzes the scientific evidence for the claims of agribusiness apologists and shows that this technology is neither proven safe nor needed to feed the world. Freely available under a creative commons license.

Julie Guthman, *Agrarian Dreams: The Paradox of Organic Farming in California*, second edition, (Oakland: University of California Press, 2014).
Julie Guthman challenges accepted wisdom about organic food and agriculture in this academic but accessible study. Many continue to believe that small-scale organic farming is the answer to our environmental and health problems, but Guthman refutes these portrayals with an analysis that underscores the limits of an organic label as a pathway to transforming agriculture. Her West Coast perspective is valuable in rounding out my picture, but she misses on a few points.

Andrew Kimbrell, Editor, *The Fatal Harvest Reader: The Tragedy of Industrial Agriculture*, (Washington, DC: Island Press, 2002).
This volume collects more than forty essays by thinkers such as Wendell Berry, Wes Jackson, Helena Norberg-Hodge, Vandana Shiva, and Gary Nabhan. As it exposes the ecological and social impacts of industrial agriculture's fatal harvest, it also details a new ecological and humane vision for agriculture. Its fatal flaw is an essay that reinforces the twisted version of what transpired in regulating the organic label. Island Press turned down The Organic Revolution just prior to publishing this one—coincidence?

Donella H. Meadows, Dennis L. Meadows, Jorgen Randers and William W. Behrens III, *The Limits to Growth*, (New York: New American Library, 1972).
ONLINE AT: http://www.donellameadows.org/wp-content/userfiles/Limits-to-Growth-digital-scan-version.pdf
Among the most influential books of the environmental movement, The Limits to Growth launched the issue of 'sustainability' into the public debate, and promoted the concept of 'systems thinking' in contrast to the linear reductionism that still dominates scientific inquiry. Though it was attacked by many who didn't understand or misrepresented its assertions, nothing that has happened in the last 30 years has invalidated the book's warnings. A 30 year update was published by Chelsea Green in 2004.

Brian K. Obach, *Organic Struggle: The Movement for Sustainable Agriculture in the United States*, (Cambridge: MIT Press, 2015)
Based on extensive research and interviews with a wide range of organic activists, including me, Obach tells the story of the transition of the organic movement to mainstream with clarity and nuance. His conclusions resonate with my own, even if he still misses some important details.

Michael Pollan, *The Omnivore's Dilemma: A Natural History of Four Meals* (New York: Penguin, 2006).
Many credit this book with launching the 21st century 'real food' movement. Pollan writes brilliantly about our relationship to food, explicating the failures of the industrial food system with its primary inputs of corn and chemicals, and presents convincing evidence of its harm to environment, animal welfare, and human health. He also takes some pot shots at the organic industry, while elevating Joel Salatin to agricultural super-star status. Despite posing a false dichotomy, Pollan does a great service to the cause of food system transformation.

Allan Savory and Jody Butterfield, *Holistic Management: A New Framework for Decision Making*, (Washington, DC: Island Press, 1998).

Allan Savory has gained some notoriety as an advocate for the use of planned livestock grazing to as a means to build soil organic matter and help avert climate chaos. I had the privilege of studying Holistic Management with Savory, and this book is the bible. This comprehensive framework draws on systems theory and ecology, and regards humans, their economies, and the environment as inseparable. It includes a common-sense decision-making framework through a democratic process that engages all 'stakeholders' in goal creation and direction.

Vandana Shiva, *The Violence of the Green Revolution*, (Penang/London: Third World Network/Zed Books, 1991)

Vandana Shiva, *Monocultures of the Mind: Perspectives on Biodiversity and Biotechnology*, (Penang/London: Third World Network/Zed Books, 1993)
Physicist Vandana Shiva is a prolific author and speaker on a range of issues surrounding opposition to agro-chemical-industrial-GMO agriculture, as well as advocating for reconstructive movements like organic farming, food sovereignty, and indigenous seed saving. These two books address her core arguments, in a manner both rational and passionate.

Eric Toensmeier, *The Carbon Farming Solution: A Global Toolkit of Perennial Crops and Regenerative Agriculture Practices for Climate Change Mitigation and Food Security*, White River Junction,VT: Chelsea Green Publishing), 2016.
The subtitle says it all. Toensmeier is a colleague and former student at the Institute for Social Ecology who has created the definitive guide to reversing climate change by growing food.

## Organizations, Publications & Web Sites

**ACRES, USA** — http://www.acresusa.com/

**Alternative Farming Systems Information Center (ASIC), National Agriculture Library** — https://afsic.nal.usda.gov/

**Chelsea Green Publishing** — http://www.chelseagreen.com/

**Ecological Agriculture Projects, McGill University** — http://eap.mcgill.ca/

**Green Mountain College, MS in Sustainable Food Systems** — http://www.greenmtn.edu/academics/graduate/msfs/

**Institute for Food & Development Policy (Food First)** — http://foodfirst.org/

**Institute for Social Ecology** — www.social-ecology.org

**International Federation of Organic Agriculture Movements (IFOAM)** — www.ifoam.org

**LEO-4000 National Sustainable Agriculture Standard** — http://www.sustainableagstandard.org/

**National Organic Program (NOP)** — http://www.ams.usda.gov/about-ams/prgrams-offices/national-organic-program

**National Sustainable Agriculture Coalition (NSAC)** — http://sustainableagriculture.net/

**Navdanya (Vandana Shiva's center)** — http://www.navdanya.org/

**Northeast Organic Farming Association (NOFA)** — www.nofa.org

**The Organic Standard** — www.organicstandard.com

**Organic Trade Association (OTA)** — www.ota.com

**Resurgence & Ecologist Magazine** — http://www.resurgence.org/magazine/

**Rodale Institute** — http://rodaleinstitute.org/

**Shambhala International** — http://shambhala.org/

**Stuart Hill (University of Western Sydney, Social Ecology)** — http://www.zulenet. com/see/chair.html

## Books & Publications by Grace Gershuny

Grace Gershuny and Joe Smillie, *The Soul of Soil: A Soil-Building Guide for Master Gardeners and Farmers*, 4th edition, (White River Junction: Chelsea Green: 1999).

Grace Gershuny and Deborah L. Martin, Editors, T*he Rodale Book of Composting: Easy Methods for Every Gardener*, (Emmaus: Rodale Press, 1992). Updated edition anticipated publication Spring 2018.

Grace Gershuny, *Start With the Soil: The Organic Gardener's Guide to Improving Soil for Higher Yields, More Beautiful Flowers, and a Healthy, Easy-Care Garden*, (Emmaus: Rodale Press, 1993).

Grace Gershuny, Compost, *Vermicompost and Compost Tea: Feeding the Soil on the Organic Farm* (2nd edition), (White River Junction: Chelsea Green, 2011).

Grace Gershuny, Editor, *Organic Farmer: The Digest of Sustainable Agriculture*, (Montpelier, VT: Rural Vermont, quarterly 1990-1994).

This publication can be obtained by interlibrary loan via the National Agricultural Library. Check https://www.nal.usda.gov/borrow-materials. In the AGRICOLA data base, enter call number S605.5 0743.

The WEB DuBois Library at the University of Massachusetts, Amherst has archived a complete set of this publication, along with a collection of the author's personal papers on organic agriculture in the Northeast. http://scua.library.umass.edu/ead/mums793. xml

The University of Vermont Bailey Howe Library has a complete set in its Special Collections, which can be viewed during opening hours. Check http://library.uvm.edu/hours.

Rutgers University (Dr. Joseph Heckman, Dept. of Plant Biology).

The Elm Farm Organic Research Center library, Newbury, England, includes a complete set, available for review by visitors during opening hours.
Check http://www.organicresearchcentre.com/ for more information.

Page 20

**The Future?**

# Newville, 1990...

NOTE: *The following was prepared by Grace Jensen, Vermont Coordinator for the Natural Organic Farmer's Association (NOFA), for presentation at the recent USDA conference in Montpelier, Vt., on the future of agriculture. We offer it here as an example of the point-of-view being expressed, with increasing effectiveness, by similiar organizations in New England and throughout the country. We'd be interested in your reactions; please send them to New England Farmer, Box 391, St. Johnsbury, Vt. 05819.*

### By Grace Jensen

This is written as a contribution to the national dialogue on the structure of agriculture, initiated by Secretary of Agriculture Bob Bergland. This nation's agricultural problems have been discussed and dissected at great length in recent years. Conferences and public discussions have been held by a variety of organizations, producing recommendations for policy changes at every level.

We have been asked by Mr. Bergland to suggest some remedies. The scenario that follows depicts what a group such as NOFA might design if it were making the decisions. It is a sketch of local agriculture in a rural Northeastern community as it could be in about ten years with a modest redirection of public effort.

The picture is not meant to be all-inclusive—many possibilities and embellishments are left out. Neither does it specifically address some of the critical problems, though various constructive proposals could be deduced from its basic premise: community control and development of the community's own resources. In this scheme, government's role is to forge links between communities and facilitate the sharing of information among them.

I magine, then, the town of Newville, largest population center of a remote Northern Vermont farm community in 1990. Less than 30,000 people live in the entire county, which has retained its unspoiled, pastoral beauty largely because of the inhospitability of its winters, coupled with its isolation from major transportation arteries.

Farming here, unlike other places in the Northeast, never was superceded as the the basis for the local economy, despite state development focus on tourism and manufacturing during the sixties and seventies. But the agricultural base narrowed from a diversified array of small farms to almost total reliance on dairy, produced mostly for out-of-state markets. Average herd size increased steadily to keep pace with escalating input costs. Although a large variety of food was still produced for on-farm use nearly everything that people in the town of Newville ate came from elsewhere.

It's thus not surprising that this rural backwater, maligned as a 'depressed area,' should have become a forerunner in recreating and demonstrating a sound, sustainable agriculture as the mainstay of its self-reliant prosperity. In the words of one of Newville's oldtimers who helped get the farmers market going, "If we can grow most of our own food up here, you can do it anywhere."

The Greater Newville Farmers Market was the first step in making locally grown food more available in town. At first, it was organized and run by a young woman who simply wanted a place to sell surplus from her large garden. The few other sellers were people like her—recent escapees from the city seeking a more satisfying way of life. They all had dreams of earning at least part of their living by growing food. Some had begun to do it, through a combination of unusual ingenuity, perserverance and hard work. Yet, they were often met with skepticism and even hostility from the 'established' community.

"You can't make a living growing produce up here," they were told.

"There's no money in sheep."

They also listened to neighbors who remembered times when many villages had root storage bans, and wool production was an agricultural staple. Even the smallest towns once had several stores, mills that were powered by running water, and numerous skilled workers to make and repair the tools farmers used. And they soon found that their biggest problem at the farmers market was meeting

*New England Farmer, January 1980.*

FURNITURE

**First published article by Grace Gershuny. The second page was retyped for legibility.**

demand – largely by older folks who remembered the days when fresh, nutritious garden produce could be had in town all Summer long.

The 'energy crisis' is old news by now; it had supplied the real impetus for the rest of the community to see the necessity for what the farmers market people were doing. Some folks even said we should thank OPEC for scaring us into a shift to renewable energy sources and local self-reliance while there still was enough oil left to phase out the petroleum-based economy gradually. It's a little scary, even now, to think of how completely we depended on oil to grow food ten years ago; how, besides being wasteful and inefficient in terms of resource use, it had been leading us to mine our soil, pollute our air and water, abandon once-productive farms, and put harmful chemicals in our food, all for the 'privilege' of jugging monstrous debt loads, working long hours for dwindling net returns, and leaving behind an industrialized food producing unit that our kids couldn't afford to inherit and took little pride in.

Today in Newville things are different. The farmers market has expanded into a many-faceted community food center. Owned and controlled by the farmers' cooperative, it is now open five days a week in Summer for retail sales, and serves as a wholesaler to local schools, restaurants and grocery stores all year long. There are large coolers for fresh produce and locally made dairy products, and a sizeable root cellar for year round storage. Regular trucking runs are made to similar facilities in other communities as well as to the large state terminal market, which supplies Vermont-produced food of all sorts to Northeastern urban centers.

The meat butchering and processing facility is designed for small commercial users as well as home meat producers, as are the cannery and the quick-freeze section. The electricity needed for all these activities is generated by a combination of wind and water power, with surplus sold back to the commercial network. A wood-fired furnace provides heat on days too cold for the solar collectors to work efficiently.

The farmers' cooperative also provides means for the bulk urchase of farm inputs, increasingly from someone right in Newville County or someplace else nearby. A grain producers' co-op in the Champlain Valley mixes feed rations to order, and a cooperative fish plant in Maine trades its pungent liquid fertilizer for Newville's popular herb-flavored cheese. Much of the technology is experimental. Local tinkerers often come up with ideas for taking some of the grunt work out of food handling, or extending the useful life of an antiquated machine. The cooperative's computer terminal is another tool the growers use frequently. Besides giving information on current prices or the projected returns on five acres of rutabagas, it allows them to share information of local interest and set up trades of labor and equipment.

The local consumer food co-op was instrumental in organizing the food center, and the consumer representatives work with the farmers to plan new operations and keep the community informed of what's available. Besides butchering, canning and freezing, individuals can bring their own grain in to be ground or use the bean cleaner. Classes are held regularly in various aspects of food production, storage and use. The food co-op features certified 'biologically grown' products, which people seem to prefer, though anything raised locally is sure to be better than the artificially ripened, pesticide-laden, week-old stuff we used to import from out West – even in Summer!

None of this was thought possible in the early seventies. People still believed we'd have cheap oil indefinitely to irrigate fields in Arizona and carry staple foods across the continent every day. It became possible because people who found pleasure in doing things for themselves didn't wait for 'experts' to tell them it was possible. It was a struggle at first even to be considered for a farm loan on less than fifty acres, to produce foods other than milk. The growers were, finally, grudgingly allowed to supply their own labor for building the food center, and had to fight a maze of red tape to include plans for a waste composting facility instead of a septic system. They must still pay their share of taxes to retire the debt on Newville's ten-year-old, expensive sewage treatment plant – which the engineers can never seem to make work right. But the state planning office now includes food processing facilities as eligible for industrial development loans. The growers narrowly won out over a scheme to manufacture plastic Vermont Christmas trees – only because they had learned how to mobilize community support from the start.

The Extension Service is again fulfilling its role of providing assistance for all the community's farmers. The state experiment station is following up suggestions to test the value of locally available waste materials as compost, and exploring ways to increase the availability of existing soil phosphorus reserves. Consultants are available to help those just getting started, as well as farmers making the transition to biological soil management after watching nitrate prices soar. Some farmers decided to diversify as an alternative to expensive manure storage systems required under clean water regulations, and have been helped to fit their available resources into newly emerging marketing opportunities. Youngsters wanting to learn about farming are matched up with accredited operating farms, where they are assured of getting competent guidance in a full range of agricultural skills in exchange for their labor.

Although these developments are still in the embryonic stage, the whole community has been noticeably invigorated. A spirit of optimism pervades Chamber of Commerce meetings, where once anxiety was commonplace. There will always be more to do, always problems to try us, always challenges to face. There are still those among us who seek short-term personal profit, even if it destroys the long-term capability of people to provide for themselves. But we no longer wait for specialists to find our answers, or assume that our own resources are inadequate to meet complex needs in an interdependent world.

The foregoing may seem like idealistic fantasy to some, but none of the possibilities depicted in Newville is unreasonable or farfetched. Many are being attempted right now – with little or no government support – by NOFA and other groups like NOFA. If you're one of the many who has begun to recognize the urgency of the food crisis we face, we hope you will join forces with us to develop sane alternatives while there is still time.

# November 1998 — Letter to the Editor, *The Ecologist*

This is the letter I sent to the editors of The Ecologist magazine in response to an article by Ben Lilliston & Ronnie Cummins published in the summer of 1998. It is based on the document I drafted for the NOP, entitled "Don't Believe the Lies," in response to some of the public comments to the first proposed rule that we were receiving early in 1998. Neither was ever published.

Dear Editor,

This is a response to the article entitled "Organic Vs 'Organic': The Corruption of a Label," which appeared in your July/August 1998 issue. A condensed version of this article appeared in the following issue. This and other information widely circulated by the Pure Food Campaign (and others) is so wildly inaccurate and misrepresented that it undermines any possible understanding by the organic community as to the real issues and legitimate concerns involved with the attempt by USDA to regulate the labeling of organic products. As someone who has been involved with the discussion about the legitimization of organic methods, for over twenty years through grassroots activism and direct participation in farmer-led certification, and for four years as one of the principal authors of the much-maligned USDA proposed rule, I can no longer quietly sit by and say nothing. Because I care deeply about the fate of the organic idea, and its potential for reversing so many harmful agricultural practices, I feel compelled to speak.

Unfortunately, there are many among your readers who will discount anything I have to say because of the fact that I am still employed by USDA. I have seen, read, and heard in person the anger felt by many people towards any activity of the US government, and the USDA in particular. To those who are still trying to sort out fact from fiction, I will try to provide clear and accurate information. One type of information about which I feel very much more qualified to talk about than the authors of this article or any other member of the public is a description of the intent of the authors of the National Organic Program proposal. It is understandable that many people find the regulatory language confusing, but you can't claim to know what the authors of the proposal were thinking unless you ask them.

There are so many fallacies and half-truths in this article it is hard to know where to start. Many of these inaccuracies are insidious in that they are based on presumptions of bad intent, and on continual repetition of innuendoes (such as characterizing "the USDA's recent attempts to degrade current high organic standards") that give them the appearance of fact. There are many places where the prejudicial attitude towards anything that might have been published by USDA is evident, starting with the opening paragraphs. The first sentence incorrectly states that the proposed rule would be "legally binding." The U.S. regulatory process requires that any new regulations first go through a lengthy review process, culminating in their publication for public comment in the Federal Register. This is why the document is called a "proposed rule." The whole idea is to present a work in progress that is intended to be changed based on public comments before it becomes "final," or legally binding. The statement that the agency "previewed the proposed federal regulations to the press on the Wednesday before Thanksgiving..." is pure fiction. That there were many who "anticipated" a weaker set of standards than is current in the industry is true, which shows only that these people needed to interpret the proposal in a way that would justify their preconceptions.

The charge that the administration "disregarded nearly every policy proposal...made by the NOSB" is grossly untrue. There was only a handful of places in which the proposed rule disagreed with or contradicted recommendations provided by the NOSB, and in general most of the proposed rule was consistent with the NOSB's recommendations. Many of the Board's specific recommendations were not addressed in the proposed rule, not because they were disregarded, but because they were too detailed and specific to be appropriate for regulations. One assumption within USDA that was not clearly communicated to the public is the extent to which these details will be filled in through program manuals. The process for developing and amending program manuals is much more fluid than the process for establishing or changing regulations, and is routinely done in consultation with the industry being regulated.

Contrary to the assertions of this article, we did not propose to permit the use of any of the "Big Three:" genetically engineered organisms (GEO's), irradiation, or sewage sludge (biosolids). The first draft of the proposed rule, which was approved by the Secretary of Agriculture and sent to the Office of Management & Budget (OMB, which must approve any significant new regulation before it can be published) the previous June (often referred to as the "June draft") contained explicit prohibitions on both GEO's (as organic crops or livestock) and irradiation. OMB insisted that we replace the prohibitions with requests for public comment on these subjects. As for "biosolids," we agreed with the NOSB's recommendation that sludge meets the definition of synthetic given in the law, and could therefore not be used unless it appeared on the National List, which it didn't. In any case, the resounding public comment against allowing any of these to be labeled as organic was clearly heard, and the Secretary of Agriculture quickly issued public assurances that the next round of regulations (which would be yet another proposed rule, not a final rule as stated in the article) would clearly prohibit all three.

The intensive confinement of animals and "a host of other conventional factory farm agricultural practices" were not proposed to be permitted either. The intent in allowing many of these "loopholes" was to build into the regulations the kind of flexibility that all organic programs now provide, so that decisions about whether a given questionable practice (such as keeping cows indoors in the winter) was actually "necessary" would have to be justified by the producer and approved by the certifier. Once again, changes insisted on by OMB eliminated a whole mechanism that established strict criteria for making exceptions to the preferred organic management practices. The frequently repeated scenario of making it possible to label as organic a product from an intensively confined, antibiotic laden, irradiated, genetically manipulated product was never a remote possibility in the regulations that were proposed.

The authors go on to identify several issues on which the proposed rule seems to be in conflict with the NOSB's recommendations. We did propose to allow animals from conventional operations to be used for organic meat and poultry if they are brought onto a farm at very early stages of life. Up until recently such leeway was commonly found in many existing organic programs, and there was some public testimony in the course of earlier NOSB meetings that a complete prohibition would unduly restrict the ability of new farmers (large or small) to begin organic livestock production. The public comment that we received suggests that organic livestock production has rapidly reached a more advanced level, so that small producers are confident that such leeway is not needed. Changing this is no big deal, and I have not heard anyone at USDA suggest that the agency might resist making this change. Similarly, the proposed allowance for some non-organic feed was higher than the level currently accepted in the industry for emergency feed exemptions–no problem to change it, and no desire to thwart the desire of producers to keep improving.

## Confusion about Label Claims and "Higher" Standards

Another issue cited by the authors as contradicting the NOSB's recommendations is the prohibition against certifiers using their seals
to represent "higher" standards. In fact, this provision agrees with
the NOSB's recommendations about use of certifier seals. One of
the main purposes of the Organic Foods Production Acts to facilitate interstate trade by establishing consistent national standards for
organic production. There continues to be a lot of confusion about
what is meant by "standards," especially when the standards reflect a
whole management system approach. Making comparisons between
whole systems according to how strict they are about one provision
or another turns the whole concept on its head. For example, one
important organic principle is to establish nutrient cycling systems,
most commonly by integrating livestock and crop production. A
program that requires only 100% organic feed for livestock may
appear to have "higher" standards, but in effect it may discourage
crop producers from keeping animals because of the difficulty in ob-
taining enough organic feed at a reasonable price. Is it better to be
"stricter" or to encourage integrated nutrient cycling practices?

Perhaps one reason for confusion about "floor" versus "ceiling" in
standards is that environmentalists and activists are unaccustomed to the
kind of market development regulations represented by this program, as
opposed to the kind of regulations that protect the public from pollution.
It makes a great deal of sense for states to be able to enact stricter standards for air and water safety than those enacted at the federal level. Regulations that set standards to facilitate interstate commerce are a different
can of worms. In this case the fight among certification groups who want
to promote their programs by marketing their certification seals based
on differences in standards is misguided, and has created a more night-
marish bureaucracy than anything the government could dream up. This
is one of the situations that the federal law was enacted to try to remedy.

To characterize the requirement that products labeled as "organic"
comply with the USDA's regulations as giving the agency a "monopoly"
on the word is idiotic, as is the claim that it would either limit free speech
rights or "criminalize dissent." The preamble to the proposed rule clearly
states that individual producers or processors can continue to make any
truthful label claims they wish, and that any accredited certifier can verify that these claims are accurate. An organization that wishes to establish

"higher" standards for its members, owners, or products can do that, and market this claim as it sees fit–fair labor practices is one I would personally like to see gain in popularity. For example, if a baby food manufacturer wants all of its ingredients to be tested to show no detectable pesticide residue it could do so, make that claim on its product labels, and request its organic certifier to verify that this standard is being met. The manufacturer's label could be promoted as meaning "no detectable pesticide residues." Under the proposed regulations, however, the USDA accredited certifier could not market its logo as a claim of "no detectable pesticide residues" if that is not a requirement of the federal organic program.

Unfortunately, this is one issue in which deliberate misinformation has been spread, and which has succeeded in further confusing things for the public. The so-called "eco-labeling" prohibition is also a case of interpreting a request for public comment as an intent to do something that nobody wants. The examples we gave of phrases that may possibly imply that a product was organically produced was included so that people would know what we were talking about, in hopes that they would give us specific terms that should or should not be considered the same as making an organic claim.

### Rethinking Basic assumptions?

The unstated assumptions at the basis of this article come closest to articulation in the frequently repeated statement that: "The numerous loopholes and provisions in the rules would open the door for large-scale agribusiness to overwhelm an alternative food system largely composed of small farmers, retailers, and processors." Many comments I've read and heard refer to the "common knowledge" that USDA is owned, lock, stock, and barrel by these agribusiness concerns, and that anything it does is therefore at their behest. The authors' lengthy enumeration of USDA's record of supporting conventional agribusiness is not news, but this does not constitute evidence that these interests had anything to do with developing the National Organic Program proposal.

Very few large agribusiness firms expressed any interest in this program, submitted public input, or tried to convince us of anything in particular during the three years when we were actually drafting the proposed rule. My colleagues on the USDA staff shared my own strong commitment to protecting the integrity of organic agriculture and the interests of small organic farmers through a regulatory process that we knew could later be influenced by more conventional interests. During the drafting process nearly all of the questions asked of any provision under discussion related to how it would affect current or potential small organic farmers, retailers or processors. Even OMB's misguided changes were, I believe, made under its mandate to minimize the burdens imposed by any new regulations. While there was little contact with conventional agricultural organizations during the drafting process, the staff consulted regularly with many organic farmer and consumer groups, such as the Organic Trade Association, Organic Farming Research Foundation, the Independent Organic Inspectors Association, and others. Most of the conventional agribusiness groups cited by the authors submitted public comment after the proposed rule was published.

The fact that the Secretary of Agriculture was convinced to sign off on a document that did explicitly prohibit the use of GEO's and irradiation as organic practices is testimony to a significant change in internal attitudes that has been happening over the past few years, thanks to an administration that is sincerely sympathetic to the general concepts upheld by organic producers. The great "expose" touted by Mother Jones is laughable because it actually shows our success in these internal discussions, despite the objections raised by representatives of APHIS and the Office of the Trade Representative.

So if the proposed rule was not a product of agribusiness interests, why was it so flawed? Many of the "flaws" perceived by the authors of this article, although repeated widely as incontrovertible fact, do not exist. To the extent that some of the proposed standards were looser than is common in industry practice, we are guilty of having erred on the side of making it easier for small farmers to be organic. There is hardly unanimity about many of these standards within the industry, either, and many examples could be given of legitimate disputes over how much flexibility, including controversies about standards promulgated by IFOAM. Staff members of the USDA National Organic Program have also had an integral role in formulating the current Codex Alimentarius organic standards, including revisions that establish the understanding that, while details of standards may differ from country to country, they need to conform with generally agreed organic principles. This is the basis on which the National Organic Program was designed.

The statement, attributed to former NOSB Chair Michael Sligh, to the effect that the USDA's proposal attempts to "shift the whole organic concept from a process-based approach (emphasizing the way something is grown) to a performance-based approach (emphasizing measurable properties of the final product)" is about as backwards as any characterization could be. It was a satisfying (if fleeting) moment for me when, during the public presentation of the proposed rule last year, Secretary of Agriculture Dan Glickman emphasized repeatedly that this regulation is about how a product is produced, not its qualities. This is the mantra that permitted us to eventually win the internal battles to prohibit GEOs and irradiation, among other things. This is why the administration was able to support a program that prohibits practices that are actively promoted elsewhere in the department, including use of agrichemicals of all sorts. I agree with Mr. Sligh that the US government's opposition to labeling of GEO's for consumers is based largely on the insistence that process standards are irrelevant. By opposing, or at least delaying, implementation of the USDA's organic program, activists who want to impose mandatory labeling for products of genetic engineering are shooting themselves in the foot.

The authors point to "a booming $4 billion industry" to buttress their arguments, citing a poll indicating that "54 per cent of American consumers said they would like to see 'organic' food production become the dominant form of agriculture in the United States." I was unaware that this question had been asked, but would certainly be among those who heartily agree–this goal is in fact among the prime motivations I had when I accepted this position with USDA. The problem here is that information about this booming industry relies largely on unsubstantiated label claims– we have no idea just how many products labeled as "organic" are even certified. The much-touted California law does not (contrary to popular belief) require certification, and figures available from that State indicate that about half of the producers that are registered as organic under California law are not certified. Many within the industry have been quietly warning about a consumer time bomb that could seriously undermine the organic market based on even one highly publicized case of fraud. This is one of the reasons that consumer groups have been among the most insistent from the beginning that the federal government step in to regulate these claims.

Finally, the authors state (in describing a situation to which their misinformation has contributed), that "millions of organic consumers–as well as certifiers, farmers and retailers–are now so disillusioned and distrustful of the USDA that they are no longer willing to accept any compromises at all." They also refer to the need to prepare for a "protracted battled with the USDA." With these attitudes of warfare and inflexible unwillingness to deal with the USDA in good faith, the prophecy becomes self-fulfilling. There can surely be no credible organic program implemented without the collaboration and cooperation of the community on whose behalf it is being established. Unfortunately, while the authors hold great promise for a privately devised national standard and accreditation scheme, too many of the different segments of the industry have a similar attitude towards each other for this to happen any faster or more painlessly than the federal process. It certainly won't be any cheaper. At least the government, imperfect as it is, really is constrained by built-in mechanisms of accountability to the public—a principle to which too many grassroots organizers give lip service alone.

The subtitle of your magazine, "Rethinking Basic Assumptions," is one that I hope your staff and your readers will take very seriously. Perhaps you believe that this only applies to other people, but I would suggest that we all must do this, and do with great care, whenever we undertake to rally the public for a cause that we believe is just.

Sincerely,

Grace Gershuny
USDA National Organic Program Staff
Barnet, Vermont, USA

# Acknowledgements

Countless friends and colleagues have supported and inspired me to do this work and write this story. Some are mentioned in these pages, but many are not. This necessarily truncated list reflects many conversations over the years with people who have offered help, supported my contrary viewpoints, read drafts, given advice, commented, and generally encouraged me to keep going, as well those who have contributed financially; many belong in several categories. They include co-workers, co-conspirators, fellow writers, reviewers, spiritual warriors, agents, editors, and cherished friends. It has been a long road, and I am grateful to all of you:

Sue Alward, Margo Baldwin, Peter Barnes, Renee Carpenter, Christine Carrington, Betsy Chodorkoff, Dan Chodorkoff, Dan Daggett, Pascual Delgado, Theresa DelPozzo, Katherine DiMatteo, Amy Ehrlich, Edward & Freida Gershuny, Janet Givens, Newcomb Greenleaf, Gwendolyn Hallsmith, Michael Hankin, Miriam Hansen, Thomas Harding, Stuart Hill, Libby Hillhouse, Stewart Hoyt, Carol Hyman, George Kalogridis, Samuel Kaymen, Mark Keating, Joan Kydd, Frances Moore Lappé, Reeve Lindbergh, Jeannie Lowell, Britt Lundgren, Daphne Miller, Dierdre Mullane, Penny Patch, Ella Reznikova, Suzanne Richman, Ted Rogers, Howie Ross, Leslie Rowell, Gunnar Rundgren, Allan Savory, Jim Schley, Marc Schwartz, Joe Smillie, Joe Spieler, Woody Starkweather, Eleana Sussman, Jonathan Teller, John Todd, Nancy Jack Todd, Jessica Govea Thorbourne, Eric Toensmeier, Brian Tokar, Shay Totten, Jill Warzer, Ben Watson, Madeleine Winfield, Bill Wolf, & Enid Wonnacott.

A special shout-out to Philip Ackerman-Leist, who gave me the opportunity to work with amazing students and colleagues in the Green Mountain College MS in Sustainable Food Systems program, and to all the brilliant social ecology students and colleagues who have given me hope and inspiration.

Not least of all, my family and close friends have formed a circle of emotional and financial support and good cheer to smooth my path: My loving partner Pete Blose, talented and beautiful daughter Opal Hoyt, wise sisters Henny Lee Gershuny and Roxanne Fand, and gal pals in the garden girls and the moon sisters.

I am also indebted to professional helpers in bringing this book to frui-tion. When I finally recovered from losing Miranda (please see my per-sonal remembrance on the following pages), my search for a compati-ble editor turned up Cathy Donohue, who has proved to be rigorous as well as friendly in getting me to clarify my narrative and keep the story flowing. Getting to publication meant finding a book designer who could wrap my carefully crafted words within a harmonious visual story. By sheer luck and good karma, Marie Hathaway came into my life just when I needed her—as a garden helper and student as well as a crackerjack web and book designer. To wrap it up, former NOFA comrade Andrea Chesman made time in her busy schedule to give this book a professional index. Any flaws you may find are my responsibility alone.

# Personal Remembrance: Miranda Constance Smith

It is no exaggeration to say that this story could not have emerged without the love and friendship of Miranda Smith. She has been integral not only to the task of figuring out how to tell this story, but to the story itself. Her influence extended far beyond my personal world, and was crucial for inspiring the courage, good humor, and pursuit of excellence needed to persevere in this project. My determination to complete this project is motivated in large part by the desire to honor her contribution and validate her faith in me.

It seems important to paint a more detailed portrait of this remarkable person for those who never had the privilege of knowing her. A vibrant, charismatic visionary, Miranda was also strongly practical and proficient as an organic grower, teacher, author and editor of farming and gardening books. She farmed in the Northeast and Southeast, as well as northern Quebec. She authored at least a dozen books, including several for Rodale Press. She had an amazing, brilliant mind and was largely self-taught in the agricultural sciences, as well as being a great cook and a serious student of nutrition and health. She was infinitely curious and interested in everyone, and had a bawdy sense of humor.

We first met in 1979, when she, along with a group of friends who worked for the National Center for Appropriate Technology (NCAT), decided to form a consulting group and move to Newport, VT. Before this she had been at the Institute for Local Self-Reliance in DC, and had consulted on urban agriculture, greenhouses and rooftop gardening projects in various places.

Miranda's pioneering work in agriculture led her to Topsfield, MA to co-manage the demonstration organic farm there with Eliot Coleman, later living and working with Robert Houriet at his organic vegetable farm in Hardwick, VT. Her journey took her to the New England Small Farms Institute (NESFI) in Belchertown, MA, where she managed their first Community Supported Agriculture farm, delighting in mentoring young farmers. She later was engaged to help develop a self-provisioning farm for a therapeutic center in the Catskills serving a severely disabled population.

After a stint in a "real job" as a gardening editor at Country Home Products Press in New Jersey Miranda moved to Florida – glad to escape winter and return to her southern roots. There she became involved with Chinese healing arts, studying with Grandmaster Fu of the Emei tradition of Qigong. She became a prodigious healer in her own right before she finally succumbed to cancer in June of 2011, just shy of her 67th birthday.

Miranda Smith, 2004

John, her final love and companion, wrote this in his blog: "Model, actress, activist and an organizing force in Greenpeace, author of a dozen books on gardening, pioneer in rooftop gardening, a leader in organic farming, scholar of Chinese healing, and so much more, she was a positive force in a sometimes cloudy world. Wherever she went she was at home. She loved travel and living in sunshine."

---

Miranda's daughter, Simone LePage, circulated a few gems billed as "things my mother taught me":

"The people who change the world in truly significant ways often weren't the ones broadcasting those changes."

"Stand up for yourself, stand up for others, stand up for what you believe but be willing to change your mind. Throw out your old beliefs no matter how attached you are to them if they no longer serve you."

When talking about her life at the end she wanted us to know that if she got more time she wouldn't spend it being noble, she would spend it having fun. "Have fun."

...and my new motto: "Damn convention."

# Index

Made in the USA
Middletown, DE
24 January 2020

83692756R00158